THE SOVIET UNION
AND THE LAW OF THE SEA

THE SOVIET UNION and THE LAW OF THE SEA

William E. Butler

The Johns Hopkins Press

BALTIMORE AND LONDON

242959

The Johns Hopkins Press, Baltimore, Maryland 21218
The Johns Hopkins Press Ltd., London

Library of Congress Catalog Card Number 73-138037

International Standard Book Number 0-8018-1221-6

To Darlene and Bill III

CONTENTS

LIST OF MAPS

ABBREVIATIONS

AJIL	*American Journal of International Law*
BFSP	*British and Foreign State Papers*
Dokumenty	*Dokumenty vneshnei politiki SSSR*
DSB	*Department of State Bulletin*
ILM	*International Legal Materials*
IM	*Izveshcheniia moreplavateliam*
LNTS	*League of Nations Treaty Series*
N. R.	*Nouveau Recueil de traités,* 16 vols. (1808–39)
Polnoe sobranie	*Polnoe sobranie zakonov Rossiiskoi imperii*
Recueil	*Recueil de traités,* 8 vols. (1761–1808)
Recueil N. S.	*Nouveaux Supplemens au Recueil de traités,* 3 vols. (1761–1839)
SDD	*Sbornik deistvuiushchikh dogovorov, soglashenii i konventsii, zakliuchennykh SSSR s inostrannymi gosudarstvami*
SGIP	*Sovetskoe gosudarstvo i pravo*
SP SSSR	*Sobranie postanovlenii soveta ministrov SSSR*
SS&D	*Soviet Statutes and Decisions*
SS RSFSR	*Sistematicheskoe sobranie zakonov RSFSR, ukazov prezidiuma verkhovnogo soveta RSFSR i reshenii pravitel'stva RSFSR*
SU RSFSR	*Sobranie uzakonenii i rasporiazhenii RSFSR*
SZ SSSR	*Sobranie zakonov i rasporiazhenii SSSR*
UNTS	*United Nations Treaty Series*
Vedomosti RSFSR	*Vedomosti verkhovnogo soveta RSFSR*
Vedomosti SSSR	*Vedomosti verkhovnogo soveta SSSR*

PREFACE

This book explores the origins and development of prerevolutionary Russian and Soviet doctrines and practices relating to certain aspects of the public international law of the sea: the legal regimes of territorial waters, internal sea waters, closed seas, continental shelf, deep seabed, and high seas. While it does not purport to be an exhaustive study of the Soviet approach to the law of the sea, it should be of interest to students of international law and Soviet foreign policy and, particularly, to those who will be concerned during the 1970s with the further codification of the law of the sea.

The importance of Soviet legislation and treaty practice has often been overlooked by Western students of maritime affairs, and the significance of doctrinal writings misunderstood or exaggerated. As a consequence, our perceptions of Soviet interests in or disaffection with the public order of the oceans have not always been accurate. By devoting considerable attention to the actual practices of the Soviet government, along with the doctrinal views set forth in Soviet international legal media, this work hopes to contribute to a better and more balanced understanding of Soviet maritime policy.

The present volume is an enlarged and revised version of a doctoral dissertation submitted to the faculty of the School of Advanced International Studies of The Johns Hopkins University. It represents a continuation of my earlier studies concerning Soviet territorial waters, initially begun at the Harvard Law School.

This book could never have been completed without the encouragement and assistance of a great number of people over the past five years. Professor Herbert S. Dinerstein gave invaluable counsel and guidance as the principal adviser to my dissertation; his appreciation of the importance of legal studies for understanding Soviet society, institutions, and foreign policy is all too rare among American students of Soviet affairs. I am also indebted to David W. Wainhouse and Francis O. Wilcox for providing much needed moral and financial support during the early years of doctoral study in Washington D.C., and to Stephen M. Schwebel and Robert M. Slusser, who served with them as members of the dissertation committee.

An appointment as Research Associate at the Harvard Law

School and Associate of the Harvard University Russian Research Center from 1968–70 enabled me to draw upon the outstanding collections of the Harvard Law School Library and Widener Library and provided the most precious commodity of all in doctoral research—time to complete the study. My debt to two members of the Law School faculty is especially great. R. R. Baxter directed my earlier studies of Soviet maritime law, and his constant encouragement and valuable comments are reflected in the present work as well. Harold J. Berman was generous beyond any reasonable expectation in ensuring that I had sufficient time for research and writing, and I have benefited incalculably from his advice and criticism during our association.

The brief remarks in the Introduction relating to the development of international law in prerevolutionary Russia I originally prepared as part of the class materials for a seminar on "Soviet, Chinese, and Western Approaches to International Law" offered at the Harvard Law School in 1968–69 by Professors R. R. Baxter, H. J. Berman, and J. A. Cohen, with the participation of W. E. Butler and Hungdah Chiu, and again in 1969–70 by Baxter, with Butler and Chiu. These remarks have been since revised in light of faculty and student criticisms, yet still they do not begin to do justice to the subject. The historical development of international law in Russia merits considerably greater attention from Western scholars, both for insight into modern Soviet approaches to international law and into the origins of "Western" international law.

I should also like to express my appreciation to Miss Myrtle Moody, of the Harvard Law School Library, for her assistance in obtaining fugitive materials and otherwise making the library collection more accessible.

The maps were expertly prepared for this volume by Mrs. Barbara Gibbons, of Belmont, Massachusetts.

The editors of the *American Journal of International Law* have kindly granted permission to draw upon my article "The Legal Regime of Russian Territorial Waters" and my note "The Soviet Union and the Continental Shelf," which appeared, respectively, in the January issues for 1968 and 1969. The editors of the *Harvard International Law Journal* also graciously permitted me to use materials from my comment "Soviet Concepts of Innocent Passage" published in the Winter 1965 issue.

Chapters 2–4 of the present volume are based upon my earlier monograph *The Law of Soviet Territorial Waters,* published by Frederick A. Praeger Inc. in 1967. The course of recent developments and access to materials not previously available to me are primarily responsible for the very substantial revisions and additions that have been made. The extensive documentary appendices translated for that volume, however, are of inestimable importance for the student of Soviet maritime policy, and frequent reference is made to them throughout the present study.

London, England   WILLIAM E. BUTLER

THE SOVIET UNION
AND THE LAW OF THE SEA

Chapter 1

GENERAL INTRODUCTION

In general, Western scholarship on Soviet international law has tended to concentrate upon trends in Soviet legal writing, to exaggerate the monolithic nature and "official" character of legal scholarship, to overlook the implications of diversity of opinion among Soviet jurists on particular issues, and to devote remarkably little attention to Soviet state practice. The inclination to look upon the USSR as a unique entity in the international system has naturally illuminated the divergencies in Soviet and Western approaches to international law while at the same time obscuring or distorting basic similarities. There has also been little appreciation or study of the continuity (or discontinuity) of attitudes, approaches, or principles in Tsarist and Soviet doctrines or practice.[1]

The study of comparative approaches to international law is especially essential in an era when the subjects of international law are unprecedented in number, when all purport to observe a single system of international law, and when the major actors claim to have distinctive views of international law and diplomacy. But applying the comparative method to international law presupposes a thorough familiarity with and understanding of the theory and especially the state practice of the objects of study. In the case of the Soviet Union, such a familiarity is impeded by the lack of research in these areas. The need for comprehensive, dispassionate, and accurate studies devoted to Soviet theory and practice in specific branches of private and public international law is particularly pressing. Only they can provide the necessary factual and legal framework for comparative research on a higher plane. Although an excellent beginning has been made with the publication of studies of Soviet treaty law and citizenship law, the need for such studies is far from being fully met.[2]

The present work undertakes to examine salient aspects of the

---

1. For a more extensive discussion of these points, see William E. Butler, "American Research on Soviet Approaches to International Law," *Columbia Law Review,* LXX (1970), 218–35.

2. See Jan F. Triska and Robert M. Slusser, *The Theory, Law, and Policy of Soviet Treaties* (Stanford, Calif.: Stanford University Press, 1962); George Ginsburgs, *Soviet Citizenship Law* (Leyden: Sijthoff, 1968).

Soviet approach to the international law of the sea, with special attention accorded to both doctrine and practice of the Tsarist and Soviet periods. This is not, it must be stressed, a comprehensive treatment of all aspects of the law of the sea. The law of the sea in time of war is beyond the scope of the study, and many of the more technical or functional dimensions of, for example, the regime of the high seas and the international law of fisheries are treated briefly or completely omitted.

Limiting the study in this manner is not intended to suggest that the areas left unexplored are less significant or deserving. Rather, it seemed more desirable to focus attention upon those elements of the law of the sea that best reflected the interplay of legal, technological, political, economic, diplomatic, and strategic considerations instrumental in shaping the Soviet approach to the regime of the seas. These subjects—the legal regimes of territorial waters, internal sea waters, closed seas, the continental shelf, the deep seabed, and the high seas—represent a broad range of transactions and relations among the Soviet Union, the international community, and the oceans and their resources. How the Soviet leadership and Soviet jurists have responded to ocean-related legal and policy choices can yield important insights into the approach of a state to international law.

Viewed from another perspective, a study of the Soviet approach to the law of the sea provides data about the interaction between a country's attitude toward the law of the sea, on the one hand, and its maritime capabilities and interests on the other. The transition of the Soviet Union from a state possessing an insignificant navy and merchant marine and whose marine interests lay primarily in coastal waters into a state possessing a formidable naval capability, a major high seas fishing fleet and merchant marine, and worldwide maritime interests has been as unexpected as it was rapid. No other country has experienced changes of such magnitude in these respects in so brief a period and, concomitantly, has been obliged to grapple with their legal and policy implications.

In order to facilitate comparison with non-Soviet doctrine and practice, this study treats each legal regime within the traditional subdivisions found in most Western treatises and casebooks. Since Soviet materials do not always fit neatly into Western categories, a certain amount of stretching and pushing, appropriately noted, has been necessary.

In exploring the topics that make up this study, the author has been guided by the proposition that the approach of a given country to international law cannot be understood without an appreciation of the historical experience and domestic legal setting in which that approach evolved. Consequently, considerable attention is devoted to historical Russian attitudes toward the legal regime of the seas and to the body of Tsarist and Soviet statutes, other normative acts and documents, treaties, and judicial decisions relating to maritime affairs.

The suggestion that historical perspective is essential to understanding contemporary Soviet approaches to international law should not be construed as an argument on behalf of historical determinism. It merely calls attention to the fact that in addition to its current body of state practice, legislation in force, and particular status in the international system, a country's attitude toward international law is also comprised of words, documents, and experiences accumulated over many centuries. Its history embodies the sum of that state's relations with other entities in the international community, its aspirations and reverses, its victories and defeats, its strengths and vulnerabilities.

For readers who are not well acquainted with the development of international law in Russia, the following background information may be helpful. It is offered in full knowledge that research in this area is wholly inadequate in order to provide some perspective for the succeeding chapters.

The Development of International Law in Prerevolutionary Russia

The Bolshevik Revolution of 1917 purported to make a complete break with Russian "bourgeois" institutions and values. For certain purposes the Union of Soviet Socialist Republics is deemed to be the legal successor of the Russian Empire, but Soviet international lawyers sharply differentiate between Tsarist and Soviet periods of international legal history. Although there is no aversion to citing prerevolutionary Russian legal writings or practices and there is obvious national pride in the "progressive role" Russia had in the formation or codification of international legal norms, Soviet jurists have been reluctant to acknowledge any organic continuity between Russian and Soviet approaches to international law.

Even though the Russian theory and practice of international law have not been the object of systematic study, it is clear that the practice of international law greatly antedated the development of publicists to clarify and systematize norms of international conduct. Russian state practice thus created its own body of law and custom, differing in many essential respects from that of other European or Asian entities, long before the emergence of a Russian jurisprudence of international law.[3]

Russia's entrance into the European family of nations is traditionally ascribed to the latter portion of the reign of Peter the Great, in the early eighteenth century. But the principles and practices identified with the growth of the law of nations were well-known in tenth-century Kievan Russia, which on at least four occasions had entered into treaty relations with the Eastern Roman Empire (Byzantium) in the aftermath of successful military campaigns.[4] The treaty of 945, which confirmed and expanded upon the earlier treaties, included provisions regulating the disposition of mutual offenses, murders, thefts, and other crimes committed by nationals of one state against those of the other. The parties agreed to extradite criminals upon the complaint of either government regardless of the protests of the accused. Nationals of the contracting parties were accorded equal or special protection of the law of the receiving state. In the event of bankruptcy of a Russian merchant, for example, the treaty gave his foreign creditors priority over Russian creditors. Should a Russian national in Byzantium die intestate, the treaties provided that his estate would be returned to his relatives in Russia, unless an heir were designated in writing, in which case the estate would go directly to that heir.

Russian treatment of aliens during this period was in many ways in advance of practices in Western Europe. Russia did not recognize the Germanic institutions of *Wildfang,* which permitted local authorities to seize a foreigner and make him a serf, or *Strandrecht,* under which shipwrecked foreigners, together with their stranded goods, belonged to the lord of the land along the coast where the boat went aground; nor did Russia recognize the widespread *droit d'aubaine,* under which the feudal lord, and later the king, confiscated the property of an alien who died within his jurisdiction. Under the Russian treaty of 911 with Byzantium, the parties undertook a positive duty to assist shipwrecked merchants of the respective states.

These treaties were contracted on the basis of equality. Oaths not to violate the instrument were sworn by both sides. The treaty of 945 is known to have been transcribed in duplicate and submitted

3. See V. E. Grabar, *Materialy k istorii literatury mezhdunarodnogo prava v Rossii (1647–1917)* (Moscow: izd-vo Akademii nauk SSSR, 1958); F. I. Kozhevnikov, *Russkoe gosudarstvo i mezhdunarodnoe pravo* (Moscow: Iurizdat Ministerstva iustitsii SSSR, 1947).

4. These treaties, concluded respectively in 907, 911, 945, and 971, are translated in S. H. Cross and O. P. Sherbowitz–Wetzor, *The Russian Primary Chronicle: Laurentian Text* (Cambridge: The Medieval Academy of America, 1953).

by the Russian envoys to their ruler for ratification and promulgation.[5]

Relations among Russian and foreign merchants were often governed by commercial treaties. In 1006 the Russians signed a commercial convention with the Volga Bulgars. The northern Russian cities of Novgorod and Smolensk contracted commercial agreements respectively in 1189 and 1229 with several German cities. In addition to commercial clauses, these treaties contained provisions treating crimes by Russians against aliens and *vice versa.*[6]

Throughout the Kievan period, diplomatic relations were carried on by embassies and envoys extraordinary. Diplomats were granted special protection by custom and by treaty provisions.

Even the Mongol conquest of Russia in about 1240, which effectively cut off much of Russia from Western influence for nearly two and a half centuries, left its imprint upon Muscovite diplomatic practice.[7] When Muscovite princes finally threw off the "Tatar yoke," Western ambassadors journeying to Muscovy discovered that the Russian concept of a government's duties toward a foreign envoy differed markedly from that in Europe. In the Russian view an ambassador was a guest of the ruler to whom he was accredited. The ruler was obliged to provide the ambassador and his suite with free transportation, lodging, food and drink, and to guarantee the ambassador's personal safety. In diplomatic ceremony great attention was paid to the exchange of lavish gifts. Russian practice also forbade a foreign emissary to be armed, even with ceremonial sword, when received in audience by the Tsar. Many of these peculiarities were abolished by Peter the Great. However, even into the nineteenth century, Western diplomats professed to detect remnants of practices traceable to the Tatar period.

As Tatar domination and influence receded, an embryonic Russian state emerged, consolidated its authority, claimed to succeed Byzantium as the head of the Eastern Orthodox Church, and slowly expanded its international relations with Europe and the Orient. In the absence of jurists, it was left to Muscovite diplomats to prescribe and generalize state practice. The creation of an Ambassadorial Department [*prikaz*] in 1549 facilitated the systematic compilation and pres-

---

5. *Ibid.,* pp. 73–77; George Vernadsky, *A History of Russia: Kievan Russia* (New Haven: Yale University Press, 1948), II, p. 317; M. Taube, "Études sur le Développement Historique du Droit International dans l'Europe Orientale," *Recueil des Cours,* XI (1926): 412–27.

6. See L. K. Goetz, *Deutsch-Russische Handelsvertrage des Mittelalters* (Hamburg: Friederichsen & Co., 1916).

7. George Vernadsky, *A History of Russia: The Mongols and Russia* (New Haven: Yale University Press, 1953), III, p. 387.

ervation of documents recording international legal practices of the period. While these documents still have not been adequately investigated, they indicate that Russia clearly had an awareness of international custom and treaty practice.

Russia recognized the privileges and immunities of ambassadors, although on occasion the arrest of a foreign ambassador was permitted as an act of reprisal. Russian diplomats in this period were involved in several disputes over the scope of exemption from customs duties, particularly with regard to distinguishing ambassadorial baggage from goods intended for sale. In 1501 Russia lodged a vigorous protest with Lithuania against duties being levied on a Russian ambassador en route to Western Europe. Similarly, in 1667 Russia received satisfaction after a prolonged quarrel with France over charges imposed upon the Russian embassy to Paris.[8]

Documents of that period also illustrate Russian attitudes toward the laws of war (wars must be "just"; a formal declaration of war must be delivered to the enemy), the concept of protectorates, the legal status of aliens, and freedom of the seas. However, even though Russian diplomats had definite ideas of norms obligatory in the conduct of states, the terminology used was often different from that of the *jus gentium* of Europe.

Peter the Great's turn toward the West was followed by a substantial importation of European international legal institutions and practices. However, authentic Russian contributions in the opposite direction occurred most dramatically when Catherine II took the first practical step in 1780 toward codifying principles of maritime warfare by developing the celebrated Armed Neutralities of 1780 and 1800. Intended as the bases of a general code for naval warfare, these principles ultimately received almost universal acceptance in the Declaration of Paris of 1856, despite some inconstancy by Catherine and her successors.

Tsar Alexander I was a founding father of the international order established at the Congress of Vienna, and for a time was an able exponent of disarmament, control of the slave trade, and the codification of international law. In 1820 he undertook what proved to be the first in a series of international arbitrations among states during the nineteenth century by serving as umpire in an Anglo–American dispute over the ownership of slaves in American territory previously occupied

8. Legal writs and processes brought against the Russian ambassador in London were interpreted by the envoy as a personal affront to the tsar and led to the enactment by Parliament in 1708 of the Act of Anne, which protected foreign diplomats from such harassment. *BFSP,* I, 903.

by British forces. Russia eventually played a very influential role in drafting the Convention for the Pacific Settlement of International Disputes of 1899.

Codification of the rules of land warfare also owes much to the initiative and interest of the Russian government. Tsar Alexander II convoked the abortive Brussels Conference of 1874 to draft a comprehensive set of rules for land warfare;[9] eventually the Brussels draft was adopted at the Hague Peace Conference of 1899, convened at the instance of Tsar Nicholas II, who had hoped the nations also would consent to his broad proposals for disarmament and the peaceful settlement of disputes.

On a less positive note, the Tsarist government contributed to the international legal principle of material "change of circumstances" as a justification for the unilateral repudiation of treaty obligations by declaring in October 1870 to be no longer bound by those articles of the Treaty of Paris of 1856 which neutralized the Black Sea or required Russia to limit its naval forces in that sea. A circular note sent by the Russian Ministry of Foreign Affairs to the other signatory powers alluded to "repeated violations" and to changes in the political situation caused by the union of the Danubian principalities—to which the Great Powers acquiesced even though the union breached other international agreements—and by developments in the technology of naval warfare introduced by iron-clad vessels.[10] While Russia obtained the concessions desired with regard to the Black Sea at a conference of 1871, the Russian ambassador signed a protocol declaring that a power may not liberate itself from the engagements of a treaty nor modify its provisions without the consent of the other parties.[11]

The development of international law as a subject of scholarly and professional inquiry and the creation of a body of international lawyers occurred much later in Russia than in Western Europe. Muscovite interest in Western military art seems to have been responsible for the first Russian exposure to European international legal scholar-

9. For a rather partisan account of Russian participation in the Brussels conference, written by a member of the Russian delegation partly to refute "turcophiles" who unfavorably contrasted Russian proposals at the conference with the behavior of Russian soldiers in the Turko–Russian War of 1877–78, see F. F. Martens, *Vostochnaia voina i briussel'skaia konferentsiia 1874–1878 g.* (St. Petersburg: Tipo. A. Benke, 1879).

10. The text of the note is published in E. A. Adamov (ed.), *Sbornik dogovorov Rossii s drugimi gosudarstvami 1856–1917* (Moscow: Gospolitizdat, 1952), p. 103.

11. *BFSP*, LXI, 1198.

ship. A German work on the science of warfare which briefly discussed the treatment of prisoners of war, published in Russian translation in 1647, is regarded as the first Russian translation of a treatise on international law.[12] Peter the Great ordered copies of Grotius' *On the Law of War and Peace* (1625), Pufendorf's *Juris Naturae et Gentium* (1672), and Wicquefort's *The Ambassador and His Functions* imported and translated. These translations were available only to state officials in manuscript form and were never published.[13] Libraries of Russian diplomats, however, did contain these and other European treatises in their original languages and, judging by official documents of the period, the diplomats obviously were acquainted with their contents.

In 1717 the first original work of an unofficial character on international law appeared in the Russian language. Written by the Russian diplomat, P. P. Shafirov, and simply entitled *Discourses,* the volume assayed the legal grounds for the war then being fought against Sweden. Shafirov severely criticized Sweden for violations of the laws of war. Among the questions Shafirov treated were: (1) status of diplomatic agents of belligerents upon the outbreak of war; (2) status of subjects of belligerents on enemy territory; (3) appeals to the population; (4) military activity of combatants and of the peaceful population; (5) capitulations; (6) status of prisoners of war; and (7) reprisals.[14]

12. Wallhausen, *Kriegskunst zu Fusz* (3 vols., 1615–17). By order of the tsar, a German manual on military art published in 1565–73 was translated in 1606–7 and reworked in 1621. Devoted primarily to technical aspects of military operations, it also dealt in part with the treatment of prisoners of war. However, the Russian translation was not published until 1777, when the manuscript was rediscovered in the Kremlin Armory.

13. Since the translators were not familiar with legal terminology, the translations of the seventeenth century were of poor quality. A complete translation of Grotius did not appear in Russian until 1956.

14. An English translation of this work, published in London in 1722, identified the author only by his initials ("P. S."). The publishers described the tract as a "discourse concerning the just reasons which his Czarist Majesty, Peter I, . . . had for beginning the War against the King of Sweden, Charles XII, *Anno* 1700, . . . and which of the two Parties most observed the Rules established among Christian and polite Nations in carrying on the War," the whole having been "drawn up in the Year 1716, . . . and printed and published the Year following 1717 . . ." Shafirov declared:

> That the Proceedings on the part of his Czarist Majesty during the whole War were suitable to all Christian Moderation and Clemency, and for the greater part according to the Custom and Maxims of all civilized and Christian Nations, and that if on certain Occasions some Rigour was used, it was mostly done by way of Reprizals for the Cruelties committed by the *Swedes* against his Czarist Majesty's Forces and Subjects: On the contrary that on the Swedish side the said War was, from the beginning till this present time, carried on, not at all in a manner used among civilized Na-

After the death of Peter the Great, there was little progress in developing a science of international law until the reign of Catherine II. No more foreign works were translated and no original Russian treatises published, although Vice-Chancellor A. P. Bestuzhev-Riumin did draw up a "Declaration" on the immunities of diplomatic agents. Nor did official literature contain vivid diplomatic documents such as those of earlier years. However, a periodical literature on international law and diplomatic history did begin to emerge, and the foundation for the teaching of international law was laid with the opening of the Academy of Sciences in 1725 and the founding of Moscow University in 1755.

Under Catherine II, Russia entered a brief period of enlightenment and intellectual stimulation from Western Europe. Although the works of Wolff and Vattel were not translated, their views were represented in the writings of a faithful follower, D. Nettel'bladt.[15] Russian diplomatic historians exploited the archives of the Ministry of Foreign Affairs to produce seminal works on the early history of Russian diplomatic and international legal practice. Two works of a theoretical character were published: V. T. Zolotinskii's *Abridgement of Natural Law* and V. F. Malinovskii's *Discourse on War and Peace.*[16] International law began to appear as part of courses in natural law given at Moscow University. By the early nineteenth century, several textbooks on natural law, incorporating discussions of international law, had been published, primarily by foreign professors invited to teach in Russia. The majority of these were published in German and Latin; only one was written in Russian, although eventually most were translated.

Most of the writings of Russian publicists cited in the present work date from the last forty years of the Russian Empire, the golden age of Tsarist scholarship in international law. By then the pressures for domestic legal reform in Russia had attained considerable success; a class of Russian jurists, many educated in Europe, emerged, and the study of international law received correspondingly greater attention from able jurists. Departments of international law were formed

---

tions, but rather with inhuman Cruelty and bitter Animosity against his Czarist Majesty.

[P. P. Shafirov], "A Discourse Concerning the Causes of the War Between Russia and Sweden," in *The Present State of Russia,* ed. [F. C. Weber] (London: W. Taylor, etc., 1722), II, pp. 235–351, 240.

15. A complete translation of Vattel was not published in Russian until 1960.

16. The latter was a pacifist tract which the peace movement rediscovered, translated, and circulated throughout Europe in the 1850s.

within the law faculties of universities at Moscow, Petersburg, Iur'ev, Kharkov, Kazan, and Kiev. In addition, international law was taught in universities at Odessa, Warsaw, Tomsk, and Helsinki. Other institutions of higher learning, such as the Petersburg Polytechnic Institute, the Moscow Commercial Institute, the Military Law Academy, and the Nikolaevsk Maritime Academy, had faculties to teach international law.

Russian international lawyers published extensively on all aspects of public and private international law; German and French influence was especially strong in Russian international legal circles, and all the major European "schools" had their Russian followers. Among the better known Russian international lawyers were T. F. Stepanov, M. N. Kapustin, D. I. Kachenovskii, A. N. Stoianov, F. F. Martens, N. M. Korkunov, L. A. Kamarovskii, and N. A. Zakharov, V. A. Ul'ianitskii, O. O. Eikhel'man, V. P. Danevskii, and P. E. Kazanskii.

The most renowned of Russian publicists, especially abroad, was F. F. Martens. Martens held the chair of international law at the University of St. Petersburg, became a member of the State Council of Foreign Affairs with the rank of Privy Councillor, was a Russian delegate to many international conferences, was a member of the Hague Permanent Court of Arbitration, served several terms as the vice-president of the Institute of International Law, received honorary doctorates from Cambridge, Oxford, and Yale, and edited a 15-volume collection of Russian treaties. He authored several treatises on international law, the most important being *International Law of Civilized Nations,* which went through five Russian editions and was widely translated abroad (but not into English).

A Note on Soviet International Legal Materials

Although one need not espouse some of the questionable methods of kremlinology, there are certain indicators and "rules" which Western analysts have found useful and reliable in studying Soviet materials. Some of these implicitly have guided the selection and analysis of data in this study. While it may be an imposition on students of Soviet affairs to outline them briefly, international lawyers not familiar with Soviet lore may find these observations helpful.

To the average Western reader of Soviet international legal media, Soviet scholarship has consisted largely of monotonous, politically oriented works, ponderous and self-righteous in style, employing stereotyped ideological and political formulas and terminology. The legal analysis of concrete problems is rudimentary, and there is often little indication that the author is familiar with Soviet or foreign professional literature or is fully conversant with the applicable legal principles. At the same time, such writings are thought to be "official," in the sense that everything published in the USSR must pass through censorship; since the government must approve of what Soviet international lawyers write, it is believed that their writings must reflect official opinion and have important predictive value for Soviet foreign policy.

Both of these impressions can be misleading. To the extent they are accurate, however, they provide an important basis for interpreting the writings of Soviet jurists.

The task of the analyst has been complicated in some respects and eased in others by the impressive increase in the quantity and quality of Soviet international legal writing since the death of Stalin. The style of legal expression is less stereotyped, the level of discourse more sophisticated, and the citation of primary and secondary sources more frequent. Many Western international lawyers, being unfamiliar with the scholastic style of discourse in socialist legal media, have erred in their appraisals of the professional competence of Soviet jurists.

The "official" character of Soviet international legal scholarship has been evaluated simplistically in the West. It is true that Soviet international lawyers do not publicly criticize or debate the legal dimensions of Soviet foreign policy and routinely endorse all Soviet behavior in international relations. It would be inconceivable for a Soviet jurist, for example, to criticize the Soviet occupation of Czechoslovakia on legal grounds, although silence can also be eloquent.

But it does not follow that the views of a Soviet jurist necessarily represent those of his government or that the Soviet government is prepared to act in conformity with principles espoused by jurists. The reaction of many Western international lawyers to the publication by a Soviet publishing house in 1961 of an English translation of a standard Soviet textbook of international law is an interesting case in point. The textbook in question was first published in the USSR in 1957 under the collective authorship of leading Soviet international lawyers. On the title page it was noted that the textbook had been approved by the USSR Ministry of Education for instructional use in the university law faculties. Some foreign observers apparently concluded the notice of approval gave the volume an official character superior to that of other Soviet publications on international law, and to this day one finds references in Western literature to "official textbooks."

Actually, there are several textbooks by different groups of authors which have been approved for instructional use. All are rather elementary, since the Soviet law student is the equivalent of an advanced college undergraduate in the United States, and these texts provide his first exposure to public international law. Although they are valuable sources for understanding Soviet legal doctrine, they must be read in conjunction with the more important specialized literature. In many cases the views contained in the textbooks are outmoded or simply not accepted by other Soviet jurists. One must make subjective, comparative judgments on the basis of the literature as a whole.

In another respect, Soviet international legal writing *is* official. Many positions taken by Soviet jurists are inspired expressly by Soviet diplomacy; a given work may in fact be the equivalent of a brief for a particular policy of the Soviet government.

The historic waters doctrine is an excellent example of the need to distinguish between the two concepts of "official." If the views of textbook writers were official in the sense that the Soviet government was prepared to assert the rights claimed by Soviet jurists, one would have expected the northern Arctic seas to have been closed to foreign vessels. Soviet jurists insisted that these "seas of the bay type" were internal waters. Yet, such a claim was not even mentioned by the Soviet government when American vessels entered those waters. Nevertheless, the doctrine of "seas of the bay type" originated in the early years of the Cold War at the behest of the government as part of a diplomatic campaign to attain a special status for these waters when it came time to draft international conventions defining the legal regime of the sea. Other examples of policy advocacy will be encountered during this study.

The use of doctrinal writings in the USSR to advocate particular policies can give an exaggerated impression of Soviet disaffection with the existing world order. It is therefore essential to ascertain whether Soviet doctrine corresponds to legislation in force and state practice. As this study seeks to demonstrate, the importance of Soviet legislation and diplomatic documents for an understanding of the Soviet approach to the law of the sea is difficult to exaggerate.

Those who follow closely the turgid prose of public Soviet media have found that abstruse, convoluted ideological terminology actually serves as a highly sophisticated system of communication through which policy is debated and criticized within the Communist world. To understand such discussions, one must be familiar with the protocol employed by Communist media: what have been the customary formulas and practices? How does a particular formulation modify or contradict previous formulations? In the present study, for example, considerable attention is given to the various formulations in Soviet textbooks and treatises regarding the nature and extent of coastal jurisdiction seaward and the existence of a right of innocent passage in international law. Changes in formulations correlated with positions assumed by Soviet diplomats during the drafting of the Geneva Convention on the Territorial Sea and Contiguous Zone. Similarly, the various formulations of the closed sea principle revealed considerable concern in Soviet legal circles over the scope and viability of that concept. The omission of the standard closed sea formulation and the insertion of an abbreviated list of historic waters in a Soviet treatise published in 1969 indicates that both doctrines are in disrepute in some quarters of the Soviet legal establishment and are undergoing substantial revision.

Other symbolic evidence is also helpful. Experienced readers of the Soviet daily press know that politically significant articles are generally printed on the inside pages at or near the bottom. When in October 1968 *Izvestia* published an article near the bottom of page two about the imminent commencement of oral argument before the International Court of Justice in the *North Sea Continental Shelf* cases, the item was intended to signal that something germane was about to be announced in the USSR. Two days later, the Soviet Union, Poland, and the German Democratic Republic signed a joint declaration on the continental shelf of the Baltic Sea which foreshadowed the substance of the Soviet judge's dissenting opinion in the cases.

It is common knowledge that editorials in the Soviet press signed "Observer" are especially reflective of the views of the Soviet leadership and unsigned editorials even more so. Certain pseudonyms also are used to signal authoritative publications. Readers of the leading Soviet legal journal, *Sovetskoe gosudarstvo i pravo,* discovered in the early 1950s that "S. Borisov" wrote particularly cogent critiques of decisions of the International Court of Justice. This turned out to be the *nom de plume* of the Soviet judge on the court, S. B. Krylov.

Less bizarre clues may be equally important. Articles by leading authorities are usually of greater significance than those of unknown persons. Yet an individual's meteoric thrust to prominence may be of political import. In 1950 the editors of *Sovetskoe gosudarstvo i pravo* signalled the beginning of a vigorous campaign on behalf of the closed sea doctrine by publicizing the defense of a doctoral dissertation on the regime of the Baltic Straits.

Articles published under institutional auspices can be an indication of contending views of ministries with regard to a given issue. The appearance in 1967 of an unsigned lead editorial in *Rybnoe khoziaistvo* condemning the seizure of Soviet fishing vessels by Argentina demonstrated that agency's concern over expansive claims to coastal jurisdiction, a concern not so widely shared at that time in other departments of the Soviet government.

A change in the composition of the editorial board of a legal journal might signify anything from a major realignment of political views to the mere retirement of an individual for purely personal reasons. A formulation of the right of innocent passage in a textbook may constitute a substantively different Soviet interpretation of an international convention or merely careless editing on the part of the authors. All judgments of this character are interpretive, subject to error, exaggeration, and misuse. A well-informed analyst should know much about the intellectual history of the Communist movement, Marxist–Leninist ideology and its transmutations, the protocol of Soviet media, the history of Soviet politics and foreign policy, the structure and operation of the Soviet legal system, and international law.

Chapter 2

THE LEGAL REGIME
OF TERRITORIAL WATERS

The boundaries and the regime of Soviet territorial waters have been shaped by several factors, the foremost of which has been national security. Russian and Soviet naval power was, until recently, not regarded as formidable. Even now the highly respected Soviet navy is not a "deep-blue" fleet capable of effectively challenging its American counterpart, although it could be in the future.[1]

The Tsarist fleet operated primarily in the Baltic and Black Seas against Sweden and Turkey, respectively. Time and again during the late eighteenth and the nineteenth centuries access to Russian ports was interrupted by hostile naval forces with comparative ease. In 1856 Russia was prohibited from keeping warships in the Black Sea as a price of terminating the Crimean War. Her modest acquisition of naval forces in the late nineteenth century, greatly exaggerated and over-rated at the time, was decimated in a single engagement with the Japanese navy during the Russo–Japanese War. As one observer commented with considerable understatement, "It is hardly ever possible in the . . . history of the Russian navy to say that that service enjoyed good fortune."[2]

During the Russian Revolution and ensuing civil war, allied naval power off Russian coasts enabled the United Kingdom, France, the United States, and Japan to intervene, although briefly and ineffectively, while the Soviet regime struggled to consolidate its authority. Later, control of the seas by the Western powers restricted Bolshevik freedom of action in pursuing revolutionary ambitions in Poland, Germany, and the Balkans.[3]

Soviet weakness in the Baltic theater was a major factor in Soviet

---

1. An excellent history of the development of Soviet naval strategy and capabilities is Robert W. Herrick, *Soviet Naval Strategy: Fifty Years of Theory and Practice* (Annapolis, Md.: U.S. Naval Institute, 1968).

2. David Woodward, *The Russians at Sea* (London: William Kimber, 1965), p. 165.

3. Soviet protests against the unauthorized entry of foreign warships into Russian ports and against the harassment of the remnants of Russian shipping appear with some frequency in diplomatic documents of the period. See, for example, *Dokumenty*, I, 80, 85, 247, 347–48.

policy toward Finland and the Baltic states from 1939–41, as well as toward Turkey in the Black Sea from the 1920's to the present. The proximity of naval forces of the North Atlantic Treaty Organization to Soviet coasts continues to evoke official protests and critical press commentary, even though the Soviet Union has itself become a large naval power.[4]

Economic considerations have been a second important factor. The Russian and Soviet merchant marine has always lacked sufficient capacity to carry all domestic seaborne trade. In the Tsarist period, Russian vessels had to be purchased primarily from abroad because the country's iron and steel producing centers were situated far from Russian coasts. Wooden sailing vessels still comprised more than one-third of the Russian merchant marine in 1914, and these were obsolete, at best suited for cabotage.[5] Soviet dependence upon foreign bottoms for maritime trade became more acute with the large-scale destruction of Russian merchant ships during World War I and their subsequent seizure by White Armies during the civil war. The shortage of vessels, coupled with a desperate need for industrial imports, explained the "warm attitude of the Soviet state toward the rules applied by bourgeois states."[6]

Coastal fisheries and other marine resources were of immediate concern to Tsarist and Bolshevik authorities. The Russian fishing industry had been concentrated primarily in inland waters and coastal seas. By 1890 the annual catch in inland waters began to decline sharply despite a vigorous consumer demand for fish products. Although rich fishery resources abounded off Russian coasts in the northern and far eastern seas, the low level of fishery technology, underdeveloped methods of processing, preserving, and transporting fish, and the lack of government incentive contributed to Russian underutilization of these fisheries in a period when foreign operations in these seas were expanding rapidly. Russian imports of fish increased five times in value from 1900 to 1913; a prime source of the imports was Norway, whose fishermen were especially active off Russia's Murmansk coast.[7] One Russian response, to be examined in detail below, was to

4. See, for example, A. Pogodin, "Bonn's Strategic Plans in the Baltic," *International Affairs* [Moscow], no. 9 (1961), 33–37.

5. Margaret Miller, *The Economic Development of Russia, 1905–1914* (2d ed.; London: Frank Cass & Co., 1967), pp. 179–80.

6. V. F. Meshera, *Morskoe pravo* (Moscow: izd-vo Morskoi transport, 1959), III, p. 5.

7. Miller, *Economic Development of Russia*, pp. 268–73. Also see V. M. Shparlinskii, *The Fishing Industry of the U.S.S.R.* (U.S. Department of Commerce Publication OTS 63–11122; Jerusalem: Israel Program for Scientific Translations, 1964), pp. 2–7.

exclude foreign fishing within specified zones. The attitude of the Soviet government toward foreign fishing in its coastal waters was even more unyielding by virtue of its concern to protect what in 1917 had become Socialist property, and prior restrictions on foreign fishing were confirmed and broadened.

A third factor has been the pattern of historical discoveries, explorations, and conquests.[8] The coasts of the White Sea were settled by Russians at least ten centuries ago. Exploration and settlement of the Arctic coasts by Russians goes back to at least the thirteenth century and possibly earlier. But the Black, Baltic, Azov, Aral, and Caspian Seas have been subordinated to partial Russian control only since about 1700. Although the far eastern shores began to be colonized late in the seventeenth century, effective Russian control dates only from the second half of the nineteenth century. While for the most part the Russian advance toward the sea was a gradual, prolonged, and tentative process, there is, nevertheless, a substantial record of Russian and Soviet explorations and expeditions on which to base claims to expanses of coastal waters.

Concept of Territorial Waters

TERMINOLOGY

In 1960 a Soviet legal scholar commented that there is no firmly established legal classification of water expanses along Soviet coasts.[9] This scholar might also have added that the problem of the legal classification of coastal waters has always plagued Russian international legal scholarship.

Russian international lawyers were strongly influenced by continental jurisprudence in the formulation and systematization of legal norms, including the law of the sea. The kind of diversity of opinion among Western publicists concerning the legal nature of territorial waters existed in Russian writings as well, but in a more complicated way.

The waters adjacent to state territory are commonly divided into two categories: (a) territorial, and (b) internal, interior, inland, or national. Within the waters of category (a), international law recog-

8. See F. A. Golder, *Russian Expansion on the Pacific 1641–1850* (Cleveland, Ohio: Arthur H. Clark Co., 1914), pp. 250–66; R. J. Kerner, *The Urge to the Sea* (Berkeley: University of California Press, 1946); Mairin Mitchell, *The Maritime History of Russia, 848–1948* (London: Sidgwick & Jackson, 1949); Yuri Semyonov, *Siberia: Its Conquest and Development* (Baltimore: Helicon Press, 1963).

9. S. A. Malinin, "K voprosu o pravovoi klassifikatsii vodnykh prostranstv," *Morskoe pravo i praktika*, XLVI (1960), 13.

nizes that foreign vessels and nationals may assert certain rights against the coastal state, particularly the right of innocent passage, whereas the coastal state exercises absolute and complete national sovereignty over the waters specified in the second category. Included within category (b) are harbors, ports, internal gulfs and bays, lakes, and rivers. Following the example of some continental publicists, Russian international lawyers posited a third category; in their view, contiguous waters should be classified as: (a) coastal; (b) territorial; and (c) inland or national.

The "inland or national" waters referred to fresh water lakes and rivers, which clearly were within the sovereign authority of the state. The distinction, however, between the "coastal" [*beregovoe*] and the "territorial" [*territorial'noe*] seas was the source of endless confusion, which Russian publicists were unable to dispel even among themselves. As one jurist lamented, "neither Russian nor foreign literature discusses the differences between the concepts of coastal and territorial seas."[10]

In Russian texts, the term "territorial" sea or waters generally referred to what in modern practice would be classified as internal waters: for example, the waters of gulfs, bays, roadsteads, and other sea waters enclosed by the possessions of a single state. Martens defined territorial waters as "that portion of coastal waters wedged into the land territory of the state."[11] The littoral state was said to enjoy "significantly greater rights" within territorial waters than those accorded by international law within "coastal" waters;[12] and in the view of several Russian scholars, the coastal state possessed the same unlimited sovereignty over the "territorial sea" as it did over land.[13]

The term "coastal" [*beregovoe*] sea in Russian literature described the contiguous belt of waters over which the littoral state exercised limited sovereignty: for example, that expanse of sea which today we call "territorial waters." To compound the confusion, many, perhaps most, Russian jurists used the terms "coastal" and "territorial" waters interchangeably, without regard to the implications of such usage.[14] Tsarist legislation was equally inconsistent in its termi-

10. V. E. Grabar, *Materialy k istorii literatury mezhdunarodnogo prava v Rossii (1647–1917)* (Moscow: izd-vo AN SSSR, 1958), p. 407.

11. F. F. Martens, *Sovremennoe mezhdunarodnoe pravo tsivilizovannykh narodov'* (5th ed.; St. Petersburg: Tipo. A. Benke, 1904–5), I, p. 391. In conformity with this definition, Martens attributed the Gulf of Finland and the Gulf of Riga to the "territorial waters" of Russia.

12. Grabar, *Materialy*, p. 407.

13. I. Ovchinnikov, "Territorial'noe more," *Morskoi sbornik*, CCXC, no. 1 (1899), 81.

14. See A. M. Gorovtsev', *Slovar' kratkoi entsiklopedii mezhdunarodnogo prava* (St. Petersburg: Tipo. Trenke i Friuso, 1909), p. 8.

nology. Among the terms to be found were: "sea waters" [*morskie vody*]; "coastal belt of waters" [*pribrezhnaia polosa vod*]; "territorial sea" [*territorial'noe more*]; "water expanse" [*vodnoe prostranstvo*]; "territorial belt" [*territorial'naia polosa*]; and others. No pattern of systematic usage was in evidence.

Soviet legislators and publicists have employed several terms for waters washing Soviet shores. These include: "coastal waters" [*pribrezhnye vody*]; "territorial belt of waters"; "sea border belt" [*morskaia pogranichnaia polosa*]; "sea belt"; "coastal waters" [*beregovye vody*]. "Territorial waters" has been used most often by Soviet legislators, although not in the majority of instances. That term was used in 8 of 22 normative acts expressly pertaining to questions of Soviet territorial waters and in 35 treaties and agreements concluded by the RSFSR, the Ukraine, and the USSR with other states prior to 1954. The term was not employed, however, in the majority of normative acts (14 of 22); in particular, it was not used in the 1927 statute on the state boundary, which after 1948 was cited by the Soviet government as having codified the 12-mile breadth of Soviet territorial waters.

In a letter of July 20, 1929, concerning territorial waters sent by the government of the Soviet Union to the Preparatory Committee for the 1930 Hague Conference on the Codification of International Law, it was noted: "As regards the difference between territorial waters and coastal zones, Soviet law has not given any interpretation of the various terms it employs in this matter."[15]

In 1954 a Soviet jurist urged his colleagues to unite in using "territorial waters" because that term predominated in Soviet treaty practice and diplomatic correspondence and "doubtless . . . will be used in our further legislation relating to territorial waters." He criticized those

15. League of Nations, Conference for the Codification of International Law, *Bases of Discussion Drawn Up for the Conference by the Preparatory Committee: Supplement to Volume II—Territorial Waters,* Doc. No. c.74(b).-M.39(b).1929.v, p. 2; *SS&D,* VI (1969), 31. The expression "territorial waters" was also employed inconsistently in Soviet diplomatic practice. A variety of formulae described the waters off Soviet coasts. In a Note of April 17, 1918, the Soviet government requested Germany to refrain from hostile actions with regard to Russian warships "sailing between Russian harbors or within the limits of Russian territorial waters." *Dokumenty,* I, 247. In this instance "territorial waters" seemed to be equated with internal waters. A Note of June 6, 1918, insisted that British warships could not be permitted "in waters contiguous to the northern coast of Russia." *Ibid.,* I, 348. A Note of June 8, 1919, to Great Britain mentioned "our territorial waters of the Gulf of Finland," implying a status of internal waters. *Dokumenty,* II, 190. In Notes of April 15, and May 4, 1920, the Soviet government distinguished between territorial and internal waters, declaring the former to extend to three nautical miles. *Ibid.,* II, 457, 500. Reference was made in Notes of June 5 and 20, 1920, to Persia to the territorial waters of the Caspian Sea, the meaning being unclear. *Ibid.,* II, 557, 580.

Soviet international lawyers "who attempt to defend the term 'territorial sea,' which has not existed and does not exist in Soviet practice and which does not predominate in international practice."[16]

Nikolaev was not engaging in idle bickering over semantic nuances. In the past many Soviet jurists had denied the existence of a 12-mile belt of territorial waters, pointing to the inconsistencies in Soviet legislative terminology. Some Soviet jurists also regarded territorial waters as part of the high seas over which the coastal state possessed certain limited rights. These writers preferred terminology which stressed the relationship between territorial waters and the high seas rather than their relationship to the coastal state.

Most Soviet writers adopted "territorial waters,"[17] and it was incorporated into Article 3 of the 1960 statute on the state boundary.[18]

The 1956 naval international law manual preferred "territorial waters" because it more correctly reflected the "nature of the waters designated and . . . the connection of the sea belt with the territory and with the 'internal sea waters' of the coastal state."[19] That term has been retained in the 1966 naval international law manual.[20]

But other jurists have pointed to the usage of territorial "sea" [*more*] in the 1958 Geneva Convention on the Territorial Sea. They find nothing in Soviet practice or legislation which obliges Soviet writers to refrain from using that term. Indeed, the 1968 Edict on the Continental Shelf of the USSR refers to the territorial "sea" instead of territorial waters.[21] However, this usage signifies merely a desire to conform to the language of the Geneva conventions and most assuredly is not intended to denote a return to legal views of the interwar period.

16. A. N. Nikolaev, *Problema territorial'nykh vod v mezhdunarodnom prave* (Moscow: Gosiurizdat, 1954), pp. 199–200.

17. Keilin, Kolodkin, Meshera, Nikolaev, and Uustal' were among those who preferred this term. However, in 1969 Nikolaev entitled his new monograph with the very term he had attacked fifteen years previously. See A. N. Nikolaev, *Territorial'noe more* (Moscow: izd-vo Mezhdunarodnye otnosheniia, 1969).

18. The official text of the Statute on the Protection of the State Boundary of the USSR, adopted August 5, 1960, appeared in *Vedomosti SSSR* (1960), no. 34, item 324. English texts are published in William E. Butler, *The Law of Soviet Territorial Waters* (New York: Frederick A. Praeger, 1967), pp. 111–25; *SS&D,* VI (1969), 45.

19. A. S. Bakhov (ed.), *Voenno-morskoi mezhdunarodno-pravovoi spravochnik* (Moscow: Voengiz, 1956), p. 56.

20. P. D. Barabolia *et. al., Voenno-morskoi mezhdunarodno-pravovoi spravochnik* (Moscow: Voenizdat, 1966).

21. See Article 1 of the Edict on the Continental Shelf of the USSR, adopted February 6, 1968, in *Vedomosti SSSR* (1968), no. 6, item 40; translated in *ILM,* VII (1968), 392; *SS&D,* VI (1970), 258. Both terms are used in Article 4 of the Fundamental Principles of Water Legislation of the USSR and Union Republics. *Izvestia,* December 11, 1970, p. 2.

DEFINITION OF TERRITORIAL WATERS

The legal nature of territorial waters (using that term henceforth in its modern sense), being distinguished both from land territory and from the high seas, occupies a somewhat transitional status. Two constructions of the legal nature of territorial waters are possible, and reflecting a similar division among Western jurists, two "schools" of thought have grown up around those constructions in Russian and Soviet jurisprudence. The first and perhaps the most influential school, led by F. F. Martens, considered territorial waters to be in the actual ownership [*sobstvennost'*] of the littoral state, a prolongation of coastal territory, and subject to its authority.[22] Martens' view was shared by Zakharov,[23] Kamarovskii,[24] and Ul'ianitskii.[25]

The second school, which was probably closer to prevailing Western views, defined territorial waters as that part of the high seas over which a coastal state may exercise jurisdiction for limited purposes relating to its national security, protection of navigation and public health, fiscal interests, fisheries, and cabotage. V. Sivers,[26] Stoianov,[27] and Grabar[28] supported this approach. A middle position was adopted by Kazanskii,[29] who considered territorial waters both a possession of the coastal state and a part of the high seas.

In Soviet literature of the interwar period, the second school predominated. Grabar wrote in the *Encyclopedia of Soviet Law* that the latter construction "has been adopted more and is more satisfactory."[30] V. A. Belli, who edited the Soviet naval international law manual in 1939, similarly defined territorial waters as part of the high

22. Martens, *Sovremennoe mezhdunarodnoe pravo*, I, pp. 386–87.
23. N. A. Zakharov, *Kurs obshchago mezhdunarodnogo prava* (Petrograd: Veisbrut, 1917), pp. 156–58.
24. L. A. Kamarovskii and V. A. Ul'ianitskii, *Mezhdunarodnoe pravo po lektsiiam* (Moscow: Universitetskaia tipo., 1908), pp. 82–84.
25. V. A. Ul'ianitskii, *Mezhdunarodnoe pravo* (Tomsk: Tipo. Sibir. t-va. pechatnogo dela, 1911), pp. 87–89. Ul'ianitskii wrote that the coastal sea is "that part of the high seas washing the possessions of the coastal state and over which it may exercise dominion [*gospodstvo*] from shore. . . . Despite coastal dominion over territorial [*sic*] waters, its territorial sovereignty over them is not unconditional. . . ." [right of innocent passage]. *Ibid.*, pp. 87–89.
26. V. Sivers, *Glavneishie svedeniia po morskomu mezhdunarodnomu pravu* (St. Petersburg: n.p., 1902), p. 5.
27. A. N. Stoianov, *Ocherki istorii i dogmatiki mezhdunarodnogo prava* (Kharkov: Universitetskoi tipo., 1875), p. 356.
28. V. E. Grabar, "Beregovoe more," *Novyi entsiklopedicheskii slovar'* (St. Petersburg: Brokganz & Efron, [1916]), V, col. 59–60.
29. P. E. Kazanskii, *Uchebnik mezhdunarodnogo prava* (Odessa: n.p., 1902), pp. 137–38.
30. Grabar, "Beregovoe more," col. 59–60.

seas subject to certain jurisdictional rights of the coastal state.[31] E. B. Pashukanis, a prominent Soviet jurist who fell victim to the purges in 1937, carefully avoided taking a position on the issue, although he recognized that two points of view existed about whether territorial waters are a constituent part of littoral state territory.[32] Pashukanis' neutrality on the issue is all the more remarkable since, as a leading Marxist legal philosopher, he might have been expected to stress the complete state ownership of contiguous waters. His failure to do so suggests that the second school was still widely accepted in Soviet international legal jurisprudence and state practice.

Following World War II, there was a renewed emphasis on the view, originally dominant in Russian legal doctrine, that territorial waters are a prolongation of land territory, wherein the territorial authority is unlimited. The most extreme position was taken in 1954 by A. N. Nikolaev who defined Soviet territorial waters as a "constituent part of the territory of the USSR, under its sovereignty and its state ownership."[33] The extreme nature of Nikolaev's definition lay not in the notion of extending state sovereignty to the territorial sea (a principle acknowledged at the 1930 Hague Conference and in Article 1 of the 1958 Geneva Convention on the Territorial Sea) but rather in the absolute and unconditional character of such sovereignty, including a denial of the right of innocent passage in international law.

Nikolaev contended that his definition of territorial waters was embodied in the following Soviet legislation: (1) Article 6 of the constitution of the USSR, which declared that waters are part of state ownership; (2) the 1927 statute on the state boundary which established a 12-mile belt of waters; (3) the 1935 Air Code of the USSR which placed air space above territorial waters under exclusive Soviet sovereignty; (4) the 1935 decree on fishing which transformed territorial waters into a marine fishery reserve of the USSR. In addition, Nikolaev maintained that the Soviet Union assumed, by right of state succession, the 12-mile limit established by the Tsarist government.[34]

---

31. V. A. Belli (ed.), *Voenno-morskoi mezhdunarodno-pravovoi spravochnik* (2 vols.; Moscow-Leningrad: izd-vo NKVMF, 1939–40), cited in Nikolaev, *Problema territorial'nykh vod,* p. 202.

32. E. B. Pashukanis, *Ocherki po mezhdunarodnomu pravu* (Moscow: izd-vo Sovetskoe zakonodatel'stvo, 1935), pp. 119–22. On the demise and rehabilitation of Pashukanis, see John N. Hazard, "Cleansing Soviet International Law of Anti-Marxist Theories," *AJIL,* XXXII (1938), 244–52; id., "Pashukanis Is No Traitor," *AJIL,* LI (1957), 385–88.

33. Nikolaev, *Problema territorial'nykh vod,* p. 204.

34. *Ibid.* According to Uustal', Russian legislation governing coastal waters remained in effect after the Bolshevik revolution until May 15, 1918, when the RSFSR created a 12-mile customs zone along the lines of the previous law

An examination of these legislative acts, however, suggests that Nikolaev's interpretation of their provisions was highly tendentious. Neither the constitution of the USSR nor the 1927 statute on the state boundary contained a reference to *territorial* waters; the 1935 Air Code did not delimit territorial waters; the 1935 decree on fishing referred only to fishing rights; and, as we shall see below, the Tsarist government had effectively established only a 12-mile customs zone, as well as a 12-mile fishing zone, on the far eastern coast. The Tsarist government did not claim exclusive sovereignty over or ownership of the water expanses affected.

Other Soviet jurists in the postwar era have generally leaned toward Nikolaev's definition of territorial waters, with some very important qualifications. The editors of the 1947[35] and 1951[36] international law textbooks, for example, affirmed coastal state sovereignty over territorial waters, but differed from Nikolaev by asserting that the coastal state may not restrict the right of innocent passage.

The 1956 naval international law manual defined territorial waters as a belt of a definite breadth extending along the coast which is a constituent part of the territory of the coastal state and subject to its sovereignty. This definition was said to accord with the practice of the majority of states.[37] Kolodkin accepted this definition with the addition of the vitally important qualification: "taking into account generally recognized norms of international law."[38]

The formulation of Article 1 of the 1958 Geneva Convention on the Territorial Sea did not provoke noteworthy comment from Soviet jurists during the drafting of the convention. The acknowledgment contained in Article 1 that the sovereignty of a state extends to the territorial sea belt adjacent to its coast was in full accord with Soviet views, and the stipulation that such sovereignty should be exercised subject to the provisions of the convention and "to other rules of international law" conformed with state practice and the writings of most Soviet jurists. International lawyers in the Soviet Union did emphasize, however, that coastal state sovereignty in the territorial sea is the source of that state's rights with respect to passing vessels, imply-

---

of 1909. See A. T. Uustal', *Mezhdunarodno-pravovoi rezhim territorial'nykh vod* (Tartu: izd-vo Tartuskogo gos. univ., 1958), pp. 157–58.

35. V. N. Durdenevskii and S. B. Krylov (eds.), *Mezhdunarodnoe pravo* (Moscow: Iurizdat Ministerstva iustitsii SSSR, 1947), p. 253.

36. E. A. Korovin (ed.), *Mezhdunarodnoe pravo* (Moscow: Gosiurizdat, 1951), p. 301.

37. Bakhov, *Voenno-morskoi spravochnik,* p. 81.

38. A. L. Kolodkin, *Pravovoi rezhim territorial'nykh vod i otkrytogo moria* (Moscow: izd-vo Morskoi transport, 1961), p. 7.

ing that should there be a conflict between sovereignty and the passage of vessels, the former must be given precedence:

Recognition of the sovereignty of a coastal state signifies recognition of those rights which that state exercises in its territorial sea. By virtue of the existence of the sovereignty of a coastal state in its territorial sea, the state has the exclusive right to publish acts concerning the regulation of the re-gime in these waters—security, sanitary, trade, navigation, and resources. The totality of norms defining the rights and duties of a coastal state and passing vessels is the legal regime of the territorial sea.[39]

BREADTH OF TERRITORIAL WATERS

Soviet international lawyers have repeatedly asserted at interna-tional conferences and in their own legal writings that the Soviet Union applied "the twelve-mile limit [of territorial waters]; that breadth had been determined by Russia half a century ago."[40] This statement con-tains two questions which merit detailed analysis. (1) Did the Soviet Union adopt and consistently apply a 12-mile limit of territorial waters throughout its history? (2) Had Russia adopted a 12-mile limit "half a century ago?" A third, related question is: why did Russia and the Soviet Union adopt their respective territorial limits at sea?

Russian claims to territorial waters. The breadth of coastal juris-diction claimed by Russia varied with the particular interest it wished to protect. The first apparent Russian assertion of a territorial sea, em-ploying the cannon shot rule, occurred in treaties concluded with France on December 31, 1786 (Art. 28);[41] with the Kingdom of the Two Sicilies on January 6, 1787 (Art. 19);[42] with Portugal on De-cember 9, 1787 (Art. 24);[43] as well as with Sweden on March 13, 1801 (Art. 25).[44] On December 31, 1787, the cannon shot rule was incorporated in Russian legislation regulating privateering.[45] How-

39. V. M. Koretskii and G. I. Tunkin (eds.), *Ocherki mezhdunarodnogo morskogo prava* (Moscow: Gosiurizdat, 1962), p. 54.
40. G. I. Tunkin, in United Nations Conference on the Law of the Sea, Geneva, 1958, *Official Records* (London: United Nations, 1958), III, p. 31. Also see the Statement of V. M. Koretskii to the Second United Nations Con-ference on the Law of the Sea, Geneva, 1960, *Official Records* (New York: United Nations, 1962), I, p. 116; and the comment of S. B. Krylov, in United Nations, *Yearbook of the International Law Commission 1955* (New York: United Nations, 1956), I, p. 156.
41. G. F. von Martens, *Recueil*, IV, 210; *SS&D*, VI (1969), 13.
42. Martens, *Recueil*, IV, 229; *SS&D*, VI (1969), 14.
43. Martens, *Recueil*, IV, 315; *SS&D*, VI (1969), 14.
44. Martens, *Recueil*, VII, 329; *SS&D*, VI (1969), 15.
45. Martens, *Recueil*, IV, 336; *SS&D*, VI (1969), 15; also translated in Henry G. Crocker, *The Extent of the Marginal Sea* (Washington D.C.: GPO, 1919), p. 620. An edict of January 26, 1779, instructed the Russian Admiralty to despatch "two warships and two frigates" to patrol the Northern Sea "from

ever, the Law on Prizes Taken by Warships, enacted in 1806, did not refer to the breadth of the territorial sea because of disagreement over whether the cannon shot rule should be applied or another rule formulated.[46]

In the reign of Alexander I, an edict of September 4, 1821, reserved fishing and sealing regions exclusively for Russia by claiming a 100-mile belt in the Bering Sea.[47] All foreign vessels were forbidden "to approach" within this distance of the Russian coast. After strenuous objections by Great Britain and the United States, the parties against whom it was directed, the edict was repealed in 1824.[48] Most Russian jurists later characterized the edict as a unjustified extension of territorial waters, although, as will be noted below, one publicist interpreted the edict as remaining in force except with respect to the United States and Great Britain.

While recognizing the cannon shot rule in the nineteenth century, Russia on several occasions refused to acknowledge the three-mile limit as a general rule of international law. In diplomatic correspondence with Great Britain over the Russian seizure of the *Lord Ch. Spenser* in the Black Sea, Vice Chancellor Nesselrode objected to the applicability of the three-mile rule: "Each state reserves the right . . . to resolve this question [the limit of territorial waters] in accordance with its own convenience and interests."[49] During the 1840s, Russian trading officials urged their government to extend territorial waters to 40 Italian miles in order to reduce the competition of foreign whalers. The Russian government declined to do so on the ground that protests would result "since no clear and uniform agreement has yet been arrived at among nations in regard to the limits of jurisdiction at sea."[50]

---

the White Sea to Cape Nord and the surrounding region" so that not a single vessel could slip by without identifying itself. The measure was prompted by raids of American corsairs on Russian shipping. F. F. Martens, *Sovremennoe mezhdunarodnoe pravo,* I, 388.

46. *Polnoe sobranie,* XXIX (1st ser.), 426.

47. English texts appear in *Parliamentary Papers, United States No. 1 (1893), Behring Sea Arbitration,* CX (1893–94); *SS&D,* VI (1969), 16.

48. With regard to the United States, by a treaty of April 17, 1824. See William M. Malloy (ed.), *Treaties, Conventions, International Acts, Protocols, and Agreements between the United States and Other Powers* (Washington D.C.: GPO, 1910), II, p. 1512; *SS&D,* VI (1969), 17.

49. F. F. Martens (ed.), *Sobranie traktatov' i konventsii, zakliuchennykh' Rossieiu s' inostrannymi derzhavami* (St. Petersburg: Tipo. A. Benke, 1898), XII, p. 67. Nesselrode is also reported to have said, "But if there is a principle on which both publicists and governments have always held a single opinion, it is the following: each state has the right and duty to take into consideration first of all the requirements of its personal security." *Ibid.*

50. Thomas W. Fulton, *The Sovereignty of the Sea* (Edinburgh: Wm. Blackwood & Sons, 1911), p. 585.

When in 1874 Britain, through the medium of a circular letter, endeavored to achieve consensus on the three-mile limit, Russia concurred that the three-mile limit was supported by practice but considered the legal view unsettled.[51]

The three-mile limit was accepted for certain purposes in Russian legislation and practice. In 1853 Russian cruisers were instructed to enforce a three-mile limit off the shores of Russian America.[52] After the abortive edict of 1821, however, the next Russian legislation relating to coastal jurisdiction appears to have been the Customs Code of 1868. Russia had been conducting customs operations under a code approved in 1857 which provided for customs supervision only on land. Since this was wholly inadequate to prevent smuggling, a committee was formed in 1867 within the Ministry of Finances to draft an appropriate amendment. Invoking the cannon shot rule, the committee proposed that "the expanse of water within three nautical miles of the Russian coast be deemed the territorial sea, subject to the effect of Russian laws." This formulation met with opposition in the state council. As ultimately approved on July 1/13, 1868, the Customs Code provided: "The expanse of water within three nautical miles of the Russian coast, both on the mainland and on islands, shall be deemed the maritime customs belt."[53] The Customs Code of 1892 retained the same provision.

The Russian Rules on Prize Law of 1869 governed "waters within cannon shot of shore batteries or extending from shore to a distance of three nautical miles." But the Statutes on Maritime Prizes of 1895 and 1914, replacing the 1869 rules, omitted a definition of the waters affected, thereby leaving the question open.[54]

In the 1860s, Russian opposition to the activities of Norwegian fishermen off the Murmansk coast resulted in a number of incidents wherein the latter were mistreated while seeking shelter on Russian shores. As a result, the governor of the Archangel *Guberniia* instructed fishing inspectors in 1866 that Norwegians were no longer to be allowed to fish "close to the Russian coast."[55] Despite the warnings of

51. H. A. Smith (ed.), *Great Britain and the Law of Nations* (London: P. S. King Ltd., 1935), II, p. 206.
52. Fulton, *Sovereignty of the Sea*, p. 585.
53. State Duma, Commission on Fisheries, "Doklad po zakonoproektu ob uporiadochenii rybnago promysla v Arkhangel'skoi gubernii," *Prilozheniia k stenograficheskim otchetam gosudarstvennoi dumy. Tretii sozyv'. Sessiia chetvertaia. 1910–1911 gg.* (St. Petersburg, 1911), V, no. 592, III/4, p. 16. This little-known report contains the best available summary of the legislative history of Tsarist enactments concerning maritime jurisdiction.
54. Ul'ianitskii, *Mezhdunarodnoe pravo*, p. 85.
55. C. B. V. Meyer, *The Extent of Jurisdiction in Coastal Waters* (Leiden: Sijthoff, 1937), pp. 243–44. The Russian instruction was published that

Norwegian authorities, the Norwegian fishermen continued to work their traditional areas, and the complaints of local Russians increased. Russia constructed a vessel to patrol the area, and in 1887 ordered the vessel to enforce a three-mile zone. In 1893 and 1896, the same limit was specified in new instructions to other cruisers, but the area affected by fishing restrictions was extended to include the entire area of the White Sea south of a line running from Sviatoi Nos to Kanin Nos at a distance of three miles from each of those points.[56]

Russian jurists were divided on the issue of the breadth of territorial waters. Most reluctantly recognized that the practice of nations "in the majority of instances testifies that at present the expanse [of territorial waters] is a distance of three miles from shore. . . ."[57] Many, however, quickly qualified this observation by adding that a state may change the outward boundary of territorial waters by domestic legislation to conform to its needs, especially given the increasing range of artillery. The most influential Russian international lawyer, F. F. Martens, completely rejected the three-mile rule as a "general obligatory law":

There is no such obligatory international law [*zakon*] and there can be none. On the contrary, the rule of Bynkershoek [cannon shot rule] is the single true measure for determining coastal state authority over that portion of the high seas washing its coast.[58]

Martens' views on this question, it must be added, were somewhat chameleonic, perhaps reflecting his close connections with government circles and his membership, with the rank of privy councillor, on the Council of Foreign Affairs.[59] In the second edition of his classic

---

same year, at the request of the Norwegian minister of the interior, by the governor of the Norwegian Province of Finnmark. The latter repeated his warning in 1871, stating that the Russian claim to exclusive fishing extended to one marine league from shore. The Russian instruction had not specified any limit. See Stefan A. Riesenfeld, *Protection of Coastal Fisheries under International Law* (Washington D.C.: Carnegie Endowment, 1942), p. 197; and, in general, V. Böhmert, "Die russische Fischereigrenze," *Zeitschrift für Völkerrecht,* xxi (1937), 441–96; xxii (1938), 257–306.
   56. Meyer, *Jurisdiction in Coastal Waters,* p. 246; Böhmert, "Die russische Fischereigrenze," p. 473; Ovchinnikov, "Territorial'noe more," p. 61.
   57. Ovchinnikov, "Territorial'noe more," p. 61; Ul'ianitskii, *Mezhdunarodnoe pravo,* p. 87; Zakharov, *Kurs obshchago mezhdunarodnogo prava,* p. 157.
   58. F. F. Martens, *Sovremennoe mezhdunarodnoe pravo,* i, p. 390.
   59. At the height of the cold war, one Western publicist portrayed Martens as an apologist for Tsarist foreign policy and implied that very little had changed in the role of international lawyers in this respect under the Soviet regime. See Arthur Nussbaum, "Frederick de Martens: Representative Tsarist Writer on International Law," *Nordisk Tidsskrift for International Ret,* xxii (1952), 60.

treatise, Martens recommended that the breadth of territorial waters be settled by international agreement since the variable and indefinite ranges of ordnance made the cannon shot rule unworkable.[60] By 1894, Martens had cast aside any reservations about the workability of the cannon shot rule.[61] Indeed, when serving as arbitrator in the *Costa Rica Packet* case between the Netherlands and Great Britain, he commenced his award with the observation: ". . . taking into consideration that the right of state sovereignty over the territorial sea is determined by the range of cannon from the low water mark. . . ."[62]

In any event, there can be no doubt that Martens greatly influenced Russian policy toward enlarging its coastal jurisdiction. In 1898 Martens was appointed the chairman of an interdepartmental commission attached to the Ministry of Foreign Affairs which was charged with resolving the issue of foreign fishing rights in the Okhotsk Sea, the Sea of Japan, and the Kamchatka [Bering] Sea. The commission decided to broaden its inquiry to include the entire problem of territorial jurisdiction and submitted a draft statute providing that:

Where the expanse of Russian territorial waters has not been determined by special international regulations or treaties, or established by long usage without any definite time limit, such waters shall extend to cannon shot range from the coast; *i. e.,* to at least six (6) nautical miles (60 degrees latitude), the distance being reckoned from the line of lowest ebb tide.[63]

However, no further legislative action was taken on the matter.

In 1906 a second committee was appointed, this time by the Naval Ministry and chaired by Vice-Admiral Hildebrandt, to examine the problem of territorial waters of northern Russia. The committee recommended that a 20-mile limit be established along the Murmansk coast and that portions of the White and Kara Seas be closed. These proposals also received no further support within the government.

During the deliberations of the Hildebrandt committee, the Ministry of Foreign Affairs abandoned the opinion which it had ventured in the 1898 committee chaired by Martens and, jointly with the Naval Ministry, decided that:

It would seem more expedient to approach resolution of the question not by a theoretical definition once and for all of a single general norm for all of

---

60. Martens, *Sovremennoe mezhdunarodnoe pravo,* (2d ed.), I, p. 376.

61. F. F. Martens, "Le Tribunal d'Arbitrage de Paris et la Mer Territoriale," *Revue Générale de Droit International Public,* I (1894), 42. Martens suggested that a 10-mile limit would better conform to the average range of ordnance and offer greater protection to coastal fishery interests.

62. For the text of the award, see *Revue Générale de Droit International Public,* IV (1897), 737; *SS&D,* VI (1970), 326.

63. *State Duma Report,* p. 17; *SS&D,* VI (1969), 21.

the sea boundaries of the Empire, but by a preliminary detailed elucidation of the practical needs of the Russian Government and Russian subjects in this respect, taking into account the local natural and cultural conditions of the various maritime regions of Russia, as well as the various state and private interests in this question; for example, with regard to customs, sanitary control, police, etc.[64]

Pursuant to this view, the Ministry of Finances submitted a proposal in 1908 to extend the maritime customs belt to 12 nautical miles. Approved on December 10, 1909, the new law subjected to supervision "every vessel" within 12 miles of shore. Apparently under the impression that a general 12-mile limit had been established by the 1909 customs law, Great Britain and Japan entered strong protests, the former declaring that the Russian law was contrary to international law, but without result. Other maritime nations apparently made no objections.

Emboldened by success, the government prepared a draft law to extend exclusive Russian fishing rights along the northern coast to 12 miles and to close portions of the White Sea for the purposes of conserving fishery stocks and reducing competition from Norwegian fishermen. The proposed law would also have infringed severely upon operations by British trawlers in the region.

An unexpected impetus to the enactment of such legislation was given by the *Onward Ho* incident. Although the language of the 1909 decree seemed quite clear, apparently many Russian officials were in doubt as to what base lines were applicable in determining the 12-mile limit. Consequently, in July 1910, a British trawler, the *Onward Ho,* was seized by a Russian cruiser while trawling between 3 to 12 miles outside the line connecting Capes Sviatoi Nos and Kanin Nos and more than 12 miles from the nearest land. Even before the official British protest reached St. Petersburg, the trawler was released because it was evident that the vessel was beyond the area under Russian customs supervision. The British claim for compensation underlined the need for a precise delimitation of coastal authority in the area.

In 1911 a second bill extending exclusive coastal fishing rights on the far eastern shores to 12 miles was introduced. Britain and Japan lobbied strenuously aginst both bills. In a reply sent early in 1911 to the Japanese protest against the 1909 customs law, the Russian Ministry of Foreign Affairs reiterated:

. . . in modern international law there exists no *generally accepted* rule concerning the limits of territorial waters within which sovereign state authority may be exercised.

64. *State Duma Report,* pp. 17–18.

The question has been given widely different solutions either by international treaties or the municipal laws of a state, and very often in an unequal manner for the various protected interests (customs regulations, fisheries, criminal or civil jurisdiction, sanitary observations, etc.).

Thus an examination of the laws dealing with the question shows that a great many states in Europe and America exercise undisputed jurisdiction within limits that exceed the so-called ordinary zone of three nautical miles. . . .

Taking into consideration the . . . provisions of laws against which no State appears to have protested, together with the fact that Russia is not bound by any international treaty fixing the 3-marine-mile zone for the territorial waters and that therefore its area cannot be measured from the viewpoint of international law except by the range of cannons on the coast (which now even exceed the 12-nautical-mile limit) the Imperial Government is unable to admit that the Russian law of December 10, 1909, conflicts with international law.

Lastly, the Imperial Ministry deems it its duty to recall to the Japanese Embassy's memory that the Institute of International Law (whose authority on such questions is unquestionable) did not hesitate to declare (as far back as 17 years ago, when it met at Paris, in 1894) that the "usually adopted" distance of three miles was absolutely insufficient.[65]

Great Britain was successful with regard to the northern coast bill, but the 12-mile zone for the far eastern coast, which did not directly impinge upon British interests, became law on May 29, 1911, entering into force at the end of that year. The United States entered no protest against either the customs or the fishing law. Its inquiries reflected a concern that Russia might attempt to enforce the customs law against all vessels found within 12 miles of shore, whether bound for a port or merely passing, without reference to whether such vessels were actually engaged, or suspected of being engaged, in smuggling. In oral communications with the Russian government, the United States merely reserved all rights of whatever nature.[66] There is no record that the 1911 decree was enforced against Japanese vessels by the Tsarist government.

It is therefore apparent that Tsarist Russia had not laid claim to a 12-mile breadth of territorial waters. Without doubt, the Russian government would have liked to make such a claim, and it carefully reserved its legal right to do so while agitating for an international agreement to resolve the issue once and for all. However, the pattern

65. Note of the Russian Minister of Foreign Affairs to the Japanese Ambassador to Russia, *Foreign Relations of the United States, 1912* (Washington D.C.: GPO, 1919), p. 1308; *SS&D,* VI (1969), 23.

66. *U.S. Foreign Relations 1912,* pp. 1298–99. A general account of the diplomatic exchanges is given by William E. Masterson, *Jurisdiction in Marginal Seas with Special Reference to Smuggling* (New York: Macmillan Co., 1929).

of Russian legislation and the records of legislative history relating to the drafting of the customs and fishing laws of 1909 and 1911 suggest that Russia was extremely apprehensive about the reactions of other powers, particularly Great Britain and Japan, and that the government carefully tried to minimize protests by creating two 12-mile contiguous zones for special fiscal and economic purposes.

If, as a prominent Japanese international lawyer has suggested, "it is clear that Russia's intention was to create a zone of territorial jurisdiction twelve miles wide. This claim was inherited by the USSR . . . ,"[67] then the most the Soviet regime could "inherit" was an unrealized intention. In reality, however, the Soviet regime succeeded to more. It acquired the heritage of Russian law and the Russian attitude toward the sea. Although Soviet maritime frontiers did not become virtually identical with those of Tsarist Russia until 1940, the Tsarist and Soviet geopolitical positions in the 1920s were sufficiently similar for the purpose of shaping maritime attitudes. Moreover, both governments were obliged to deal from a position of maritime weakness.

Soviet claims to territorial waters: 1917–45. Revolution, civil war, a campaign against Poland, and the consolidation of economic and political order had been the major preoccupations of the Soviet leadership until 1920–21, when the regime began to conclude peace treaties and frontier agreements with neighboring states. The first legislative act concerning coastal jurisdiction was enacted May 15, 1918. A decree "On the Establishment of the Border Guard," it provided that "the expanse of waters within twelve nautical miles of the line of lowest ebb tide" of the sea coast was to be the maritime customs belt "within whose limits all Russian and foreign vessels are subject to supervision by the border guard."[68] This decree replaced the customs law of 1909, which until then had remained in force.

Under a decree of May 24, 1921, Soviet nationals were granted exclusive fishing rights within 12 miles of the coast from the Finnish border to the northern tip of Novaia Zemlia and within the entire White Sea; that is, the White Sea and Cheshskaia Bay were closed to aliens for the purpose of commercial fishing.[69] This decree, it will be recalled, affected British and Norwegian fishing interests most directly. Moreover, the Soviet government had acted to protect a region

67. Shigeru Oda, *International Control of Sea Resources* (Leyden: Sijthoff, 1963), p. 15.

68. *SU RSFSR* (1918), no. 44, item 539; *SS&D*, vi (1969), 25.

69. *SU RSFSR* (1921), no. 49, item 259; *SS&D*, vi (1969), 26. The British government did not recognize the validity of the decree, and British and Norwegian trawlers continued to fish in the prohibited zone. See Uustal', *Mezhdunarodno-pravovoi rezhim territorial'nykh vod,* p. 159.

toward which the Tsarist government had been exceedingly timid. The fishing decree carefully avoided the term "territorial waters" in delimiting coastal fishing jurisdiction.

On March 2, 1923, the Soviet regime abrogated all treaties, concessions, contracts, and other conditions affecting commercial fishing or sealing in the far east which had been contracted prior to the date of the reunification of the Far Eastern Republic with the RSFSR (November 14, 1922). The right of fishing in territorial waters of the RSFSR henceforth was to be leased to Russian or foreign nationals, although certain bays and mouths of rivers were reserved exclusively for Russian nationals or local national groupings. This decree, although using the term "territorial waters," carefully refrained from specifying the breadth of the waters available for leasing.[70]

The approach embodied in the fishing decrees was followed throughout the interwar period in other normative acts regulating or extending coastal jurisdiction. The first Statute on the Protection of the State Boundary of the USSR, approved September 7, 1923, charged the border guard (the Unified State Political Administration, or OGPU) with preventing the "plunder of our water resources" within the 12-mile belt established by the fishing decrees of 1921 and 1923 (Art. 5[e]). The statute further created a 12-mile maritime frontier belt within which "special rights" were granted to the border guard, and within which vessels or individuals "shall be subject to certain restrictions provided for by the present Statute" (Art. 8). The nature of these special rights and the kind of claim being asserted was further clarified in Article 25, which referred to the "12-mile maritime frontier belt of the high seas washing the coast of the USSR."[71] In a note to Article 25, an exception was created for the Gulf of Finland, the only place where Soviet territorial waters had been delimited, in this case by the 1920 peace treaty with Finland. Here the authority of the Soviet border guard did not exceed four miles—the limit of territorial waters. Thus, the maritime frontier belt was fixed only in those areas where a claim to territorial waters had not been previously asserted. The 1927 statute on the state boundary retained the same position on this question.[72]

An Instruction for the Navigation of Vessels in Coastal Waters Within Artillery Range of Shore Batteries in Peacetime, of July 5,

70. *SU RSFSR* (1923), no. 36, item 378; *SS&D,* vi (1969), 27.

71. V. V. Egor'ev *et al., Zakonodatel'stvo i mezhdunarodnye dogovory Soiuza SSR i soiuznykh respublik o pravovom polozhenii inostrannykh fizicheskikh i iuridicheskikh lits* (Moscow: Iurizdat nkiu RSFSR, 1926), p. 427; *SS&D,* vi (1969), 28.

72. *SZ SSSR* (1927), no. 62, item 625; *SS&D,* vi (1969), 30.

1924, provided that "within the limits of territorial waters merchant vessels of the USSR and merchant vessels of foreign powers, with the exception of special zones . . ." shall have the right of unhindered navigation.[73] Foreign warships were allowed to navigate in territorial waters as well, but not to anchor, to conduct training exercises, and so forth. Again, the breadth of territorial waters was not specified. The reference in the instruction to "artillery range of shore batteries" led some Western international lawyers to assume that by expressly permitting free passage in time of peace a broad zone of territorial waters defined by cannon shot range had been created.[74] The provisions of the instruction, however, do not support such an interpretation.

A 10-mile zone wherein the use of wireless radio equipment is restricted was established by a decree of July 24, 1928,[75] superseding a similar decree of January 16, 1923.[76] Although the term "territorial waters" was used in both decrees, it clearly was not coterminus with the 10-mile zone, nor was it otherwise defined or delimited.

Further examples of the identical situation may be found in the 1929 Merchant Shipping Code,[77] the decree on the sanitary protection of the boundaries of the USSR of August 23, 1931,[78] the 1935 Air Code,[79] and others.

During the interwar period, Soviet jurists also concurred with this interpretation of Soviet legislation. Grabar circumspectly observed in 1927 that a state may extend its "powers with regard to the contiguous coastal sea to a distance of up to twelve nautical miles from shore in those instances where there is no obstacle in prior treaty agreements. . . ."[80] His carefully chosen language implied that only the creation of special zones would be permissible. More directly to the point, V. Egor'ev wrote in 1932:

In some instances the expression "territorial waters" is encountered in internal provisions of laws, together with the terms "maritime belt" or "waters of the USSR," but also without indicating their breadth, which, therefore, remains precisely outlined only for the Gulf of Finland.[81]

73. Egor'ev, *Zakonodatel'stvo i mezhdunarodnye dogovory,* p. 433; *SS&D,* VI (1969), 58.

74. Gilbert Gidel, *Le Droit Public de la Mer* (Paris: Recueil Sirey, 1934), III, p. 114.

75. *SZ SSSR* (1928), no. 48, item 431; *SS&D,* VI (1969), 30.

76. *SU RSFSR* (1923), no. 6, item 93; *SS&D,* VI (1969), 28.

77. *SZ SSSR* (1929), no. 41, item 365.

78. *SZ SSSR* (1931), no. 55, item 355.

79. *SZ SSSR* (1935), no. 43, items 359(a) and (b).

80. Grabar, "Beregovoe more," col. 61.

81. V. Egor'ev, in E. F. Rozental' (ed.), *Morskoe pravo SSSR* (Moscow: Vneshtorgizdat, 1932), p. 109.

Sheptovitskii cautioned that "the 12-mile coastal maritime belt of the USSR should not be confused with territorial waters, which the USSR has only along the coasts of the Gulf of Finland. . . ."[82] And in the naval international law manual of 1939, Belli pointed out that "legislation of the USSR does not define the breadth of territorial waters of the Soviet Union . . . ," but ". . . establishes border and customs zones, fishing zones, zones for the use of wireless radio equipment, fortified zones, and zones closed to navigation."[83]

In at least one reported criminal proceeding, a People's Court in Vladivostok used the term "territorial waters" as synonymous with internal waters in convicting a British officer of arrogation, again suggesting the great confusion over the nature and breadth of Soviet claims.[84]

During the period 1917–45, the Soviet Union or its constituent republics contracted at least 27 bilateral or multilateral treaties, agreements, and protocols containing explicit references to "territorial waters." In all instances but two, the instruments defined neither the nature nor the breadth of the territorial waters in question. In the Soviet–Norwegian Treaty on Trade and Navigation of December 15, 1925, the parties came close to equating the Soviet 12-mile fishing zone along the northern coast with territorial waters in granting Norway most-favored-nation treatment to fish within that zone.[85] A fishing agreement allowing Great Britain to fish within 3 miles of Soviet coasts of the same region expressly provided that the views "held by either contracting Government as to the limits in international law of territorial waters" would not be prejudiced by the agreement.[86]

The RSFSR–Finnish peace treaty of October 14, 1920, defined the breadth of territorial waters of both contracting parties in the Gulf of Finland as "four nautical miles from the coast and, in an archipelago, from the furthest islet or rock protruding above sea level."[87] The

---

82. M. Ia. Sheptovitskii, *Morskoe pravo* (Leningrad: Gostransizdat, 1936), p. 35.

83. Belli, *Voenno-morskoi spravochnik,* pp. 10–13, as cited in Nikolaev, *Problema territorial'nykh vod,* pp. 202–3. The same view reportedly was supported by A. D. Keilin and P. P. Vinogradov, *Morskoe pravo* (Moscow: izd-vo Morskoi transport, 1939).

84. Case of Siutor (1926), reported by V. Egor'ev in Rozental', *Morskoe pravo SSSR,* p. 109.

85. Article 31. *SDD,* III, 114–28; *LNTS,* XLVII, 9–37; *SS&D,* VI (1969), 29.

86. Article 2. *SDD,* VI, 43–45; *SS&D,* VI (1969), 37.

87. Article 3. *SDD,* I, 76–92; *LNTS,* II, 5–79; *SS&D,* VI (1969), 26. On August 3, 1930, this definition of territorial waters was incorporated in a decree, "On the Water Expanses of the Gulf of Finland to Which the Authority of Agencies of the USSR and RSFSR Extends." *SZ SSSR* (1930), no. 44, item 450.

treaty further provided for a number of specific exceptions, as a result of which the breadth of territorial waters in certain places in the Gulf of Finland was one and one-half miles. The Soviet–Finnish Agreement Concerning the Aaland Islands, of October 11, 1940, followed the same pattern in fixing the territorial waters of the islands at three nautical miles.[88]

In the postwar period Soviet jurists generally overlooked interwar legislation and treaty practice and placed great emphasis upon the statement of the Soviet observer, V. Egor'ev, to the 1930 Hague Conference for the Codification of International Law. Egor'ev's statement was said to have been an official view of the Soviet government, although upon careful reading it seemed to conform more to Soviet law and practice of the 1920s than to mirror Soviet dissatisfaction with the existing state of the law. While he clearly disputed the existence of a general international legal rule governing the breadth of territorial waters, Egor'ev also was concerned that the "rights of usage" be protected—that the zonal approach of the Soviet government in asserting jurisdiction over coastal waters not be upset:

The positive law on this question displays very wide divergencies. Whether you consult legislation, treaties, or diplomatic correspondence, there is great divergence as to the exercise of rights in territorial waters and in adjacent waters. These rights are sometimes exercised over belts of three miles, six miles, or twelve miles in width. The historic reasons which have been advanced by certain countries are disputed by others, and in any case they cannot upset the existence of certain facts. There are certain countries which have to ensure these rights in waters which are not generally used for navigation, and therefore it appears that we should confine ourselves to a general statement that rights of usage which are established in this manner ought not to be upset.[89]

Soviet claims to territorial waters: 1946–60. Soviet legislative and treaty practice with regard to the breadth of territorial waters in this period was essentially the same as that of the previous period. Prewar maritime legislation remained in force, and Soviet international treaties and agreements containing references to territorial waters or otherwise pertaining to their regime did not define the breadth of such waters. Nor did fishery legislation enacted by the USSR in 1954 and 1958 define the breadth of territorial waters, although the 12-mile

88. Article 2. *SDD*, x, 17–18; *SS&D*, vi (1969), 40. A 12-mile customs zone was created in the Gulf of Finland by a Soviet–Finnish Customs Convention of April 13, 1929. *SDD*, v, 41–46; *LNTS*, xcvi, 93–115; *SS&D*, vi (1969), 79.

89. League of Nations, *Conference for the Codification of International Law, Committee No. 2—Territorial Waters.* c.r. 13, April 3, 1930, pp. 23–24.

fishery zone was preserved.[90] Soviet diplomatic practice and doctrinal writings on international law did undergo significant transformation.

An international law textbook prepared by the USSR Academy of Sciences and published in 1947 declared that the question of the breadth of territorial waters was one of the most controversial in international law. The usual norms, it was noted, were from 3 to 6 miles, but states often created special contiguous zones of up to 12 miles.[91] Soviet legislation of the interwar period was carefully described as asserting "jurisdiction" over coastal waters. Although characterizations such as Belli's were avoided, no contention was made that the USSR claimed a belt of territorial waters of 12 miles.

In a treatise issued in 1948, Kozhevnikov outlined the "viewpoint of the Soviet Government on the question concerning the regime of the territorial sea." He described (inaccurately) the 1921 fishing decree as fixing a 12-mile maritime belt along the Soviet coast, cited the Anglo–Soviet diplomatic correspondence in connection with that decree, and quoted the statement of the Soviet observer to the 1930 Hague conference. The overall impression was that the USSR continued to insist upon the right to fix its territorial waters at 12 miles and was prepared to compromise on a lesser limit for certain purposes by way of convention. His tone was conciliatory and nonassertive, and there was no attempt to review thoroughly prewar Soviet legislation or writings of publicists.[92]

By 1951, the situation had changed somewhat. The customary norm of the breadth of territorial waters was now said to extend from 3 to 12 miles; and the same interwar Soviet legislation "as a whole . . . corresponds to the regime of territorial waters, and this belt is considered to be such waters."[93] In the foreword to a 1953 translation of a leading British treatise on maritime law, S. B. Krylov flatly asserted that the USSR had a 12-mile limit and omitted any reference to contiguous zones.[94] By 1954, Nikolaev asserted what has now become a

90. Uustal' wrote that the 1954 decree referred in Article 1 to "territorial waters of the USSR of a breadth of 12 nautical miles." Uustal', *Mezhdunarodno-pravovoi rezhim territorial'nykh vod,* p. 161. Unfortunately, the text of the decree is not available; however, the 1958 statute makes no such claim, although the expression "territorial waters" is used. For the complete text of the 1958 statute, see E. N. Kolotinskaia, *Pravovaia okhrana prirody v SSSR* (Moscow: izd-vo MGU, 1962), p. 80.

91. Durdenevskii and Krylov, *Mezhdunarodnoe pravo,* pp. 253, 258.

92. F. I. Kozhevnikov, *Sovetskoe gosudarstvo i mezhdunarodnoe pravo* (Moscow: Iurizdat Ministerstva iustitsii SSSR, 1948), pp. 215–16.

93. Korovin, *Mezhdunarodnoe pravo,* pp. 301, 307.

94. S. B. Krylov (editor's introduction), in A. P. Higgins and C. J. Colombos, *Mezhdunarodnoe morskoe pravo* (Moscow: izd-vo Inolit, 1953), p. ix.

standard formula in Soviet doctrinal writing, that the USSR has claimed a 12-mile limit since 1917.[95]

As East–West relations deteriorated into the Cold War, a number of incidents occurred in the Baltic Sea and off the far eastern coasts with regard to Soviet enforcement of its coastal jurisdiction. The most thoroughly documented instances concerned Swedish vessels,[96] but the legal aspects of the assertion of Soviet jurisdiction, apart from one peculiarity related to the Baltic region itself, seem to have been essentially the same for Danish, Norwegian, and Japanese vessels.

On several occasions between 1948 and 1950, Swedish vessels were apprehended by Soviet patrol boats—in one case, for allegedly infringing a coastal defense zone, and in others for illegally fishing within 12 miles of Soviet coasts. The location of the vessels in every instance was in dispute. In a Note of May 4, 1950, the Soviet government asserted that it was exercising jurisdiction on the basis of the 1927 statute on the protection of the state boundary of the USSR, which as we have seen established a maritime frontier zone of 12 miles, and on the basis of the 1935 decree on fishing, which fixed a fishing zone of 12 miles. Sweden apparently equated the frontier zone with a claim to territorial waters in its reply of July 24, 1950, to which the USSR replied, in consonance with its long-held opinion on the subject, that there were no generally recognized rules of international law regulating the breadth of territorial waters, emphasizing that no new extension of Soviet territorial waters had taken place since 1927. Assuming the vessels actually had penetrated the 12-mile zone and were engaged in illegal fishing, the assertion of Soviet jurisdiction would seem to have been proper under the legislation in force. Moreover, the Soviet Union appeared to be interpreting and applying that legislation just as it had during the interwar period. However, since the Scandinavian countries had characterized the Soviet assertion of jurisdiction as a claim of complete sovereignty over the 12-mile belt, the Soviet government was obviously not averse to enforcing that claim either.[97]

95. Nikolaev, *Problema territorial'nykh vod,* p. 61. But Uustal' more accurately conceded that Tsarist Russia had only created a customs zone by its law of 1909. He instead tried to trace the Tsarist 12-mile claim to "repeated official declarations" that coastal states had the right to fix a 12-mile belt of territorial waters. Uustal', *Mezhdunarodno-pravovoi rezhim territorial'nykh vod,* p. 162.

96. Leonard B. Schapiro, "The Limits of Russian Territorial Waters in the Baltic," *British Year Book of International Law,* xxvii (1950), 439; Gene Glenn, "The Swedish-Soviet Territorial Sea Controversy in the Baltic," *AJIL,* l (1956), 942.

97. It has been argued that the Soviet Union did not succeed to a 12-mile belt of territorial waters in the Baltic Sea when the Baltic states were incorpo-

In the far east, according to Japanese sources, more than one thousand Japanese vessels were seized by Soviet authorities in 1945–62. Presumably the great majority of these were taken for allegedly violating the fishing decree of 1935 or the post-1956 bilateral fishing agreements.

Although it exercised supervision in its maritime frontier zone and enforced a 12-mile fishing limit, it is noteworthy that the USSR did not assert a 12-mile belt of territorial waters in a series of aircraft incidents involving the United States. In each instance the USSR vaguely alleged a violation of its territory,[98] but when requested to indicate precisely where the maritime boundary was located, Soviet authorities were unresponsive. The United States thereupon advised the Soviet government that while American aircraft and vessels were instructed not to come closer than "twelve miles to Soviet held territory . . . the United States Government . . . does not recognize the claim of the Soviet Government to territorial waters in excess of three miles from its coast."[99]

---

rated into the USSR in 1940 and hence could not enforce such a limit against other Baltic powers:

> Since none of the Baltic states to whose territory the Soviet Union has succeeded ever possessed or claimed a territorial belt of twelve miles this is sufficient [assuming territorial waters is the full equivalent of state territory] to dispose in law of the present claim of the Soviet Union.

Alternatively, if sovereignty is:

> more properly to be regarded as an extension of the sovereignty which is exercised over coastal lands, or as a right appurtenant to the sovereignty of the appurtenant mainland, then such extension cannot lawfully take place in defiance of the vested rights of other states. . . .

Schapiro, "Russian Territorial Waters," pp. 240, 248; a similar position is taken by H. A. Reinkemeyer, *Die sowjetische Zwölfmeilenzone in der Ostsee und die Freiheit des Meeres* (Köln: Heymann, 1955). Although Soviet jurisprudence supported the full sovereignty theory, Soviet legislation and practice conformed to the second theory. The Soviet government proceeded on the basis that the Baltic republics were admitted to the union as juridical equals and automatically were entitled to the protection of prevailing boundary regulations. See Uustal', *Mezhdunarodno-pravovoi rezhim territorial'nykh vod,* p. 161. However, the present author has been unsuccessful in locating a specific enactment extending either the 1927 statute or the 1935 decree to the Baltic coast. Prior to their absorption in 1940, Latvia and Estonia enforced a 12-mile customs zone (re-enacting the 1909 customs law of the Russian empire) and, together with Lithuania, the Soviet Union, and other Baltic states, policed a 12-mile zone against contraband alcohol under an agreement of 1925.

98. See, for example, the incidents of April 8, 1950, and March 13, 1953. The relevant Soviet Notes are published in *DSB,* xxii (1950), 668; xxvii (1953), 577.

99. See especially the incident of July 29, 1953. The diplomatic correspondence is published in *American Foreign Policy 1950–1955: Basic Documents*

The disparity between Soviet state practice and doctrinal writings is probably to be explained by the work then in progress in the United Nations International Law Commission to prepare a draft convention on the regime of the territorial sea. The talents of the Soviet international legal community were enlisted to help obtain international consensus for a broader territorial sea and a general regime more favorable to Soviet interests. During discussions in the commission, the Soviet representative asserted that the USSR had embodied the 12-mile rule in its own legislation and suggested that the draft convention should allow the breadth of the territorial sea to be "determined by the national legislation of each coastal state."[100] Ultimately, the commission decided to leave final determination of the breadth of the territorial sea to an international conference, observing that, while international practice on the subject was not uniform, international law would not permit an extension of the territorial sea beyond 12 miles. The Geneva Conferences on the Law of the Sea of 1958 and 1960 were unable to reach a satisfactory disposition of the issue, and to this day it remains unresolved.

Two considerations apart from historical commitment were paramount in the formulation of the Soviet position on the breadth of the territorial sea at the 1958 Geneva conference. The three-mile limit was considered wholly inadequate for coastal defense. Claiming that "imperialist powers had used the sea lanes" for aggressive actions against the USSR, and noting that in World War II "fascist Germany used the sea for military operations against the Soviet state," it was "clear that in a similar situation a three-mile breadth of territorial waters would be inadequate for the defense of our security." Economic interests were believed to be disadvantaged by the three-mile limit as well: "Exploration of the marine wealth of coastal seas by foreigners represents a threat to our national economy just as it does to our security."[101]

Both of these interests were shared, in the opinion of the Soviet leadership, by the less developed nations. In his initial address to the first committee of the 1958 Geneva Conference on the Law of the Sea, G. I. Tunkin stressed that relationship. The attitude of the Soviet Un-

---

(Washington D.C.: GPO, 1957), II, p. 1984. However, in an exchange of Notes accompanying the signing of the Anglo-Soviet fishing agreement of 1956, the Soviet government declared that the "width of the territorial waters of the Soviet Union and their regime have been defined" by the 1927 statute on the state boundary, implying a 12-mile limit. See *UNTS*, CCLXVI, 209.

100. S. B. Krylov, in United Nations, *Yearbook of the International Law Commission 1955*, I, p. 156.

101. Uustal', *Mezhdunarodno-pravovoi rezhim territorial'nykh vod*, p. 158.

ion concerning the delimitation of the territorial sea "was prompted not only by the fact that it had itself adopted the twelve-mile limit, but also by its policy of helping small and economically less advanced countries to develop their national economies and improve their standards of living."[102] The Soviet position gained considerable propaganda support from apprehensions voiced by American officials that a rule other than the three-mile limit would "materially reduce the area of the high seas on which our fleets could operate. . . ."[103]

The deliberations of the Geneva Conferences on the Law of the Sea have been fully reported elsewhere.[104] For our purposes it is sufficient to note that the proposal of the Soviet delegation provided:

Each state shall determine the breadth of its territorial waters in accordance with established practice within the limits, as a rule, of three to twelve miles, having regard to historical and geographical conditions, economic interests, the interests of the security of the coastal state and the interests of international navigation.[105]

In introducing the Soviet proposal, Tunkin reiterated the long-standing Russian and Soviet position that there was no rule in international law governing the breadth of the territorial sea and that states should be allowed some flexibility in resolving that question in conformity with their diverse interests. However, the expression "as a rule," designed to allow a territorial sea of greater than 12 miles in "exceptional cases" and probably intended to appeal to the Latin American states, seemed to make the entire issue academic. Most critics felt, with justification, that the Soviet formulation was completely open-ended and subject to great potential abuse. The proposal was rejected at the plenary meeting of the conference by 47 votes to 21, with 17 abstentions.[106]

102. Tunkin, in *1958 Official Records*, III, 32.
103. Arthur Dean, "The Geneva Conference on the Law of the Sea: What Was Accomplished," *AJIL*, LII (1958), 611; also see Dean's Statement to the Senate Foreign Relations Committee, *DSB*, XLII (1960), 251, cited in Koretskii and Tunkin, *Ocherki mezhdunarodnogo morskogo prava*, p. 90. Another argument frequently heard in Soviet media was that imperialist powers advocate a minimal breadth of territorial sea in order to "carry on intelligence without hindrance and to exert pressure on small states. . . ." P. D. Barabolia and N. D. Lesnikov, "Novoe polozhenie ob okhrane gosudarstvennoi granitsy soiuza SSR," *Morskoi sbornik*, no. 2 (1961), 13.
104. For a convenient summary, see Marjorie Whiteman (ed.), *Digest of International Law* (Washington D.C.: GPO, 1963–), IV, p. 79.
105. Doc. A/CONF.13/C.1/L.80. *1958 Official Records*, III, 233; *SS&D*, VI (1969), 44.
106. *1958 Official Records*, II, 40. The Soviet delegation also supported an eight-power proposal sponsored by Asian, Middle Eastern, and Latin American countries to allow states to fix a territorial sea of up to 12 miles. Those states

Although a Convention on the Territorial Sea was adopted by the 1958 Geneva conference, the issue of the breadth of the territorial sea was not resolved. A second Geneva conference convened in 1960 expressly to settle that issue adjourned without success. At the second conference, intensive efforts were undertaken to reconcile coastal fishing interests with those of a narrow territorial sea. On March 21, 1960, the USSR submitted a proposal virtually identical to the eight-power proposal introduced at the 1958 conference:

Every state is entitled to fix the breadth of its territorial sea up to a limit of twelve nautical miles. If the breadth of the territorial sea is less than this limit, a state may establish a fishing zone contiguous to its territorial sea, provided, however, that the total breadth of the territorial sea and the fishing zone does not exceed twelve nautical miles. In this zone a state shall have the same rights of fishing and of exploitation of the living resources of the sea as it has in its territorial sea.[107]

Later in the conference, the USSR withdrew this proposal in favor of one submitted by 18 less developed countries and embodying the essential features of the Soviet formulation, with certain additions.

The initial Soviet proposal offers an interesting contrast to its position at the first Geneva conference. By 1960, the USSR had abandoned the open-ended formulation in favor of a flat maximum limit of 12 miles. However, the various criteria enumerated in the 1958 proposal were also eliminated, thereby allowing states to fix a 12-mile limit without offering historical, economic, or other justifications. In addition, the 1960 Soviet proposal expressly provided for a fishing zone strictly limited to 12 miles. The USSR eventually voted in favor of the somewhat broader 18-nation proposal, which was defeated in the committee of the whole by 39 votes to 36, with 13 abstentions.

Although the Soviet proposal was clearly tailored to win the support of the less developed countries, it was markedly more conservative than the proposal advanced in 1958 and, as the 18-power proposal demonstrated, was also too conservative for the Latin American, Middle Eastern, Asian, and African powers. The reasons for the hardened Soviet attitude can only be the object of speculation. In the two-year period between 1958 and 1960, the Soviet Union began to deploy its relatively new high seas fishing fleet off foreign coasts, and Soviet authorities may have realized that broad fishing zones or territorial waters were not necessarily in the Soviet interest. More fundamentally,

---

with a lesser territorial sea could create a fishing zone of up to 12 miles. *Ibid.,* p. 128.

107. A/CONF.19/C.1/L.1. *1960 Official Records,* II, 164; *SS&D,* VI (1969), 44.

however, it is likely that the Soviet Union did not in fact want a general rule of international law that would sanction a breadth of territorial waters in excess of 12 miles. To be sure, the USSR would have looked favorably upon the widespread use of the "special exception" clause. It is also possible that the Soviet Union hoped, by adopting a more modest position than the less developed nations and a more extreme position than the Western maritime powers, to encourage a compromise on the basis of its own proposal.

Shortly after the 1960 Geneva conference adjourned, the Soviet Union adopted a series of normative acts codifying the results of the Geneva conferences and, on October 20, 1960, formally ratified the 1958 Convention on the Territorial Sea and Contiguous Zone, with two reservations not relevant here;[108] the convention entered into force on October 1, 1964.[109] Since, in the Soviet view, the breadth of territorial waters could not be resolved by an international conference, each state was entitled to adopt its own limit in accordance with its interests. On August 5, 1960, the Soviet Union enacted into law for the first time a 12-mile belt of territorial waters which at the line farthest seaward "shall constitute the state boundary of the USSR at sea,"[110] unless a different breadth is established by international agreements. Several exceptions to the 12-mile rule exist. Under the 1940 peace treaty with Finland, a 3-mile limit was established at the northern extremity of Suursaari Island in order to ensure freedom of passage for vessels sailing to the north.[111] A Soviet–Finnish agreement of May 20, 1965, established a breadth of territorial waters of less than 12 miles in the Gulf of Finland.[112] A median line presently constitutes the boundary in the Bering Strait and in the straits between the Japanese Island of Hokkaido and the Soviet Kurile Islands.[113]

Soviet claims to territorial waters: 1961–69. The failure to reach agreement on the breadth of territorial waters has resulted in a deluge of unilateral state claims to territorial waters of 12 miles or more. A recent incomplete tabulation shows 11 states claiming territorial waters in excess of 12 miles and at least 40 states claiming 12 miles.[114]

Soviet jurists no longer suggest that states may determine their

108. *Vedomosti SSSR* (1964), no. 43, item 472.
109. *UNTS,* dxvi, 205.
110. Article 3. Statute on the Protection of the State Boundary of the USSR, *Vedomosti SSSR* (1960), no. 34, item 324; *SS&D,* vi (1969), 45.
111. *SDD,* x, 10–17.
112. English texts of the agreement are published in *ILM,* vi, 729; *SS&D,* vi (1969), 53.
113. Barabolia, *Voenno-morskoi spravochnik,* p. 47.
114. *Marine Science Affairs* (Washington D.C.: gpo, January 1969), pp. 248–51.

territorial waters in accordance with their interests. Rather, they observe that state practice is to fix territorial waters between 3 and 12 miles, depending upon economic or security interests.[115] The implication is clear that the USSR is increasingly intolerant of claims exceeding 12 miles.

Soviet ministries have progressed considerably further in their perception of the applicable international norm. In a lead editorial prompted by the boarding of Soviet fishing vessels within the 200-mile Argentine fishing zone, a spokesman for the USSR Ministry of Fisheries declared that ". . . the extension of territorial waters beyond the limits of 12-nautical miles from shore is considered inadmissible."[116] On the other hand, jurists associated with the USSR Ministry of Defense have taken a view more in accord with coastal defense, suggesting that although the United Nations International Law Commission had determined that modern international law does not permit extension of territorial waters beyond 12 miles, "this did not receive legal sanction."[117]

The Soviet government took the initiative in 1967 to lay the groundwork for a new international conference in order to obtain consensus on the 12-mile limit.[118] In this connection Soviet jurists recently have written that the practice of states and international legal doctrine "fully justify the position of the Soviet Union on the extent of territorial waters, namely, that 12-miles is their maximum limit."[119]

Soviet enforcement of its own 12-mile limit continues to be strict. In the first 7 months of 1968, Soviet patrol vessels detained 19 vessels and 133 Japanese nationals for border violations.[120] Seizures of Norwegian vessels are also not uncommon.

THE BASE LINE OF TERRITORIAL WATERS

Early Tsarist legislation did not specify from what point the breadth of territorial waters should be measured. By the late nine-

115. Barabolia, *Voenno-morskoi spravochnik*, p. 29.
116. *Rybnoe khoziaistvo*, no. 3 (1967), 1; translated in *ILM*, VIII (1969), 896; *SS&D*, VI (1969), 45.
117. P. D. Barabolia and V. T. Tsyganov, "Territorial'nye vody pribrezhnykh gosudarstv," *Morskoi sbornik*, no. 8 (1966), 69.
118. *Ocean Science News*, X, no. 30 (1968), 1.
119. A. L. Kolodkin, "Territorial Waters and International Law," *International Affairs* [Moscow], no. 8 (1969), 81; also see Nikolaev, *Territorial'noe more*. Volkov wrote that the absence of a fixed international legal norm limiting the breadth of territorial waters and fishing zones "creates a favorable basis for coastal states which are attempting to illegally extend their exclusive fishery jurisdiction to areas of the high seas." A. A. Volkov, *Morskoe pravo* (Moscow: izd-vo Pishchevaia promyshlennost', 1969), p. 102.
120. *Commercial Fisheries Review*, XXX, no. 10 (1968), 66–67; also see *New York Times*, August 31, 1969, p. 5.

teenth century, Russian practice was to compute the appropriate distance from the low water mark, or the line of lowest ebb tide.

The principle was incorporated respectively into instructions issued to a Russian cruiser in 1896,[121] in the draft statute on Russian territorial waters prepared by the Martens Commission in 1898,[122] the customs law of 1909,[123] and the 1911 rules on fishing in the Maritime Province.[124]

Under the 1960 statute on the state boundary, the breadth of Soviet territorial waters is calculated from the normal base line on the mainland and around islands or from the farthest point seaward of the internal sea waters of the USSR.[125] Because of the special configuration of the coasts and an insignificant difference in the ebb and flow of the tide, the breadth of Soviet territorial waters in the Gulf of Finland (where there are reefs) has been measured from the farthest islands or rocks protruding above the surface. This method was originally prescribed in Article 3 of the 1920 peace treaty between Finland and the RSFSR and later embodied in the 1930 USSR decree on the extension of USSR and RSFSR authority in the Gulf of Finland. Although the decree lost force as a result of post-World War II changes in the state boundary along the Gulf of Finland, Soviet jurists believe the principle is still applicable today.[126]

Soviet legislation is silent as to whether artificial structures which affect the shape of the sea boundary should be taken into account in determining the breadth of territorial waters or whether only the natural shore line may be used. Uustal' believed that artificial structures should be taken into account, especially around ports, since this would improve the security of the coastal state. However, when a port is located directly on the edge of territorial waters but not within territorial waters, the base line of territorial waters is to be measured from the port structures extending farthest seaward.[127]

121. Ovchinnikov, "Territorial'noe more," p. 61.

122. *State Duma Report,* p. 17; *SS&D,* vi (1969), 21.

123. William E. Butler, *The Law of Soviet Territorial Waters* (New York: Frederick A. Praeger, 1967), p. 9; *SS&D,* vi (1969), 22.

124. *Polnoe sobranie* (3d ser.), xxxi, 449–52; *SS&D,* vi (1969), 24.

125. Article 3. *Vedomosti SSSR* (1960), no. 34, item 324; also see the decree of May 15, 1918, on the establishment of the border guard, *SU RSFSR* (1918), no. 44, item 599; *SS&D,* vi (1969), 25; as well as the 1927 statute on the state boundary, *SZ SSSR* (1927), no. 62, item 625; *SS&D,* vi (1969), 30. The straight base line method of computing the breadth of territorial waters has never been sanctioned by Soviet legislation nor applied in practice to Soviet coasts. Also see Volkov, *Morskoe pravo,* p. 100.

126. Nikolaev, *Problema territorial'nykh vod,* p. 207; Uustal', *Mezhdunarodno-pravovoi rezhim territorial'nykh vod,* p. 169.

127. Uustal', *Mezhdunarodno-pravovoi rezhim territorial'nykh vod,* p. 181. Volkov considered permanent port installations (breakwaters, piers, moor-

Bays. The problem of delimiting territorial waters in bays is exceedingly complex. The general rule has been that if the entrance to a bay does not exceed a given breadth, then the base line of territorial waters is a straight line between the two farthest points of the entrance seaward, and the waters within the bay are internal waters of the coastal state. If the entrance to a bay exceeds the given breadth, then the territorial waters follow the sinuosity of the coast line within the bay.[128]

In Russian international legal writing, the closing line for bays was said to be "two cannon shots or six miles," assuming that the entrance and the shores of the bay belonged to one and the same state. If a second state had dominion over any portion of the bay, the state having dominion over the entrance did not have a right of ownership over the bay.[129] This statement of the rule generally conformed to the prevailing view in Western scholarship at the time.

A number of international conventions in the early nineteenth century fixed the closing line at 10 miles, and this limit received considerable support at the Hague Codification Conference of 1930.[130] Most Soviet jurists supported the 10-mile rule,[131] although some considered the question unresolved.[132] Notwithstanding sentiment for the 10-mile line, Soviet jurists greeted the decision of the International Court of Justice in the *Anglo-Norwegian Fisheries* case with acclaim and revised their views accordingly. The court held, according to Soviet jurists, that there was no generally recognized rule in international law limiting the breadth of the entrances of bays to 10 miles or less.[133] Thereafter, Soviet international lawyers maintained that the breadth of the entrance of an internal bay may not exceed twice the breadth of that country's territorial sea, whatever it may be.[134]

Prior to 1960, Soviet legislation had not defined or otherwise dealt with the legal status of bays or their base lines. In the fishing convention concluded with Japan on January 23, 1928, Japanese nation-

---

age) that are an integral part of a port as a segment of the coast for the purpose of measuring the breadth of territorial waters. Volkov, *Morskoe pravo,* p. 101.

128. There are numerous exceptions and refinements to this rule, depending upon the size and shape of the bay, as well as upon historical and prescriptive factors. A superb description of the applicable principles is Aaron L. Shalowitz, *Shore and Sea Boundaries* (Washington D.C.: GPO, 1962–64), I, pp. 31–59.

129. Ul'ianitskii, *Mezhdunarodnoe pravo,* pp. 145–46.

130. Durdenevskii and Krylov, *Mezhdunarodnoe pravo,* p. 247.

131. *Ibid.;* Korovin, *Mezhdunarodnoe pravo,* p. 295.

132. Sheptovitskii, *Morskoe pravo,* p. 37.

133. S. Borisov, "Mezhdunarodnyi sud o territorial'nykh vodakh," *SGIP,* no. 8 (1952), 52. S. Borisov was a pseudonym of S. B. Krylov.

134. F. I. Kozhevnikov (ed.), *Mezhdunarodnoe pravo* (Moscow: Gosiurizdat, 1957), p. 201.

als were barred from fishing in specified bays and those bays which
"penetrate into the mainland for a distance (measured along the deepest channel) that is more than three times the width of the entrance."[135] The 10-mile closing line was used in the 1930 Anglo–
Soviet fishing agreement.[136]

The 1960 statute on the state boundary incorporated the provisions of the 1958 Geneva Convention on the Territorial Sea regulating
this question. The base line is a straight line not exceeding 24 miles
drawn from shore to shore of bays, inlets, coves, and estuaries whose
entire coasts belong to the USSR.

Historic bays constitute an exception to these rules.

Archipelagoes. A specialist in international law with the United
States Navy recently commented:

Russia and its satellites as well as some of the new and irresponsible nations
would favor limiting the high seas in any way conceivable. The archipelago
concept just happens to be another encroachment on the high seas that favors the Russian philosophy.[137]

An archipelago is a formation of two or more islands (islets or
rocks) which geographically may be considered as a whole. In some
archipelagoes the islands may be clustered together, while others may
be strung out over great expanses of water. In other cases they may be
near the coast (coastal archipelago) and considered part of the mainland, or they may be situated in the ocean (mid-ocean) and considered
independent units. Instead of each island possessing its own territorial
waters, a straight base line is drawn around the perimeter of the island
or group of islands, touching upon the prominent points. The territorial waters are measured seaward from that base line, and all waters
enclosed within the base line are considered to be internal waters. In
recent years the Philippines and Indonesia have sought to apply the
archipelago theory.

Although the archipelago principle as applied by Indonesia and
the Philippines has been endorsed in Soviet international legal writing
and although Soviet jurists assert that "international law recognizes
the sovereign right of each state to fix the length of such straight base
lines at its own discretion" in accordance with the judgment of the International Court of Justice in the *Anglo-Norwegian Fisheries* case,[138]

135. Article 1 of Annex A. *SDD,* v, 89–106; *SS&D,* vi (1969/70), 148.
136. *SDD,* vi, 43–45; *SS&D,* vi (1969), 37.
137. John R. Brock, "Archipelago Concepts of Limits of Territorial Seas,"
Naval War College Review, xix, no. 4 (1966), 35.
138. V. M. Chkhikvadze *et al.* (eds.), *Kurs mezhdunarodnogo prava v
shesti tomakh* (Moscow: izd-vo Nauka, 1967–), iii, pp. 187–89. The USSR for-

such endorsement is something less than enthusiastic. In the most authoritative treatment of the question in Soviet literature, Zhudro concluded that there must be an organic connection, resulting from a political, administrative, and economic unity, within the archipelago islands. Moreover, even though the length of archipelago base lines is not limited by international law, such lines may not be of an unreasonable or willful nature or based on political motives.[139] Zhudro avoided the question of innocent passage through archipelago waters, but other Soviet jurists have emphasized the existence of such a right.[140] Uustal' has recommended that straight base lines of archipelagoes be limited to a maximum of 24 miles.[141]

Soviet legislation does not treat the delimitation of archipelagoes, thereby creating the assumption that the principle is not applied to Soviet waters. However, one jurist has suggested that the water expanse lying between the islands of Saarema, Hiuma, Vörmsi, and the mainland of the Estonian SSR would be an appropriate place to invoke the archipelago principle.[142] (See Map 1.)

Ice-covered water expanses. The difficulty in fixing a base line for territorial waters in seas permanently covered by ice raised the issue of whether such ice should be considered the equivalent of land and the territorial waters be measured from the seaward edge of the ice.

Martens rejected the notion that the Kara Sea, which is frozen over for nine months of the year, could be considered an extension of Russian territory: ". . . ice has yet to be equated with dry land. . . ."[143] However, the Tsarist decree of 1911 regulating fishing in the Maritime Province did provide that territorial waters were to be measured from the low water mark or "from the edge of the ice along the coast."[144]

Uustal' believes that permanent ice enclosing the islands and the mainland in polar regions is an inseparable part of the mainland and the islands and should be used to fix the base lines for territorial wa-

---

mally recognized the Indonesian declaration applying the archipelago concept. *Pravda,* February 13, 1958. In the early 1960s the Indonesian navy detained a Soviet hydrographic survey ship for violating Indonesian "internal" waters near Natuna Island. The Soviet ship was interned in an Indonesian port but later escaped. See Sayre A. Swarztrauber, *The Three-Mile Limit of Territorial Seas: A Brief History* (Washington D.C.: American University, unpublished Ph.D. diss., 1970), p. 454.

139. A. K. Zhudro, "K voprosu o razgranichenii territorial'nykh vod i vnutrennykh vod gosudarstv v arkhipelagakh," *Morskoe pravo i praktika: sbornik materialov,* xcvii (1963), 3–9.

140. Chkhikvadze, *Kurs mezhdunarodnogo prava,* iii, p. 187.

141. Uustal', *Mezhdunarodno-pravovoi rezhim territorial'nykh vod,* p. 182.

142. A. T. Uustal', "Iskhodnaia liniia territorial'nykh vod Estonskoi SSR," *Sovetskoe pravo* [Tallin], no. 2 (1969), 108; *SS&D,* vi (1969), 56.

143. Martens, *Sovremennoe mezhdunarodnoe pravo,* i, p. 384.

144. *Polnoe sobranie* (3d ser.), xxxi, 449–52.

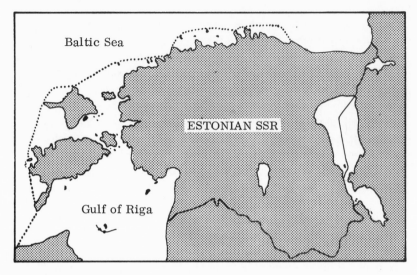

Map 1. *Base Line of Estonian Territorial Waters Proposed by Soviet Jurist and Based on Archipelago Principle*

ters in the Arctic.[145] His opinion was shared by Soviet jurists in the 1930s[146] but has no basis in Soviet legislation or state practice.

The outward line of territorial waters is the state boundary of the Soviet Union at sea. In those areas where Soviet territorial waters adjoin the territorial waters of a neighboring state, the maritime lateral state boundary is established pursuant to agreements concluded with those states. Examples of such agreements include that of February 15, 1957, with Norway,[147] a protocol of March 18, 1958, with Poland,[148] and the agreement of May 20, 1965, with Finland.[149]

The latter agreement was made necessary by ambiguities in the 1940 Soviet–Finnish peace treaty and by the fact that the USSR computed its 12-mile limit from the low water mark or the outward boundary of internal sea waters, whereas Finland measured its 4-mile limit from base lines beyond Finnish reefs, making it difficult for navigators to know precisely whose waters they were in.[150]

145. Uustal', *Mezhdunarodno-pravovoi rezhim territorial'nykh vod*, p. 184.

146. E. A. Korovin, "SSSR i poliarnye zemli," *Sovetskoe pravo*, no. 3 (1926), 46; V. L. Lakhtin, "Rights Over the Arctic," *AJIL*, xxiv (1930), 703–17. Glaciers are included as part of the USSR state water reserve in Article 4 of the Fundamental Principles of Waters Legislation of the USSR and Union Republics.

147. *SDD*, xix, 36; *UNTS*, cccxii, 326; *SS&D*, vi (1969), 50.

148. *UNTS*, cccxl, 94; *SS&D*, vi (1969), 52.

149. *UNTS*, dlxxi, 31; *ILM*, vi (1967), 727; *SS&D*, vi (1969), 53.

150. P. D. Barov, "Razgranichenie morskikh vod i kontinental'nogo shel'fa v finskom zalive," *Morskoi sbornik*, no. 8 (1966), 79.

Right of Innocent Passage

The exercise of coastal state jurisdiction, in the interests of international commerce and navigation, is generally held to be limited by the so-called right of innocent passage with respect to those vessels "as pass on the seas upon their lawful occasion."[151] Considerable diversity of opinion has existed among international lawyers concerning the nature of the right of innocent passage, the vessels to which it appertains, and the conditions under which it may be exercised. This has been equally true within Soviet international legal writing, state practice, and legislation.

INNOCENT PASSAGE IN SOVIET LEGISLATION AND TREATY PRACTICE

Tsarist legislation did not treat the problem of innocent passage. Since the Soviet regime in its early years desired both to protect Russian coasts from incursions by hostile naval vessels and to broaden foreign trade (which required "opening fatherland ports to foreign flag vessels"),[152] the regime of navigation in Soviet territorial waters had to be shaped accordingly. The 1920 Russian–Finnish peace treaty secured the right for Russian passenger and merchant vessels to use all channels open to Finnish vessels in the latter's territorial waters, conditioned upon the observance of provisions governing the pilotage of vessels.[153] Other peace treaties proscribed, "except in instances provided for in international law," the launching, passage, or navigation of any warships belonging either to organizations or groups whose object was to make war or to countries which were in a state of war with either of the contracting parties.[154] Commercial agreements contracted in 1924–27 with Italy, Sweden, Germany, Norway, Turkey, and others contained provisions, conditional on reciprocity, affecting the passage, rights, and duties of vessels belonging to the contracting parties.

The first and, until 1960, the only normative act to mention innocent passage (*mirnyi prokhod*—literally, "peaceful passage") was the Instruction for the Navigation of Vessels in Coastal Waters Within Artillery Range of Shore Batteries in Peacetime, of July 5, 1924. It provided that both Soviet and foreign merchant vessels shall have the

---

151. C. John Colombos, *The International Law of the Sea* (6th ed.; London: Longmans, 1967), pp. 131–32.

152. Meshera, *Morskoe pravo*, III, p. 5.

153. *SDD*, I, 76–92; *LNTS*, II, 5–79; *SS&D*, VI (1969), 26.

154. Peace Treaty between Russia and Estonia, February 2, 1920. *SDD*, I, 100–16; *LNTS*, XI, 29–71; *SS&D*, VI (1969), 57; Peace Treaty between Russia and Latvia, August 11, 1920. *SDD*, I, 35–49; *LNTS*, II, 195–231.

right to unhindered passage, except in special zones, within the limits of territorial waters.[155] This instruction was replaced in 1936 by the Rules for the Entrance of Vessels into Areas of Restricted Movement, whose text is not available, but which apparently made no explicit reference to innocent passage.[156]

The 1927 statute on the state boundary did not mention the right of innocent passage; however, it did consolidate the scope of coastal authority over the passage of foreign vessels. All nonmilitary vessels without distinction of flag were subject to supervision by the Unified State Political Administration (Art. 23). Within a 12-mile maritime frontier zone, all nonmilitary vessels could be boarded and searched by border guard officers; masters of vessels being searched were obliged to submit all documents in their possession relating to the vessel and its cargo (Art. 25). Nonmilitary vessels could be detained: (a) if the master failed to present all relevant documents concerning the vessel and cargo; (b) if the vessel received or discharged cargo or persons in territorial waters without proper authorization; or (c) if the vessel engaged in hunting, fishing, or other maritime trade in a prohibited area, or in an unrestricted area without proper authorization (Art. 26).[157]

In 1960, as part of widespread reforms in several areas of Soviet legislation and in response to the 1958 Geneva Convention on the Territorial Sea, the Soviet Union enacted a new Statute on the Protection of the State Boundary of the USSR and promulgated new rules governing the passage of foreign warships in Soviet territorial waters.

The new statute contained the first thorough exposition of the right of innocent passage through Soviet territorial waters, although "the Soviet Union never denied this international legal principle in the past."[158] The provisions of the 1960 statute pertaining to innocent passage may be summarized as follows:[159]

(a) Foreign nonmilitary vessels enjoy a right of innocent passage through the territorial waters of the USSR. Passage is defined as navigation through territorial waters for the purpose of traversing them without entering internal waters, of proceeding to internal waters, or of departing from internal waters for the high seas. Passage is considered innocent if a vessel follows a customary navigational course or a course recommended by competent agencies while observing the

155. Article 2. Egor'ev, *Zakonodatel'stvo i mezhdunarodnye dogovory,* p. 433; *SS&D,* VI (1969), 58.

156. Uustal', *Mezhdunarodno-pravovoi rezhim territorial'nykh vod,* p. 61.

157. *SZ SSSR* (1927), no. 62, item 625.

158. Barabolia and Lesnikov, "Novoe polozhenie," p. 16.

159. *Vedomosti SSSR* (1960), no. 34, item 324; *SS&D,* VI (1969), 63.

established regime of territorial waters, and in areas not closed to navigation (Art. 15).

(b) Foreign warships are to pass through territorial waters and enter internal waters of the USSR in accordance with the previous authorization of the Soviet government in the manner provided for by special rules for the visits of foreign warships. Foreign submarines permitted entrance to Soviet territorial and internal waters must navigate on the surface (Art. 16).

(c) Foreign warships and nonmilitary vessels, while present in Soviet territorial waters, must observe radio, port, customs, sanitary, and other rules established for navigation (Art. 17).

(d) Nonobservance by nonmilitary vessels of the rules for innocent passage because of damage or entry in distress must be communicated immediately to the authorities of the nearest Soviet port. Sending a false signal for the purpose of illegal entry into Soviet territorial waters or arrival in such waters is considered to be a violation of the state boundary, and the offending vessel is subject to detention (Art. 18).

(e) Maritime trade (fishing, crabbing, hunting, etc.) by foreign vessels is prohibited in Soviet territorial waters except as provided for by agreements with other states. Foreign vessels are also prohibited from performing hydrographic work and research in these waters. Violation entails detention of the vessel and prosecution of those responsible under the criminal codes of the union republics (Art. 19).

(f) For the purposes of the statute, violators of the state boundary of the USSR include foreign warships and nonmilitary vessels in territorial waters which violate the established rules of entrance (Art. 26).

(g) With respect to foreign nonmilitary vessels, the Soviet border guard has the right: (a) to request a vessel to show its national flag if it is not raised and to inquire as to the purpose of entrance into Soviet territorial waters; (b) to request a vessel to change course if it is in an area temporarily or permanently closed; (c) to stop a vessel and conduct an inspection when the vessel is in a closed area, is moving outside established channels or a recommended course, lies adrift, anchors, does not reply to signals for an inspection or for a change in course, or when a vessel violates rules established by the statute. An inspection includes verification of ship's and navigational documents, documents of the officers and crew, passengers, and cargo, and, in necessary instances, of the ship's quarters; (d) to take from the vessel and to detain persons who have committed crimes and who are subject to criminal responsibility under all-union and union republic legislation and to transfer them to the appropriate agencies. These measures may not be applied to a person on board a foreign vessel traversing Soviet territorial waters who has committed a crime prior to the entrance of the vessel in the territorial waters if the ship is proceeding from a foreign port, restricts its passage to territorial waters, and does not enter internal waters; (e) to pursue and detain ship-violators of the Soviet state boundary (Art. 36). Article 36 does not apply to foreign warships.

(h) Any foreign nonmilitary vessels in Soviet territorial waters may be detained by the border guard and brought to the nearest port: (a) for violation of zones permanently or temporarily closed; (b) for loading or unloading cargo or persons in unauthorized places without the permission of competent agencies; (c) for conducting maritime trade or hydrographic work and research in Soviet territorial waters; (d) for intentionally damaging navigation markers, cables, and other submerged or protruding objects belonging to the Soviet Union; (e) when the vessel's master does not present ship's and cargo documents; (f) for refusal of the vessel to obey instructions of Soviet authorities; (g) in all other instances of violation of rules established in the statute (Art. 37).

WRITINGS OF RUSSIAN AND SOVIET JURISTS

Prior to 1917, Russian jurists, apparently without exception, endorsed the right of innocent passage as a principle of international law. F. F. Martens wrote:

... the authority of the coastal state over both coastal and territorial seas should not be understood to mean the complete exclusion of such waters from the national arteries of international commerce. . . . If any merchant vessel only passes through the line of the coastal or territorial sea, it does not thereby come within the jurisdiction of coastal authority.[160]

Perhaps because it was a customary principle of international law, innocent passage seems to have been ignored in the early writings of Soviet jurists.[161] By the mid-1930s, with the doctrinal recognition of international custom as a legitimate though subordinate source of international law, Soviet jurists undertook to explain or reconcile the customary and legislative norms of innocent passage. Their efforts by no means produced identical results but rather reflected different approaches to legal analysis and the changing requirements of Soviet foreign and commercial policy.

160. Martens, *Sovremennoe mezhdunarodnoe pravo*, I, p. 392; Ul'ianitskii, *Mezhdunarodnoe pravo*, p. 88. The context of Martens' remark, however, implied that he may have had reservations about innocent passage for warships.
161. However, Korovin wrote in 1926 that "all vessels, without distinction, have a right of innocent passage in the territorial sea. . . ." E. A. Korovin, *Sovremennoe mezhdunarodnoe publichnoe pravo* (Moscow: Gosizdat, 1926), p. 63.

In 1936 Sheptovitskii acknowledged without qualification that the right of innocent passage was a "generally recognized principle of the regime of territorial waters." He defined innocent passage as "navigation not violating the rules established in the maritime belt for the safety of navigation nor the political and economic interests of the coastal state." The expression "political and economic interests" included the right to declare areas prohibited to vessels under national or foreign flags but not "in general to prohibit the passage of foreign vessels."[162]

The right of innocent passage was also endorsed in the early post-World War II era.[163] As late as 1951, it was possible to find the unqualified statement that "the passage of foreign merchant vessels through territorial waters may not be prohibited by the coastal state,"[164] although the reference to "merchant vessel" itself connoted a change in attitude. In another volume published that same year, however, V. N. Durdenevskii emphasized the obligation of the passing foreign merchant ship to respect coastal state legislation, while conceding that the practice of states and international legal custom recognized a right of innocent passage for foreign merchant vessels through territorial waters.[165] Again, the absence of a reference to Soviet legislation and treaty practice, as well as the limitation of the right to merchant vessels, signaled a change in Soviet attitude probably traceable to the increasing tension of the Cold War.

In 1954 Nikolaev advanced a more extreme interpretation of the applicable international rule:

It is commonly stated in textbooks of international law that the authority of the coastal state in territorial waters is limited by the so-called right of innocent passage of foreign vessels, both merchant and military . . . as it contravenes the sovereignty of the state over territorial waters and gives an opportunity to aggressive blocs to commit hostile actions against the coastal state under the guise of the "right of innocent passage."[166]

Nikolaev referred to the "admittance" [*dopusk*] of foreign vessels to Soviet territorial waters and concluded that

foreign nonmilitary vessels may freely pass through the territorial waters of a coastal state if this passage is not only innocent, but is necessary from the viewpoint of customary navigation; but the coastal state may legally pro-

162. Sheptovitskii, *Morskoe pravo*, p. 34; Pashukanis, *Ocherki po mezhdunarodnomu pravu*, p. 120.
163. Durdenevskii and Krylov, *Mezhdunarodnoe pravo*, p. 256.
164. G. I. Imenitov, *Sovetskoe morskoe i rybolovnoe pravo* (Moscow: Gosiurizdat, 1951), p. 21.
165. Korovin, *Mezhdunarodnoe pravo*, pp. 302–3.
166. Nikolaev, *Problema territorial'nykh vod*, p. 47.

hibit the navigation of foreign nonmilitary vessels in its territorial waters if this navigation is not called for by navigational necessity.[167]

Other Soviet international lawyers, however, did not support Nikolaev's view. In an otherwise favorable review of Nikolaev's book, Durdenevskii pointed out that in both doctrine and practice the Soviet Union consented to restrict its sovereignty over territorial waters by recognizing the right of innocent passage.[168]

Nevertheless, divergent and circumspect definitions of innocent passage appeared in Soviet legal media. Bakhov adopted an equivocal position, noting that "Soviet legislation does not prohibit the admittance of foreign merchant vessels into USSR territorial waters" and concluding that Soviet legislation is in accordance with generally recognized principles of international law. Foreign vessels must follow a recommended course of navigation, avoid closed zones, and strictly observe the rules of fortified zones. The USSR was said to possess an indisputable right of jurisdiction over foreign nonmilitary vessels within its territorial waters.[169]

A 1957 international law textbook contained an important change. The customary element of innocent passage received a different emphasis in a new formulation: "International practice shows that coastal countries do not customarily make the innocent passage of foreign merchant vessels through their territorial waters subject to special permission."[170] The term "right" [*pravo*] was no longer used in connection with passage; states were described as permitting innocent passage and as exercising their "rights" in regulating or prohibiting such passage.

Even though the 1958 Geneva Convention on the Territorial Sea was ratified by the Soviet Union in 1960, Soviet jurists writing in that year and later continued to express diverse conceptions of innocent passage. Rodionov[171] and Shmigel'skii declared, without any reference whatsoever to the Geneva convention, that states may not hinder the innocent passage of merchant vessels nor interfere in the internal order of a passing ship.[172] Lisovskii based his discussion of innocent passage on Soviet legislation and on the 1930 Hague conference.[173]

167. *Ibid.,* p. 51.
168. *SGIP,* no. 7 (1954), 142.
169. Bakhov, *Voenno-morskoi spravochnik,* pp. 85–87.
170. Kozhevnikov, *Mezhdunarodnoe pravo,* p. 210.
171. Rodionov, in D. B. Levin and G. P. Kaliuzhnaia (eds.), *Mezhdunarodnoe pravo* (Moscow: Gosiurizdat, 1960), p. 168.
172. G. L. Shmigel'skii and V. A. Iasinovskii, *Osnovy sovetskogo morskogo prava* (Moscow: izd-vo Morskoi transport, 1959), p. 30.
173. V. I. Lisovskii, *Mezhdunarodnoe pravo* (2d ed.; Kiev: izd-vo Kievskii universitet, 1961), pp. 154–56. The treatment of this question has not been

Other writers cited Article 15 of the 1960 statute on the state boundary as being dispositive, without referring to the Geneva convention.[174] A. K. Zhudro,[175] A. N. Siling,[176] and N. I. Petrenko,[177] however, acknowledged that the legal regime of territorial waters was regulated by the Geneva convention.

Some Soviet writers continued to define innocent passage only as "sailing through territorial waters for the purpose of traversing them without entering internal waters or leaving them for the high seas." This is an exceedingly narrow reading of the Geneva convention definition of innocent passage. The better view among Soviet jurists is that passage to and from internal waters of the coastal state also comes within the modern rule of innocent passage.[178]

Extensive analyses of innocent passage and the Geneva convention are found in a monograph by A. L. Kolodkin and an essay by P. D. Barabolia. Kolodkin's treatment is basically descriptive of the correlative rights and duties of the coastal state and the passing vessel. He stressed the necessity for strict observance of a coastal state's laws and regulations for a passage to be considered innocent. The primary purpose of the rights and duties of the coastal state and of the passing vessel, wrote Kolodkin, is to protect the innocent character of passage. Consequently, the master of a passing vessel has a duty to ensure that no act is committed by the vessel which in any degree infringes upon the political or defense interests of a coastal state and which could strain relations between the state to which the vessel appertains and that to which the territorial waters belong.[179] This obligation is said to be in addition to that provided by Article 17 of the Geneva convention requiring passing vessels to observe laws and rules of the coastal state and other norms of international law.

The paramount obligation to which Kolodkin referred apparently inheres in the very *raison d'etre* of innocent passage, for according to Soviet jurisprudence the right of innocent passage "was founded on the general consent of coastal states to grant this right and was re-

substantially modified in the 1970 edition. See Lisovskii, *Mezhdunarodnoe pravo* (Moscow: izd-vo Vysshaia shkola, 1970), pp. 152–58.

174. Shmigel'skii and Iasinovskii, *Osnovy sovetskogo morskogo prava* (2d ed.; 1963), pp. 33–35; F. I. Kozhevnikov (ed.), *Mezhdunarodnoe pravo* (Moscow: izd-vo IMO, 1964), p. 218.

175. A. K. Zhudro (ed.), *Morskoe pravo* (Moscow: izd-vo Transport, 1964), p. 94.

176. A. N. Siling, *Morskoe pravo* (Moscow: izd-vo Transport, 1964), pp. 60–62.

177. Levin and Kaliuzhnaia, *Mezhdunarodnoe pravo* (2d ed.; 1964), p. 195.

178. Chkhikvadze, *Kurs mezhdunarodnogo prava*, III, pp. 198–99.

179. Kolodkin, *Pravovoi rezhim territorial'nykh vod*, p. 32.

lated to the development of technology and the establishment of international sea lanes."[180]

Barabolia is one of the few Soviet international lawyers to acknowledge that the right of innocent passage of nonmilitary vessels in territorial waters had been recognized in international law by the majority of states since "feudal" times, although he criticized bourgeois theories which describe innocent passage as a "universal" and "unrestricted" right. Such erroneous theories were the result of regarding the territorial sea as part of the high seas instead of under coastal state sovereignty.[181]

INNOCENT PASSAGE OF FISHING VESSELS

The extension of the right of innocent passage to commercial fishing and sealing vessels has been troublesome because most states reserve fishing rights in territorial waters exclusively for their own nationals. Shmigel'skii concluded in 1959 that foreign fishing vessels which did not have the right to exploit their trade in Soviet territorial waters might enter such waters only in the event of distress of storm, damage, or when sailing to or returning from their areas of operation.[182] Sobakin, as well as Shmigel'skii and Iasinovskii, found additional support for this rule in Article 19 of the 1960 statute on the state boundary.[183]

The 1958 Geneva Convention on the Territorial Sea, however, did not so restrict innocent passage for fishing vessels. The convention provided in Article 14(5) that passage of foreign fishing vessels shall not be considered innocent "if they do not observe such laws and regulations as the coastal state may make and publish in order to prevent these vessels from fishing in the territorial sea." Therefore, unless a foreign fishing vessel violates the coastal state regime of territorial waters, there is no reason to treat it differently from any other passing vessel or to assume its passage is not innocent unless it falls into the categories of activity suggested by Shmigel'skii. The 1966 naval international law manual departed from Shmigel'skii's view, noting that foreign fishing vessels have a right of innocent passage unless they violate rules prohibiting fishing in territorial waters.[184]

180. Koretskii and Tunkin, *Ocherki mezhdunarodnogo morskogo prava,* p. 43.

181. *Ibid.,* p. 109.

182. Shmigel'skii and Iasinovskii, *Osnovy sovetskogo morskogo prava* (1959), p. 31.

183. *Ibid.* (2d ed.), p. 33; Levin and Kaliuzhnaia, *Mezhdunarodnoe pravo* (1964), p. 220.

184. Barabolia, *Voenno-morskoi spravochnik,* p. 31; an identical view is expressed by Volkov, *Morskoe pravo,* p. 103.

An official definition of the conditions of innocent passage for Soviet fishing vessels is contained in a little known Instruction on the Navigation Procedure for Vessels of the Commercial Fishing Fleet of the USSR, the Conduct by Them of Commercial Fishing on the High Seas, and the Duties of Executive Personnel with Regard to its Fulfillment, adopted January 16, 1961.[185] According to this instruction, Soviet fishing vessels may pass through territorial waters and fishing or other special zones (unless passage is expressly prohibited) of foreign states if: (a) the provisions of the 1958 Geneva Convention on the Territorial Sea are observed; (b) the laws and rules prescribed by the coastal state are obeyed; and (c) the vessel is put into "passing condition,"—that is, gear has been freed of fish and other marine products and stowed away in the hold or placed under a tarpaulin; auxiliary sloops are in place, tied down, and covered; derricks and cranes have been secured and other fishing mechanisms have been covered; all commercial fishing operations, processing, and catching of commercial marine life has ceased; and any loading or unloading operations or refueling has been completed (Art. 11). Thus, in the Soviet view, a fishing vessel must not only refrain from fishing in territorial waters but also must not give the appearance of performing nor in any way be prepared to perform such fishing operations.

PASSAGE OF FOREIGN WARSHIPS IN TERRITORIAL WATERS

In recent years Soviet jurists have been of one mind on the question of previous authorization from the coastal state for the passage of warships through its territorial waters.[186] They affirm that no generally recognized, obligatory rules exist with respect to the right of innocent passage of warships.

Contemporary writers have experienced difficulty in attempting to establish the existence of previous authorization in interwar Soviet practice. The Instruction for the Navigation of Vessels in Coastal Waters Within Artillery Range of Shore Batteries, of July 5, 1924, pro-

---

185. V. F. Meshera (ed.), *Normativnye dokumenty po morskomu pravu* (Moscow: izd-vo Transport, 1965), pp. 133–34; translated in *ILM*, VIII (1969), 333; *SS&D*, VI (1969), 71.

186. Article 35 of the 1964 USSR Customs Code defines a warship as:

> any vessel (or auxiliary vessel) sailing under a military or border guard flag, under the command of a person in military service and on the staff of a military command, as well as a vessel which in accordance with a special statement of the USSR Ministry of Defense, performs tasks of a military-operational nature. The Commander bears responsibility for observing the provisions of the Customs Code.

Article 36 extends the provisions of Article 35 to foreign warships visiting Soviet ports. *Vedomosti SSSR* (1964), no. 20, item 242.

vided that "warships of foreign powers have the right to sail in territorial waters, but should not anchor, conduct exercises, seizures, firings, etc."[187] Pursuant to the 1927 statute on the state boundary, Provisional Rules for Foreign Warships Visiting USSR Waters were promulgated on March 28, 1931.[188] Although the rules required previous authorization for visits by foreign warships, they were applicable by their terms only to arrivals in Soviet ports and internal waters. Consequently, when the instruction of July 5, 1924, was superseded by a new set of rules which apparently contained no reference to innocent passage,[189] the passage of foreign warships in Soviet territorial waters was regulated by international custom and prior Soviet practice.

M. Ia. Sheptovitskii presumably reflected the current status of Soviet practice under the 1931 rules when he wrote that authorization was needed only to enter internal waters.[190] V. N. Durdenevskii also stated:

Foreign warships also may pass in territorial waters without receiving previous authorization therefor and without a prior notification concerning the passage. . . . The practice of states shows that in peacetime states generally do not hinder the passage of foreign warships in their territorial waters.[191]

Durdenevskii's formulation was an accurate reflection of Soviet state practice respecting the innocent passage of foreign warships during the interwar period and in the post-World War II era until 1960. The rather frequent protests of the Soviet government occasioned by unauthorized visits of foreign naval vessels to Soviet waters were generally careful to distinguish between the right of passage in territorial waters and the right to enter internal waters.

On January 14, 1918, the Executive Committee of the Vladivostok Soviet protested to the Japanese Consul General in that city against the arrival of Japanese merchant ships and warships in the port "without consent and even without any warning" as "violating the right of the Russian Republic."[192] A German flotilla entered Russian "territorial waters" in the area of Murmansk on July 26, 1921, without per-

187. Egor'ev, *Zakonodatel'stvo i mezhdunarodnye dogovory*, p. 433; *SS&D*, vi (1969), 58.
188. Bakhov, *Voenno-morskoi spravochnik*, pp. 106–9. Harben erroneously referred to "undisclosed" Soviet rules concerning warships. See William N. Harben, "Soviet Positions Concerning Maritime Waters," *JAG Journal*, xv (1961), 149.
189. Uustal', *Mezhdunarodno-pravovoi rezhim territorial'nykh vod*, p. 61.
190. Sheptovitskii, *Morskoe pravo*, p. 51.
191. Durdenevskii and Krylov, *Mezhdunarodnoe pravo*, p. 257.
192. *Dokumenty*, i, 80; also see *ibid.*, p. 85.

mission or warning and was fired upon by shore batteries. Protesting the conduct of the German vessels, the Soviet government declared:

In conformity with norms of international law and custom no foreign vessel has the right to enter the territorial waters of another state without authorization. These provisions and customs the more so affect foreign warships, whose approach must be specially notified and authorization for entrance obtained from the appropriate state.[193]

American naval vessels were authorized to enter Soviet ports on the Black Sea in connection with the operations of the American Relief Administration. However, in certain instances American vessels were expected to notify Soviet port authorities in advance of their arrival.[194]

On May 12, 1922, the RSFSR protested the seizure of a Greek vessel by Turkish warships within Russian territorial waters as violating "customary norms of international law."[195] The incident was said to have occurred within "three versts of shore."[196]

The government of Japan was formally notified on February 9, 1923, that, "in conformity with international custom and to avoid any misunderstandings," the generally accepted norm of international law requiring warships to obtain prior authorization to visit the ports of another state "also extends to all ports of the RSFSR situated on the coast of the Pacific Ocean."[197]

In January 1924, Soviet authorities formally protested two separate incidents of American warships entering Soviet harbors in violation of "customarily recognized rules for the entrance of warships into foreign ports."[198]

Beginning in 1925, the Soviet government from time to time

193. *Dokumenty,* IV, 258. It is obvious that here "territorial waters" meant internal waters.

194. *Dokumenty,* V, 72, 717. Later American vessels were instructed to obtain specific authorization for each visit. *Dokumenty,* VI, 147.

195. *Dokumenty,* V, 380.

196. *Dokumenty,* V, 533. A verst is about 3500 feet.

197. *Dokumenty,* VI, 182. This Note was sent when a Japanese cruiser continued to remain in Vladivostok after the evacuation of Japanese occupation forces from the Maritime Province. In May 1923, a Japanese squadron of destroyers anchored without authorization at Petropavlovsk to "observe the correctness of fishing in the area." Two Japanese destroyers attempted to place navigational markers in the mouth of the Amur River in July 1923. A second note of protest was sent by the USSR in October of that year in response to these actions. *Dokumenty,* VI, 490, 612. In June 1924, a further incident occurred when Japanese destroyers fired upon Soviet vessels setting channel markers in the Amur. Again the USSR protested the presence of warships "in Soviet waters" without permission. *Dokumenty,* VII, 371.

198. *Dokumenty,* VII, 50.

sought to extend the requirement of prior authorization to Soviet territorial waters as well. In a Note of August 3, 1925, the anchoring of a Japanese destroyer without permission "in the territorial waters of the USSR" was said to contravene the "spirit of good will" between the two countries. Japan responded that the destroyer had anchored beyond the 3-mile limit of territorial waters.[199] A similar incident of July 12, 1925, was characterized as a "violation of international law" in a Soviet Note sent on December 11 of that year. In this instance the USSR equated the 12-mile fishing zone with territorial waters.[200]

When on January 5, 1926, the Soviet government protested the entrance of a French military transport vessel into Batumi without preliminary notification, the French government stated that such notification had not been required by Soviet authorities in the past and that the French navy had no official knowledge of any change in Soviet practice.[201]

It is therefore clear from the published record of Soviet diplomatic correspondence that, with the single exception concerning Japan, the USSR considered it necessary for foreign warships to have prior authorization or to give previous notification only when entering internal waters of a coastal state. In virtually every case Soviet authorities invoked customary international law to support their view, and in only one instance prior to the enactment of the Provisional Rules of 1931 was specific reference made to the existence of any applicable Soviet legislation.

In 1939, however, Keilin and Vinogradov expressed a view that was to predominate in Soviet international legal media after the war as

---

199. *Dokumenty*, VIII, 468.

200. *Dokumenty*, VIII, 702. On May 4, 1931, the USSR vigorously protested the anchoring of a Japanese warship in Avachinsk Bay within three miles of Petropavlovsk as a flagrant violation of the "law of the USSR and of international law." *Dokumenty*, XIV, 310.

201. *Dokumenty*, IX, 9. In a reply dated March 8, 1926, the Soviet government declared that on April 3, 1925 an English translation of the Hydrographic Administration Circular No. 18 had been transmitted to the French Embassy in Moscow. The circular related to the entrance of foreign vessels into Soviet ports. On August 5, 1925, additional documents were transmitted, including an (untitled) circular issued by the People's Commissariat of Military and Naval Affairs. Paragraph 5 of the latter circular, as quoted in the Note of March 8th, stipulated:

> Warships (foreign) shall be permitted in open ports only after the previous authorization of our Government. If there are no definite instructions concerning the free access of a warship, a vessel which has arrived without warning should be detained at the entrance of the port until clarification of the reasons for its arrival.

Curiously, this circular was not mentioned in diplomatic correspondence with other states in connection with similar incidents later in time.

the correct but not generally accepted position—that is, that foreign warships must obtain the prior consent of the coastal state in order to pass through the territorial waters of that state.[202]

In his dissenting opinion to the Judgment of the International Court of Justice in the *Corfu Channel* case, Judge S. B. Krylov concluded that "the right to regulate the passage of warships through its territorial waters appertains to the coastal State."[203] In support of his view, Krylov cited the absence of an international convention regulating the question, the divergent practices of states in general and hence the absence of international custom, and the opinions of leading French and American scholars who opposed the recognition of such a right.

The most ambitious attempt to base the principle of previous authorization in Soviet state practice was made by Nikolaev. Conceding that the Provisional Rules of 1931 were not explicit, he commented: ". . . it is possible to conclude from the general intent of these Rules that the authorization procedure provided by them related to territorial waters inasmuch as they are a part of USSR waters."[204] Nikolaev also referred to other official Soviet documents, such as the Telegram of December 11, 1924, to the United States protesting that the "entrance of an American warship into the territorial waters of the Soviet Union without appropriate authorization . . . contravenes international law."[205]

Keilin supported the doctrine of previous consent on the ground that the coastal state has no interests in allowing the passage of foreign warships which are comparable to the commercial benefits accruing from the passage of merchant vessels.[206]

The draft Articles on the Territorial Sea and Contiguous Zone submitted by the International Law Commission to the United Nations General Assembly contained a provision permitting the coastal state to make the passage of warships through the territorial sea subject to previous authorization or notification.[207] A proposal to delete this article from the convention was defeated, but a Danish proposal to omit the term "authorization" was adopted. Even this amended version

202. See Kozhevnikov, *Mezhdunarodnoe pravo,* p. 212.

203. International Court of Justice, *Reports of Judgments, Advisory Opinions and Orders, The Corfu Channel Case (Merits), Judgment of April 9, 1949* (Leiden: Sijthoff, 1949), p. 74; *SS&D,* vi (1969), 60.

204. Nikolaev, *Problema territorial'nykh vod,* p. 214.

205. *U.S. Foreign Relations 1924,* p. 681; *SS&D,* vi (1969), 59. In this case too "territorial waters" meant internal waters.

206. A. D. Keilin, *Sovetskoe morskoe pravo* (Moscow: izd-vo Vodnyi transport, 1954), p. 64.

207. *Yearbook of the International Law Commission 1956,* ii, 276.

failed to achieve the necessary votes, leaving the status of innocent passage of warships regulated only by Article 23 of the convention, which stated:

> If any warship does not comply with the regulations of the coastal state concerning passage through the territorial sea and disregards any request for compliance which is made to it, the coastal state may require the warship to leave the territorial sea.[208]

The Soviet Union has taken several steps to consolidate its position on the issue. First, it entered a reservation to Article 23, declaring that a coastal state "has the right to establish a procedure of authorization for the passage of foreign warships through its territorial waters."[209] Second, it explicitly provided for an authorization procedure for foreign warships in Article 16 of the 1960 statute on the state boundary. Third, the ambiguous Provisional Rules of 1931 regulating visits by foreign warships were replaced by a new set of rules in 1960.[210]

Under the 1960 rules, consent for the passage of foreign warships into Soviet territorial waters must be requested through diplomatic channels 30 days prior to the proposed visit. The request must specify the number, class, and name of the ship, the proposed port of call, the purpose of the passage, the length of stay in port, the rank and name of the commander, and the number and types of aircraft on board. Maximum duration of a visit is seven days, unless extended by special permission. No more than three vessels may enter any one port or area of territorial waters at the same time. Foreign warships in Soviet territorial waters are prohibited from conducting research, surveys, and soundings (except those necessary in channels open to all navigation), from making photographs, drawings, sketches, or lists of port areas and fortifications, from sending out armed launches, sloops, or ship's boats, from firing any kind of weapon (except salutes), laying or sweeping mines, using smoke screens, creating artificial fog or any type of underwater explosion, and from polluting waters. These provisions also apply to naval auxiliary vessels and armed ships for the protection of fisheries. A first violation of any of the provisions entails a warning; a second or continuing offense, a request to leave Soviet

---

208. *UNTS*, DXVI, 205. The Soviet Union and Bulgaria had proposed a new article that would have obliged the coastal state not to hamper the innocent passage through its territorial sea of merchant and other ships, "other than warships," of any nationality. *1958 Official Records*, III, 223; *SS&D*, VI (1969), 62.

209. *Vedomosti SSSR* (1964), no. 43, item 472; *SS&D*, VI (1969), 63.

210. Barabolia, *Voenno-morskoi spravochnik*, pp. 69–75; translated in Butler, *Law of Soviet Territorial Waters*, p. 126; *SS&D*, VI (1969), 65.

waters. Foreign warships carrying heads of state or heads of diplomatic representations accredited to the government of the USSR follow a procedure of notification rather than of authorization.

These rules do not apply to foreign warships seeking refuge because of damage or distress of storm; however, compulsory pilotage regulations apply in all instances.

Special attention was directed in the 1966 naval international law manual to the provisions requiring foreign submarines to navigate exclusively on the surface and to observe the rules for entry established for surface warships. Violation of either requirement is labeled a grave infringement of Soviet sovereignty and of generally recognized norms of international law. Because of observed instances of foreign submarines entering Soviet territorial waters for purposes of reconnaissance, the "Soviet Ministry of Defense has issued instructions that henceforth foreign submarines discovered violating the state boundary of the USSR and in a submerged position shall be destroyed."[211]

Soviet legislation and the Geneva convention. The chairman of the Soviet delegation to the Geneva Conference on the Law of the Sea summarized the results of the Convention on the Territorial Sea with respect to the right of innocent passage as follows:

It is generally recognized under international law that merchant and other nonmilitary vessels have the right of unhindered passage through the territorial waters of a foreign state, provided they use the customary shipping routes. The coastal state has the right to lay down any rules it wishes regarding the passage of warships, including a requirement that preliminary notification be given or permission obtained.[212]

As embodied in Soviet legislation adopted in 1960, this interpretation of the convention creates certain difficulties. That warships have a right of innocent passage under the text of the convention is a plausible interpretation, although it may be and has been argued that the majority of delegates at Geneva did not intend warships to have this right.[213] Article 14 under Subsection A, "Rules Applicable to All Ships," states that "ships of all states . . . should enjoy the right of innocent passage. . . ." There is no restriction on warships; Article 14(6) specifically directs that the submarine navigate on the surface while in foreign territorial waters. Moreover, the fact that many na-

211. Barabolia, *Voenno-morskoi spravochnik,* p. 50; *Pravda,* August 29, 1961; *SS&D,* vi (1969), 74.

212. G. I. Tunkin, "The Geneva Conference on the Law of the Sea," *International Affairs* [Moscow], no. 7 (1958), 48.

213. Max Sørenson, "Law of the Sea," *International Conciliation,* no. 520 (November 1958), 244; Philip C. Jessup, "The United Nations Conference on the Law of the Sea," *Columbia Law Review,* LIX (1959), 234–68.

tions filed reservations when the article permitting states to require previous authorization was deleted from the convention strongly suggests they recognized that the deletion amounted to approval of the right of passage.[214]

Some Soviet jurists have rejected the argument that the deletion of draft Article 24 from the final convention implied that foreign warships have the right of innocent passage through territorial waters. The reservation made to Article 23 by the Soviet Union was not intended to make "an exception to Article 23, but to make it more precise:"

> It is important for the development of international maritime law, inasmuch as it reflects the aspiration to codify rules regulating the right for states themselves to resolve the question of the procedure for the admittance of foreign warships into their territorial waters—a right in essence accepted . . . by universal practice.[215]

It is further contended in Soviet media that Article 23 of the convention, setting forth the conditions in which a coastal state may require a warship to leave the territorial sea, defined only the duties of warships and not their rights.[216] And since Article 17 of the convention requires the observance of laws and rules of the coastal state relating to transport and navigation, and Article 23 requires foreign warships to observe the rules of the coastal state, these rules may include the requirement of previous authorization or previous notification. Moreover, the convention did not exclude a procedure of authorization for foreign warships.[217]

In reality, however, Soviet legislation has the effect of denying rather than restricting the right of innocent passage. The requirement of 30 days advance notice of the proposed passage and the discretion to withhold authorization transforms the passage of warships in Soviet territorial waters into a privilege. Even were the requirement of authorization dispensed with, 30 days notice would effectively limit the right of passage in derogation of the principle of freedom of navigation.[218]

The Vil'kitskii Straits incidents. Since 1963, United States naval

214. Volkov seems to take this view, for although he believes Article 23 is inconsistent with "international legal practice and the legislation of many states," he interpreted that article as granting warships the right of innocent passage and treated the Soviet reservation as a normal response of taking exception to the rule. Volkov, *Morskoe pravo,* p. 104.

215. Chkhikvadze, *Kurs mezhdunarodnogo prava,* III, 210.

216. Koretskii and Tunkin, *Ocherki mezhdunarodnogo morskogo prava,* p. 109.

217. Levin and Kaliuzhnaia, *Mezhdunarodnoe pravo* (1964), p. 195; Uustal', *Mezhdunarodno-pravovoi rezhim territorial'nykh vod,* p. 71.

218. A. N. Nikolaev, a member of the Soviet delegation to the 1958 Geneva Conference on the Law of the Sea, met this objection by arguing that "the

and coast guard icebreakers have been conducting oceanographic research in the Kara, Laptev, East Siberian, and Chukotsk Seas bordering the northern coastline of the Soviet Union. In 1965, and especially in 1967, these vessels were to sail the entire northeast passage across the top of Russia, a feat never accomplished by an American ship. When polar ice prevented the vessels, in 1967,[219] from proceeding around Severnaia Zemlia, the United States notified the Soviet Union through diplomatic channels on August 24 that in order to complete their voyage the vessels (the *Edisto* and the *Eastwind*) would have to pass through the Vil'kitskii Straits separating the south of Severnaia Zemlia from the Taimyr Peninsula.[220] (See Map 2.)

The western entrance of the Vil'kitskii Straits is actually divided into two straits by a group of five small islands, the Geyberg Islands. The strait north of the Geyberg Islands is about 22½ miles wide, and the southern strait is about 11 miles wide.[221] Since all of the land and islands mentioned are Soviet territory and since the USSR claims a 12-mile limit for territorial waters, the straits each comprise Soviet territorial waters. On August 24, and again on August 28, as the two icebreakers proceeded toward the straits, the Soviet government declared that passage through the Vil'kitskii Straits would be a violation of Soviet frontiers.[222]

Although a foreign vessel has apparently never passed through the straits without Soviet approval and icebreaker assistance, and although the northern sea route is still a regional shipping route, the Soviet claim to exclude the American vessels, so far as public accounts of the diplomatic exchanges reveal, was not based upon a temporary suspension of the right of innocent passage through the area nor upon "historic rights" to the waters.[223] Rather, a radio message from the

---

paramount interests of a state should not be subordinated to a desire for haste in some other quarters." *1958 Official Records,* III, 130.

219. In 1965 the *Northwind* actually sailed around the northern tip of Severnaia Zemlia and could have completed the passage when inexplicably it was ordered to abort the mission and return. Richard Petrow, *Across the Top of Russia* (New York: David McKay, 1967), pp. 352–53.

220. *DSB,* LVII (1967), 362. The Soviet government was formally notified of the planned voyage shortly before it was publicly announced in the United States on August 16, 1967.

221. Donat Pharand, "Soviet Union Warns United States Against Use of Northeast Passage," *AJIL,* LXII (1968), 927.

222. *DSB,* LVII (1967), 362.

223. The opinion of many Soviet jurists that the northern seas have the status in international law of either closed seas or of historic bays would mean that the waters in question are internal waters through which there is no right of innocent passage. References by the Soviet government to the 12-mile breadth of territorial waters indicated that the closed sea and historic bay theories are not applied to this area in practice.

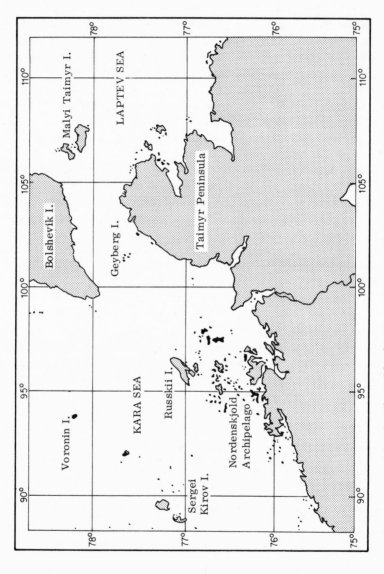

Map 2. The Vil'kitskii Straits between the Kara and Laptev Seas

Ministry of the Maritime Fleet of the USSR directly to the American icebreakers declared:

> . . . Vil'kitskii Straits are within USSR territorial waters. Therefore sailing of any foreign navy ships in the straits is subject to regulations of safety of USSR frontiers. For passing the straits according to the above regulations military ships must obtain preliminary permission of USSR Government through diplomatic channels one month before expected date of passage.[224]

A warship is defined in the 1958 Geneva Convention on the High Seas as being:

> a ship belonging to the naval forces of a state and bearing the external marks distinguishing warships of its nationality, under the command of an officer duly commissioned by the government and whose name appears in the Navy List, and manned by a crew who are under regular naval discipline.[225]

The two U.S. Coast Guard icebreakers were each armed with standard equipment, two five-inch .38 calibre guns at the bows and carried a crew of 20 officers, 195 enlisted men, and 5 civilian oceanographers.[226] Under United States law, the Coast Guard is "a military service and a branch of the armed forces of the United States," ordinarily within the jurisdiction of the Treasury Department, "except when operating as a service of the Navy." Transfer of service to the navy occurs either upon a declaration of war or "when the President directs."[227]

It is not known whether the icebreakers were operating as naval vessels or whether the officers and crew were subject to regular discipline; the oceanographic research being performed came within the U.S. Oceanographic Program, which is the ultimate responsibility of the secretary of the navy.[228] However, these distinctions between operations of the Treasury and Navy Departments may be superfluous, for under Soviet law the term warship comprehends both naval and border guard vessels.[229] The border guard of the Soviet Union is roughly the equivalent of the coast guard in the United States. The

---

224. The text of the telegram appeared in R. D. Wells, "The Icy 'Nyet'," *United States Naval Institute Proceedings,* xciv (1968), 78.

225. *SDD,* xxii, 222; *UNTS,* cccl, 82. See Article 8(2).

226. *New York Times,* August 31, 1967.

227. 14 U.S. Code, sections 1 and 3.

228. Pharand, "Soviet Union Warns the United States," p. 932.

229. Article 36, USSR Customs Code. *Vedomosti SSSR* (1964), no. 20, item 242.

armament carried by the icebreakers also probably influenced Soviet authorities to classify them as warships.[230]

Thus, under Soviet law and perhaps under the Convention on the High Seas as well, the icebreakers were warships which had not conformed to the procedure for previous authorization sanctioned by the Soviet reservation to the Convention on the Territorial Sea, by the 1960 statute on the state boundary, and by the 1960 rules for visits of warships to Soviet territorial waters.

In the American view, "a right of innocent passage exists for all ships through straits used for international navigation between two parts of the high seas" whether or not they may be overlapped by territorial waters.[231] Under the circumstances, the United States found it necessary to cancel the proposed navigation of the northeast passage. While the incident obliged the Soviet Union tacitly to concede that the northern seas have the status of high seas, it also forced the United States to respect the Soviet claim to a 12-mile limit for territorial waters and tacitly to recognize the capability of the USSR to enforce its previous authorization procedure for foreign warships.

It is puzzling that the voyage of the icebreakers should have been structured to ensure a confrontation over the issue of passage if ice conditions made it impossible to avoid the Vil'kitskii Straits. Had the planned circumnavigation, for example, been organized under nongovernmental auspices and the armament removed from the icebreakers, the legal position of the Soviet government would have been significantly more difficult to sustain.

The Soviet attitude in the Vil'kitskii Straits incident, as well as toward the whole question of innocent passage for warships, is probably founded upon national security considerations, on the fact that the northern sea route is essentially a Soviet-developed and administered undertaking, and on the conviction that the predominance of Western naval power will somehow be offset by conditioning passage upon coastal-state consent. The support for the Soviet view expressed by many nations at the Geneva conference who did not enter reservations to Article 23 suggests that international consensus still is lacking on passage for warships, notwithstanding a strict reading of the convention. Whether its newly acquired status as a ranking naval power will transform the Soviet apprehension of innocent passage for warships into a more tolerant attitude is not predictable at the moment, but such a change would not be a surprising development.

230. In 1965 A. N. Shelepin, a prominent member of the Communist Party of the Soviet Union, described the *Northwind* as a "military icebreaker." See *Krasnaia zvezda,* July 25, 1965, p. 3.

231. *DSB,* LVII (1967), 362; also see Pharand, "Soviet Union Warns the United States," pp. 933–35.

Criminal and Civil Jurisdiction

Russian jurists have held diverse views on the extent of coastal-state jurisdiction over passing foreign vessels. Although Martens, as we have seen, conceived of territorial waters as an extension of coastal territory, he regarded a vessel traversing territorial waters as subordinate only to the laws of the state whose flag the vessel flies. According to Martens, a foreign merchant vessel must visit or stop within the waters of the coastal state for a "more or less prolonged time" in order for coastal jurisdiction to appertain.[232] Ul'ianitskii believed crimes committed on vessels passing through territorial waters were only subject to coastal-state jurisdiction when the "results" of the crime extended beyond the vessel.[233]

There is no special law in the Soviet Union regulating criminal jurisdiction in territorial waters. Article 4 of the 1958 All-Union Fundamental Principles of Criminal Legislation extended the full scope of territorial jurisdiction to "all persons who commit crimes on the territory of the USSR."[234]

Inasmuch as Soviet territorial waters are under the full sovereignty of the Soviet Union, this article applies to all crimes committed on board foreign vessels while in waters of the USSR. On its face, Article 4 is inconsistent with a decree of May 24, 1927, which governs the procedure of arrests on foreign merchant vessels:

Appropriate authorities of the RSFSR shall have the right to make arrests of criminals on foreign merchant vessels only in those instances when the crime was committed by them wholly or partly on the shore or when the consequences of such crimes may give rise to serious complications on shore.[235]

Soviet authorities, however, customarily refrain from interfering, in accordance with international practice, if the crime committed does not threaten the security or public order of the Soviet Union or the humane principles of Soviet socialist law.[236]

The decree of May 24, 1927, has been interpreted by one jurist to mean that if a crime committed on a passing vessel were directed against the Soviet state, its nationals, or other persons not on board

---

232. Martens, *Sovremennoe mezhdunarodnoe pravo*, ii, 250.
233. Ul'ianitskii, *Mezhdunarodnoe pravo*, p. 89.
234. The RSFSR Criminal Code incorporates the provisions of Article 4, as do the criminal codes of the other union republics. See Harold J. Berman and James W. Spindler (trans.), *Soviet Criminal Law and Procedure: The RSFSR Codes* (Cambridge: Harvard University Press, 1966), p. 146.
235. *SU RSFSR* (1927), no. 52, item 348; *SS RSFSR*, xiv, 396; *SS&D*, vi (1969), 79.
236. Zhudro, *Morskoe pravo*, p. 108.

the vessel, or against their property, the consequences of the crime would be considered to have transcended the vessel. Since Soviet legislation provides "no restriction to the contrary," a fugitive on a vessel traversing Soviet territorial waters who has previously committed a crime on Soviet territory and is being sought by Soviet authorities may be arrested and brought to responsibility.[237]

The Criminal Code of the RSFSR contains numerous provisions directly pertaining to the regime of territorial waters: smuggling (Art. 78); illegal exit from or illegal entry into the USSR (Art. 83); violation of rules of safe movement and transport operation (Art. 85); damaging routes of communication and means of transport (Art. 86); failure of a vessel's master to render aid to a victim of disaster (Art. 129); violation of veterinary rules (Art. 160); violation of rules established for combating plant diseases and pests (Art. 161); illegally engaging in fishing or other water extractive trades (Art. 163); illegally engaging in hunting of seals and beavers (Art. 164); blasting in violation of rules for the protection of fish stocks (Art. 165); illegal hunting (Art. 166); illegally displaying the state flag of the USSR or of a union republic on a merchant vessel (Art. 203); failure to render aid upon collision of a vessel or failure to communicate the name of the vessel (Art. 204); damaging of marine telegraph cable (Art. 205); violation of rules governing transport (Art. 213); and violation of rules established for the purpose of combating epidemics (Art. 222).

The 1960 statute on the state boundary empowered ships and other vessels of the border guard to detain any foreign nonmilitary vessel situated on the territorial or internal waters of the Soviet Union or in the Soviet part of the waters of border rivers and lakes and to convoy it to the nearest port or harbor when: (a) the vessel is situated in regions permanently or temporarily closed for navigation as announced in *Notices to Mariners;* (b) the vessel embarks or disembarks people, or loads or unloads cargo, in places not established for this purpose, if these actions are performed without the permission of competent agencies; (c) the vessel illegally engages in maritime or river trade or hydrographic work and research in Soviet territorial or internal waters; (d) the officers or crew of vessels deliberately damage navigational barriers, cables, or other submerged or protruding objects belonging to the USSR; (e) the vessel's master does not present his ship's or cargo documents; (f) the vessel refuses to submit to instructions from appropriate authorities of the Soviet Union; and (g) in other instances when the vessel is in Soviet territorial waters, internal

237. Uustal', *Mezhdunarodno-pravovoi rezhim territorial'nykh vod,* pp. 139–40.

waters, border rivers or lakes in violation of the 1960 statute.[238]

Persons who have committed a "criminal transgression"[239] and are subject to criminal responsibility under USSR and union republic legislation may be detained and taken from a vessel by the border guard unless the foreign vessel is passing through Soviet territorial waters, proceeding from a foreign port, and does not enter internal waters, and the crime was committed prior to the vessel's entering territorial waters.[240]

A. N. Nikolaev cited a 1940 Statute on the Procedure of Investigation of Maritime Average as extending Soviet jurisdiction to territorial waters, suggesting that if during the course of an investigation the indicia of a criminal transgression are discovered, the port master shall inform the procurator and may detain a foreign vessel in port.[241] However, the statute only mentioned "waters" of the USSR, not territorial waters; it would seem to have related only to internal waters.

Foreign nonmilitary vessels may be detained by Soviet authorities for unseaworthiness if certain elementary requirements of safety are not fulfilled.[242] Other legislation provides for administrative or criminal responsibility for violation of fishing, use of wireless radio equipment, customs, and sanitary rules.

No statistics are available with respect to the frequency of proceedings under the aforementioned legislation. Most of the reported offenses involve fishing violations. Soviet maritime law textbooks frequently mention the arrests and convictions of British fishing trawlers during the 1920's and again in the early 1950's. Other incidents involving Norwegian, Danish, Swedish, and Japanese nationals have been reported by Western media.[243]

Civil jurisdiction is exercised under the 1961 All-Union Fundamental Principles of Civil Legislation, the union republic civil codes, and special legislation relating to civil law and foreign trade rela-

238. Article 37. *Vedomosti SSSR* (1960), no. 34, item 324; *SS&D*, VI (1969), 86–87.

239. *"Ugolovnoe prestuplenie,"* literally a "criminal crime." The expression appears to exclude the detention of persons for offenses which are only administratively punishable.

240. Article 36. *Vedomosti SSSR* (1960), no. 34, item 324; *SS&D*, VI (1969), 86.

241. Order of the People's Commissariat of the Maritime Fleet, no. 190, April 15, 1940. Volkov claims that in every instance of arrest or an investigation on board a foreign vessel, coastal state authorities must, at the request of the master, notify the consular officer of the flag state in advance and facilitate the establishment of contact between the consul and the vessel's crew. No authority is cited for this proposition. Volkov, *Morskoe pravo,* p. 105.

242. Meshera, *Morskoe pravo,* III, 28.

243. Glenn, "Swedish-Soviet Territorial Sea Controversy," p. 942.

tions[244] in accordance with Article 20 of the 1958 Geneva Convention on the Territorial Sea. The USSR has long adhered to the view that state-owned vessels are immune from coastal-state jurisdiction. Accordingly, a reservation was entered to Article 20 of the Geneva convention stipulating that levy of execution or arrest of a state vessel for the purpose of any civil proceedings while the vessel is lying in the territorial sea or passing through the territorial sea after leaving internal waters may occur only with the consent of the state whose flag the vessel flies.[245]

Foreign warships enjoy extraterritoriality in Soviet territorial waters. No action of an administrative or judicial character may be taken against them for violations of Soviet legislation and rules.

RIGHT OF HOT PURSUIT

The doctrine of hot pursuit holds that a nonmilitary vessel may be pursued from territorial waters and seized upon the high seas when the vessel or a person on board has violated the laws of a foreign state while in its territorial or internal waters. This exception to the usual rule of immunity of vessels on the high seas appears to be founded upon the belief that pursuit "is a continuation of an act of jurisdiction which has begun, or which, but for the accident of escape, would have begun, within the territory itself," and that pursuit must be permitted for the efficient exercise of littoral jurisdiction.[246]

Although the substance of the principle was still in dispute among publicists in the twentieth century, Russian revenue vessels had been authorized under Article 286 of the Customs Code of 1892 to pursue any vessel not submitting to a request to stop within the maritime customs belt [three miles] beyond this belt into neutral waters.[247] The legislation and the doctrine underlying it were promptly invoked by Russia to justify the capture of two American sealing vessels, the *James Hamilton Lewis* and the *C. H. White,* beyond Russian territorial waters for allegedly sealing illegally within those waters. The ensuing dispute was submitted to an arbitrator, who held in 1902 that:

whether the seizure took place 20, or only 11 miles from land, it was made outside Russian territorial waters; that the contention that a ship of war

244. The 1964 RSFSR Civil Code is translated in W. Gray and R. Stults, *Soviet Civil Legislation* (Ann Arbor, Mich.: University of Michigan Law School, 1965); A. K. R. Kiralfy, *The Civil Code and The Code of Civil Procedure of the RSFSR 1964* (Leyden: Sijthoff, 1966).
245. *Vedomosti SSSR* (1964), no. 43, item 472; *SS&D,* VI (1969), 89.
246. Colombos, *International Law of the Sea,* p. 168.
247. Ovchinnikov, "Territorial'noe more," p. 61. In 1888 Russian authorities pursued and seized a Canadian vessel for fishing and sealing within Russian territorial waters. Lord Salisbury declared the principle and application of

might pursue outside territorial waters a vessel whose crew had committed an unlawful act in the territorial waters . . . was not in conformity with the law of nations, since the jurisdiction of the State could not be extended beyond the territorial sea unless by express consent.[248]

Russia probably derived scant satisfaction from the arbitrator's reported repudiation of his statement, since it was conceded that pursuit in each case had been both commenced and carried out on the high seas.[249]

In 1925 the Soviet Union signed, with other Baltic states, a Convention for the Suppression of Contraband Liquors providing that a vessel suspected of carrying contraband which escapes beyond a special zone up to 12 miles in breadth may be pursued by the territorial authorities on to the high seas.[250] The Soviet–Finnish customs convention of April 13, 1929, contained a similar provision.[251] This same principle of pursuit was incorporated into Article 27 of the 1927 statute on the state boundary.

At the present time, the right of hot pursuit from Soviet territorial waters is defined by Article 36 of the 1960 statute on the state boundary, incorporating the provisions of Article 23 of the 1958 Geneva Convention on the High Seas. The border guard of the Soviet Union may continue to pursue nonmilitary foreign vessels upon the high seas if the pursuit commences in Soviet territorial or internal waters and is conducted without interruption until the pursued vessel enters its own territorial waters or those of a foreign state.

Enforcement of Article 36 by Soviet authorities against an American merchant ship, the *SS Sister Katingo,* on July 15, 1964, in the Black Sea resulted in a protest from the United States government. The vessel sailed from the Soviet port of Novorossisk without permission, which had not been granted because of a dispute over stevedoring charges. A Soviet patrol vessel followed the *Sister Katingo* outside the harbor, ordered it to return to port, and upon its failure to comply

the doctrine of pursuit fully justified. J. B. Moore, *History and Digest of International Arbitrations* (Washington D.C.: GPO, 1898), I, pp. 824–25.

248. Moore, *International Arbitrations,* I, p. 927; Philip C. Jessup, *The Law of Territorial Waters and Maritime Jurisdiction* (New York: G. A. Jennings Co., 1927), pp. 108–9.

249. John Westlake, *International Law* (2d ed.; Cambridge: The University Press, 1910), I, p. 178.

250. *SDD,* v, 46–53; *LNTS,* XLII, 73. On the same date, August 19, 1925, the USSR, Finland, and Estonia signed an agreement defining the areas subject to control under the convention. *SDD,* v, 53–54. The agreement was supplemented by a protocol of April 22, 1926. *SDD,* v, 54–55. All three instruments were ratified by the Soviet Union on July 10, 1929, and entered into force October 10, 1929.

251. *SDD,* v, 41–46; *LNTS,* XCVI, 93; *SS&D,* VI (1969), 79.

fired three rounds across its bow. The vessel was then boarded and searched and the master fined for violating Soviet law. While conceding the Soviet authorities had acted within their "strictly legal rights" to pursue, board, and search, the United States objected that the methods used were "excessive" and "outside the norms of acceptable behavior."[252] The Soviet reply, if any, has not been made public.

Special Zones

The Soviet attitude toward the theory of contiguous zones has been closely related to their concept of territorial waters. Those writers who interpreted Soviet legislation as extending jurisdiction for particular purposes described such extensions in terms of contiguous zones. Imenitov, for example, viewed the 1935 decree on fishing as creating a contiguous zone wherein fishing by foreign vessels or nationals was prohibited.[253] Belli, Egor'ev, Sheptovitskii, and others interpreted the entire prewar pattern of Soviet maritime legislation on the basis of the theory of contiguous zones, and Soviet practice suggested that the government was careful to enforce Soviet law on a "zonal" basis. Non-Soviet writers have drawn similar conclusions independently.[254] The 1947 international law textbook, reflecting the traditional Soviet attitude toward the breadth of coastal jurisdiction, stated that there was no international rule concerning the breadth of contiguous zones.[255]

At present, Soviet jurists unanimously accept the doctrine of full sovereignty of the Soviet state over its territorial waters: "In the USSR there are no contiguous zones in the common understanding of that term."[256] However, the status of fishing zones is still the subject of controversy. Siling has pointed out that the fishing zone differs from the contiguous zone in that the former protects exclusively economic interests of the coastal state whereas the latter relates primarily to the

---

252. *DSB*, LI (1964), 145–46; *SS&D*, VI (1970), 332.
253. Imenitov, *Sovetskoe morskoe i rybolovnoe pravo*, p. 21.
254. Z. Ohira, "Fishery Problems Between Soviet Russia and Japan," *Japanese Annual of International Law*, II, (1958), 1–19: Reinkemeyer, *Die sowjetische Zwölfmeilenzone*.
255. Durdenevskii and Krylov, *Mezhdunarodnoe pravo*, p. 258.
256. Levin and Kaliuzhnaia, *Mezhdunarodnoe pravo* (1960), p. 171. Koretskii contended the establishment of special zones was a circuitous means of extending sovereign rights:

> Rights exercised in such zones were the same as those possessed by the coastal state in the territorial sea and the effort to justify those claims on the ground that they were necessary solely for purposes of administration, control and jurisdiction carried no weight because these were precisely the functions discharged by a state in virtue of its sovereignty.

1958 Official Records, III, 67.

legal order of the coastal state. Fishing zones may be established irrespective of the breadth of the territorial sea, of freedom of commercial navigation, and of innocent passage. A foreign vessel has rights in a contiguous zone, whereas a fishing zone establishes special rights which appertain only to vessels and nationals of the coastal state.[257] Expressing a contrary view, Zhudro discussed fishing zones under the heading of "contiguous zones" and noted that in practice states exercise the right to establish such zones even though the fishing zone is not expressly mentioned in the Convention on the Territorial Sea.[258]

Most of the headings below would be subsumed under the section on contiguous zones in a Western treatise on the law of the sea. In Soviet literature these are regarded as rights which a coastal state may exercise within its territorial waters. Following the practice of Soviet jurists in this respect by including cabotage, we discuss below those rights which in Soviet writings are said to belong to the coastal state, bearing in mind that Soviet publicists do not necessarily regard this list as exhaustive.

REGULATION OF NAVIGATION

The regulation of navigation is considered one of the most important basic responsibilities of the coastal state in its territorial waters. Competent agencies of the USSR are authorized to establish zones or areas in which navigation, anchoring, or marine fishing and hunting are prohibited in Soviet territorial waters. The establishment and the boundaries of such zones are announced in *Notices to Mariners*.[259] Article 22 of the Law on Criminal Responsibility for Crimes Against the State imposes criminal responsibility for violation of rules for the safe movement and use of water transport which results in an accident or in grave consequences.[260]

Pilot services are governed by Chapter V of the 1968 Merchant

257. Siling, *Morskoe pravo,* p. 62; A. A. Volkov concurred:

> Some authors erroneously equate the volume of rights of a coastal state in the fishing and contiguous zones. In reality fishing zones are areas of special competence of coastal states in which their volume of rights is incomparably greater than in contiguous zones.

A. A. Volkov, "Pravovoi rezhim rybolovnykh zon," *Sovetskii ezhegodnik mezhdunarodnogo prava 1963* (Moscow: izd-vo Nauka, 1965), p. 218; Volkov, *Morskoe pravo,* pp. 114–15. It follows, in Volkov's view, that there are no "international legal norms defining the procedure for establishing fishery zones or a single system for computing their breadth; *ibid.,* p. 116.

258. Zhudro, *Morskoe pravo,* p. 114.

259. Article 9, 1960 statute on the state boundary. *Vedomosti SSSR* (1960), no. 34, item 324.

260. *Vedomosti SSSR* (1959), no. 1, item 8.

Shipping Code of the Soviet Union.[261] The Ministry of the Maritime Fleet and other concerned agencies and departments establish the areas in which the use of a Soviet pilot is compulsory, irrespective of the flag or nature of the vessel; foreign warships visiting Soviet territorial waters are also included.[262] In certain zones the services of a pilot may be required even though the passing vessel is not en route to a Soviet port. Navigation along the coast near Vladivostok, for example, is not permitted without a pilot, unless the vessels obtain instructions from the chief military pilot at Vladivostok.[263] The master of a Soviet port may prohibit vessels from being piloted when safe passage is jeopardized by poor visibility, storm, earthquake, or "other special circumstances."[264]

Icebreaker services are available pursuant to rules issued on September 14, 1944.[265]

Soviet jurists have sometimes advocated a broader concept of the "regulation of navigation" than is usually suggested by Western practice. In defending, for example, the controversial view that foreign warships must obtain the authorization of the government of the USSR prior to entering Soviet territorial waters, a Soviet publicist invoked the provisions of the 1958 Geneva Convention on the Territorial Sea. Since Article 17 of the convention requires the observance of laws and rules of the coastal state relating to navigation and Article 23 requires foreign warships to observe the rules of the coastal state, it followed— declared the Soviet lawyer—that a procedure of authorization regulated navigation and consequently must be observed by foreign warships.[266]

The Soviet Union is a party to most of the major international conventions relating to safe navigation.[267]

USE OF WIRELESS RADIO EQUIPMENT

A Soviet decree of July 24, 1928, restricted the right of warships and nonmilitary vessels to use their wireless radio equipment within

261. *Vedomosti SSSR* (1968), no. 39, item 351; *SS&D*, vi (1969), 94; William E. Butler and John B. Quigley (trans. and ed.), *The Merchant Shipping Code of the USSR (1968)* (Baltimore: The Johns Hopkins Press, 1970), p. 63.

262. Article 8, 1960 Rules for Visits by Foreign Warships to USSR Territorial Waters and Ports. Butler, *Soviet Territorial Waters*, p. 126; *SS&D*, vi (1969), 65.

263. Mitchell P. Strohl, *The International Law of Bays* (The Hague: Nijhoff, 1963), p. 334. Pilotage is also compulsory in the Vil'kitskii, Shokal'skii, Laptev, and Sannikov Straits. *IM* (1970), no. 20; *SS&D*, vi (1969), 94.

264. Article 83, USSR Merchant Shipping Code.

265. *IM* (1970), no. 15.

266. Levin and Kaliuzhnaia, *Mezhdunarodnoe pravo* (1964), p. 195.

267. Iu. Kh. Dzhavad (ed.), *Mezhdunarodnye soglasheniia po morskomu sudokhodstvu* (2d ed.; Moscow: izd-vo Transport, 1968), pp. 49–70.

"ten miles from shore" when in Soviet internal waters or in the "maritime sea belt." Nonmilitary vessels are prohibited from exchanging radio messages with shore stations unless they are in distress, are rendering aid to another vessel in distress, are being led through the ice, or must complete an especially important exchange with port authorities.[268]

All radio messages from warships and nonmilitary vessels must be open. No cypher or code other than international signal codes may be used. The local commander of Soviet naval forces is authorized to limit the duration and wave length of radio messages sent by foreign warships. The 1928 decree further provides that violators are subject to criminal prosecution under the criminal codes of the union republics.

Until 1960, violation of the decree was punishable by deprivation of freedom for a term of up to two years or by a fine not exceeding one thousand rubles under Article 75–3 of the 1926 Criminal Code of the RSFSR.[269] The 1960 RSFSR Criminal Code does not contain an offense equivalent to Article 75–3.

The major reason for adopting the 1928 decree appears to have been national security. Being highly dependent upon foreign vessels to carry Soviet commerce until comparatively recently, the Soviet government was concerned that foreign vessels might clandestinely lend support to counter-revolutionary or other groups hostile to the Bolshevik regime. Presumably the curtailment of radio exchanges would have facilitated detection and monitoring of any illicit activity.[270]

On two occasions the provisions of the 1928 decree were the subject of protests by other governments. At the time of its promulgation, the French government declared that the Soviet decree placed, in comparison with the regulations of other states, such severe restrictions as to interfere with normal navigation. Accordingly, France reserved its rights regarding the application of the decree to French warships. In reply the USSR noted that French practice and legislation "contain provisions broadening the boundaries for the exercise by the coastal state of its corresponding rights in the said waters as against norms adopted by other states."[271]

268. *SZ SSSR* (1928), no. 48, item 431; *SS&D*, vi (1969), 95.
269. Also see Article 197–2 of the 1927 Ukrainian Criminal Code; Article 208–1 of the 1928 Georgian Criminal Code; Article 237–1 of the 1927 Azerbaidzhan Criminal Code; Article 100–1 of the 1927 Armenian Criminal Code; Article 93–1 of the 1927 Turkmen Criminal Code. In the latter code, the maximum penalty was one year deprivation of freedom or compulsory tasks or a fine not exceeding 200 rubles.
270. On the security aspect of this decree, see Nikolaev, *Problema territorial'nykh vod*, p. 221.
271. *Dokumenty*, xii, 28.

In June 1932, Japan complained that the Soviet decree prevented Japanese fishing vessels from receiving timely weather reports, and as a result, several vessels suffered shipwreck. The Soviet government was requested to modify the 1928 decree so that weather data could be more easily obtained. In an essentially nonresponsive retort, the Soviet government pointed out that vessels in distress or rendering aid to others in distress were not bound by the restrictions on wireless transmissions and that in certain cases special written permission could be obtained from Soviet port authorities waiving the restrictions. Japan resubmitted its request in a Note of September 20, 1932, but without success.[272]

CUSTOMS

Article 23 of the 1960 statute on the state boundary provided that customs control is to be carried out by agencies of the USSR Ministry of Foreign Trade in accordance with legislation in force and agreements with other states.

A new Customs Code became effective on July 1, 1964.[273] Under Article 21 of the code, vessels are subject to customs control when they arrive in port. Customs inspection is not, therefore, conducted in territorial waters but in internal (port) waters, even though passengers and cargo technically enter the Soviet Union upon crossing the seaward boundary of territorial waters.

Foreign warships are exempted from customs inspection pursuant to Article 36 of the new code. All other foreign vessels are subject to customs inspection unless international agreements with the Soviet Union provide otherwise.

Within Soviet territorial waters, the border guard is empowered, together with customs agencies, to suppress the import or export of objects, materials, currency, and negotiable valuables whose import or export is contrary to law. This function would appear to relate especially to the smuggling of articles across the frontier where there is no customs control point.

The 1964 code itself, it should be noted, contains no references to territorial waters or to a special customs zone. Customs jurisdiction is exercised within territorial areas delimited by other legislation. This is a significant departure from practice under the Tsarist regime. The Russian Customs Code of 1892, for example, provided in Article 283 that the maritime customs belt shall be the expanse of water within 3 miles of the Russian coast, "within whose limits all vessels, both Rus-

272. *Dokumenty*, xv, 704.
273. *Vedomosti SSSR* (1964), no. 20, item 242.

sian and foreign, are subject to the supervision of customs author-ities."[274] In 1909 the customs regulations were amended to the effect that within 12 nautical miles, measured from the extreme low-water mark of the Russian coast, every vessel was subject to supervision by those Russian authorities responsible for guarding the frontiers of the empire. The RSFSR enacted an identical provision in 1918.

Considerable confusion arose over the scope of the 1909 amend-ment. Interpreted literally, the law authorized supervision not only of vessels actually engaged in or suspected of being engaged in smuggling but also of vessels passing innocently within 12 miles of shore. Great Britain and Japan, assuming the worst, strenuously protested the de-cree on the ground that the limits of the territorial sea were universally admitted by international usage to be 3 nautical miles. The United States merely registered its concern that the law be applied as a reve-nue measure and not interfere with legitimate American shipping. The responses of the Russian government did little to clarify the issue. Rus-sia cited American and British legislation creating a customs zone be-yond territorial waters as justification for its action, but this was cou-pled with the insistence that in modern international law there existed no generally accepted rule on the breadth of territorial waters. There is no record of an international protest against Russian enforcement of the 1909 law.[275]

From 1929 until 1941, the USSR was a party to a 1925 con-vention among the Baltic states aimed at suppressing contraband liq-uor.[276] A special 12-mile zone was fixed within which border guard vessels of all contracting parties were authorized to exercise customs supervision over all privately owned ships. Also during the interwar period, the USSR enforced, by agreement with Finland,[277] a 12-mile customs zone in that portion of the Gulf of Finland where Soviet terri-torial waters extended to 4 miles.

Contrary to the view of most Western jurists, Soviet jurists con-tend that Soviet merchant vessels, as state property, should not be sub-ject to control in foreign customs zones on the ground that interna-tional law recognizes the immunity of state-owned property and its exemption from any enforcement action of local authorities. Customs control is classified as an enforcement action. Its exercise with regard to Soviet merchant vessels is deemed to be a violation of the sover-

---

274. Cited in Nikolaev, *Problema territorial'nykh vod,* p. 58.
275. Masterson, *Jurisdiction in Marginal Seas,* pp. 286–302.
276. *Supra* note 250. According to Uustal', the treaty was terminated by the outbreak of World War II. See Uustal', *Mezhdunarodno-pravovoi rezhim territorial'nykh vod,* p. 92.
277. *SDD,* v, 41–46; *LNTS,* xcvi, 93; *SS&D,* vi (1969), 79.

eignty and equality of states and of the principle of the immunity of state property.[278]

SANITARY PROTECTION

The Soviet Union applies the International Sanitary Regulations adopted at the fourth assembly of the World Health Organization on May 25, 1951, as amended in 1955 and 1956. Sanitary protection of the Soviet state boundary is carried out by the Sanitary and Epidemiological Service, under the USSR Ministry of Health, in accordance with a Soviet decree of 1931[279] and under rules adopted by the Ministry of Health on August 20, 1959.[280] In the event of a threat of an especially dangerous infection spreading in Soviet territory or in an adjacent state, the competent agencies are empowered to close temporarily the threatened portion of the boundary and to place a quarantine over the area.[281]

SUNKEN PROPERTY AND SALVAGE

The raising of sunken property in Soviet territorial or internal sea waters is governed by Chapter VI of the 1968 Merchant Shipping Code of the Soviet Union.[282] The owner of sunken property is allowed one year from the date of sinking to notify the nearest Soviet commercial or fishing sea port of his intention to raise the property. In consultation with other state agencies concerned, the port will determine when and how the salvage operation is to be performed and shall notify the owner. If the sunken property creates an obstacle to navigation, marine hunting and fishing, or hydrotechnical and other work, the owner is obliged to raise the property at the request of the port within the period specified. If the owner is unknown, the port shall publish the period for raising the property in *Notices to Mariners* or, if the flag of a sunken vessel is known, shall notify the USSR Ministry of Foreign Affairs.

The port may refuse to permit the owner to salvage the property with his own equipment or that of a salvage company. In such event, the port shall raise the property at the owner's expense. If the sunken property constitutes an immediate threat to the safety of navigation, or

278. Uustal', *Mezhdunarodno-pravovoi rezhim territorial'nykh vod*, p. 93.
279. *SZ SSSR* (1931), no. 55, item 355; *SS&D*, vi (1969), 100.
280. Cited by Zhudro, *Morskoe pravo*, p. 112. The Statute on State Sanitary Supervision in the USSR is translated in *SS&D*, v, nos. 3–4 (1969), 109.
281. Article 23, 1960 statute on the state boundary; *SS&D*, vi (1969), 98.
282. *Vedomosti SSSR* (1968), no. 39, item 351; *SS&D*, vi (1969), 108. Butler and Quigley, *Merchant Shipping Code of the USSR (1968)*, p. 66.

the owner does not raise the property within the established period, the port may promptly raise, destroy, or otherwise remove it. The salvage of military property (not necessarily Soviet property) is to be carried out by the USSR Ministry of Defense.

The owner loses all rights to sunken property unless he notifies the proper authorities or raises the property within the periods established in the code. If the port raises the property, the owner has two years to claim it, upon payment of all costs, expenses, and losses connected with the operation. If the property must be sold, the owner is entitled to the proceeds, less all relevant expenses.

The 1968 code contains three major changes from the former legislation. First, it expressly refers to salvage in Soviet territorial waters (the 1929 code applied to property sunk "within the limits of port waters"); second, administration of salvage operations has been shifted from the border guard to the port authorities; third, salvage of Soviet-owned vessels no longer need be performed exclusively by Soviet agencies. These modifications reflect a general tendency to bring Soviet practice in this sphere much closer to the practices of Western nations.

Awards for the salving of lives or property in Soviet territorial waters are governed by Chapter XV of the 1968 Merchant Shipping Code. Although Soviet legislation does not expressly restrict the performance of salving operations in territorial waters to Soviet nationals, foreign vessels and citizens are nonetheless said to be barred from such activity on the basis of "general principles."[283] A Soviet–Danish salvage agreement of October 9, 1965, allows the salvage vessels of either party to answer distress calls in the territorial or internal waters of the other party in the Baltic region.[284]

HYDROGRAPHIC AND OTHER RESEARCH IN TERRITORIAL WATERS

Foreign vessels are prohibited from carrying out hydrographic work and research in Soviet territorial and internal sea waters under penalty of detention by the border guard.[285] The restrictions upon foreign warships are more precise. When in Soviet territorial waters, foreign warships and their personnel may not perform research and investigations, including soundings and fathomings which are not essential for safe navigation or anchorage in the Soviet port, nor photo-

283. Uustal', *Mezhdunarodno-pravovoi rezhim territorial'nykh vod*, p. 116.
284. An English text appears in *Baltic and International Maritime Conference Bulletin*, no. 6 (1965), 11885; *SS&D*, VI (1969), 112.
285. Articles 19 and 37(c), 1960 statute on the state boundary. *SS&D*, VI (1969), 112.

graph, sketch, draw, copy, or compile descriptions of ports, fortifications, and other military installations.[286]

These rules derive from the complete sovereignty of the USSR over its territorial waters. Although the 1960 RSFSR Criminal Code does not expressly provide a penalty for illicit hydrographic research, Soviet authorities doubtless would find Article 65 (espionage) to be relevant.

RIGHT TO COASTING TRADE (CABOTAGE)

In the absence of an international agreement to the contrary, a littoral state may exclude foreign vessels from engaging in coastal trade along its coasts. Originally, *cabotage* referred to vessels sailing in the territorial seas between ports of the same state located on the same sea coast. Now it has come to mean sea trade between any two ports of the same state, irrespective of whether the ports are located on the same sea or coastline.

In 1897 Russia reserved the coasting trade between the Baltic and the Black Sea, or between either sea and Siberian ports, as well as the trade between Russian ports on the same sea, to its own vessels.[287] This monopoly principle had immediate appeal to the Soviet government, and was incorporated into Article 71 of the 1929 Merchant Shipping Code of the USSR.

Pursuant to the 1968 Merchant Shipping Code, carriage and towage between Soviet ports on the same sea *(petit cabotage)* or on different seas *(grand cabotage)* is reserved to vessels sailing under the Soviet flag. For the purposes of cabotage, the following are considered to be one sea: the Black Sea and the Sea of Azov; the White Sea and the Northern Arctic Ocean; the Sea of Japan, the Okhotsk Sea, and the Bering Sea. Foreign flag vessels, however, are permitted to engage in either type of cabotage under circumstances prescribed by the USSR Council of Ministers.[288] Soviet jurists stress that any foreign ship admitted to Soviet cabotage is wholly subordinate to local navigation rules while in Soviet territorial waters or ports.[289]

COASTAL FISHING ZONE

The mobility of fishing resources has made it unfashionable to speak of man-made limits arbitrarily drawn to allocate those resources.

286. Articles 16(a) and (b), 1960 rules for visits by foreign warships. *ŞŞ&D,* vi (1969), 68.
287. Colombos, *International Law of the Sea,* pp. 383–84.
288. Article 2. *Vedomosti SSSR* (1968), no. 39, item 351; *SS&D,* vi (1969), 113; Butler and Quigley, *Merchant Shipping Code of the USSR (1968),* p. 39.
289. Nikolaev, *Problema territorial'nykh vod,* p. 234.

Nevertheless, in the case of Tsarist and Soviet Russia the question of coastal fisheries has been intimately connected with the whole subject of expanding coastal jurisdiction seaward.

Tsarist regulation of coastal fisheries. In early times Russia was more concerned about freedom of commerce than about coastal fisheries.[290] Prior to 1917, nearly 87 percent of the total Russian catch came from inland fresh water lakes and rivers, the Caspian Sea, and the Sea of Azov. Approximately 3 percent was obtained from the northern seas and 10 percent from the far eastern coast. Yet, in relying primarily upon inland fisheries, Russia was a leading producer and consumer of fish. As late as 1893, the total value of the Russian catch was the second largest in the world.[291]

By the mid-1890s, indiscriminate fishing of inland waters and of the Caspian Sea resulted in a steady decline of the annual catch at a time when consumer demand continued to grow. In the early twentieth century, Russia was obliged to import 400,000 metric tons of fish annually from countries that were exploiting fishery stocks off Russian coasts.[292] Russian sealing and hunting of marine life was also comparatively modest in contrast with the activities of Great Britain, Germany, and Japan.

The decline of inland and Caspian fisheries could easily have been accommodated by a more intensive exploitation of the far eastern and northern fishing grounds. In 1899 a prominent Russian scientist, N. M. Knipovich, proved the feasibility of trawl-fishing in the Barents Sea. Foreign entrepreneurs were quick to take advantage of the discovery, but Russia lagged far behind. By 1911, the Russian catch off the Murmansk coast amounted to less than 20 percent of the annual total catch.[293] Russia's failure to exploit its coastal fisheries has been attributed to a number of factors, all of which doubtless played a role: lack of government incentive and investment; the low state of Russian fishery technology; relative isolation of the fishing grounds from rail transport; inadequate techniques for refrigerating or preserving fish.

---

290. In an exhaustive study of early Russian fishery development, Böhmert found no evidence that Russia either asserted exclusive fishing rights or was engaged in fishery disputes with other states over coastal fishing grounds. See Böhmert, "Die russische Fischereigrenze." However, in 1620 Tsar Mikhail Fedorovich promulgated an edict proscribing trade with foreigners in the coastal region of the Ob River. *Akty istoricheskie, sobrannye i izdannye arkhheografi-cheskoiu kommissieiu* (St. Petersburg, 1841), III, pp. 87–88, 151.

291. Miller, *Economic Development of Russia,* pp. 268–73.

292. See Michael M. Ovchynnyk, "Development of Some Marine and Inland Russian Fisheries, and Fish Utilization," *Atlantic Ocean Fisheries,* ed. G. Börgstrom and A. J. Heighway (London: Fishing News Ltd., 1961), pp. 267–81.

293. Shparlinskii, *Fishing Industry of the U.S.S.R.,* p. 5.

The abortive Imperial edict of 1821 is the first example of Russian legislation aimed at reserving coastal fishing to Russian nationals. Under the edict, the "pursuits of commerce, whaling, and fishing" within the delimited area were "granted exclusively to Russian subjects" and all foreign vessels were forbidden "to approach within less than 100 Italian miles" of Russian coasts and islands upon penalty of confiscation of vessel and cargo.[294] The purpose of the edict was to protect and enlarge the monopoly of trading privileges originally granted to the Russian–America Company in 1799. The Tsar himself had purchased shares in the firm. In the face of strenuous protests from Great Britain and the United States, Russian warships were instructed to confine enforcement activities to the coast and to the interception of illicit trade with Russian settlements. After long negotiations, agreements were concluded with the United States in 1824[295] and Great Britain in 1825[296] guaranteeing that citizens or subjects of those countries would not be "disturbed or restrained" in navigation or fishing in any part of the Pacific Ocean.

Most observers concluded that the treaties of 1824 and 1825 had the effect of repealing the edict of 1821. At least one Russian jurist, however, implied that the edict remained in force except for Britain and the United States, to whom special fishing privileges had been granted by treaty.[297]

Foreign whaling operations off the far eastern coast were the source of anxiety to the Russian government in the 1840s. American whaling vessels appeared in force in the Sea of Okhotsk in 1840–42. Fifty foreign whalers operated these waters in 1841; by 1854, some 525 foreign whalers were reported. In 1843 and again in 1846, the Russian government rejected pleas from the Russian–America Company to establish a 40-mile whaling zone. An instruction issued to cruisers on December 9, 1853, prohibited foreign whalers from approaching within 3 miles of Russian shores but otherwise expressly affirmed the right of foreigners to take whales in the Sea of Okhotsk.[298]

Friction over whaling and fishing in the Sea of Okhotsk arose be-

---

294. *Parliamentary Papers,* cx (1893–94); *SS&D,* vi (1969), 16. The edict was apparently enforced only once. In 1822 the United States brig *Pearl* was seized en route for Sitka by a Russian sloop; it was released in 1829 without compensation.

295. Malloy, *Treaties, Conventions, International Acts,* ii, p. 1512; *SS&D,* vi (1969), 17.

296. *BFSP,* xii, 38.

297. Zakharov, *Kurs obshchago mezhdunarodnogo prava,* p. 157.

298. P. A. Tikhmenev, *Istoricheskoe obozr'nie obrazovaniia Rossiisko-amerikanskoi kompanii i d'istvii eia do nastoiashchago vremeni* (St. Petersburg: E. Veimar, 1861–63), ii, pp. 130–39.

tween the United States and Russia in 1868 and 1882. In 1868 an American whaling vessel in the Sea of Okhotsk allegedly was ordered to leave that sea by an armed Russian cruiser. In response to American inquiries, Russia denied the existence of an instruction to cruisers allowing restrictive measures affecting the whale fishing in the Sea of Okhotsk and affirmed the right of whaling outside Russian waters. In 1882 Russia did enact a regulation prohibiting foreign vessels from trading, hunting, or fishing within the sea boundary line of the Russian coast or islands in the Sea of Okhotsk, the Bering Sea, or the northeastern part of Asia without a special permit from the Governor–General of Eastern Siberia at Vladivostok. Diplomatic correspondence relating to the regulation implied that the zone in question was three miles wide.[299]

Meanwhile, intensive Norwegian fishing off the northern coasts of Russia had led to complaints of the mistreatment of Norwegian fishermen. As previously noted, under a series of acts promulgated by local authorities, Russia enforced a three-mile fishing zone and constructed cruisers to police the area. In an instruction of 1893, Russian cruisers were ordered to prohibit foreign fishing in Russian sea territory along the northern coast—that is, all bays, fjords, and roadsteads on the Russian coast facing the Arctic Sea, the entire White Sea south of a line running from Sviatoi Nos to Kanin Nos, and within the Barents and Kara Seas, three miles off the coast of the outermost islands, reefs, or shoals protruding above the surface of the water.[300]

In 1891 and 1892, Russian cruisers, acting under the 1882 regulation on far eastern fisheries, seized several Canadian and four American vessels in the Bering Sea on charges of whaling and sealing in Russian waters. Both Great Britain and the United States protested.[301] The case of the American vessels was finally submitted to arbitration in 1900,[302] and Russia conceded a wrongful seizure in the case of two of the vessels. The arbitrator found the seizure of the remaining two to be unlawful on the ground that Russia herself had admitted that the seizure occurred outside Russian territorial waters; in so doing, the arbitrator held the doctrine of hot pursuit to have been improper.[303]

299. *U.S. Foreign Relations 1868,* I, 462, 465, 467, 469, 470–74, 485–86; *ibid., 1882,* 447–50, 452–53.

300. Meyer, *Jurisdiction of Coastal Waters,* pp. 243–46, 249; *SS&D,* VI (1969), 19.

301. For the British correspondence, see *BFSP,* LXXXVI (1893–94), 184–276; LXXXVII (1894–96), 1058.

302. Malloy, *Treaties, Conventions, International Acts,* II, p. 1532.

303. For the text of the four awards, see *Revue Générale de Droit International Public,* X (1903), documents 1–13.

While these claims were pending, Russia enacted sealing conservation measures in 1893, whereby all vessels were prohibited from sealing within 10 miles of the Russian coast and within 30 miles of the Komandorskii Islands and Tulenev (Robben) Island.[304] Russia reassured Great Britain that this measure was not intended to dispute the generally recognized rules on territorial waters. The measure was said to be exceptional and provisional, designed to meet the passing emergency of diminishing seal stocks. Britain denied the Russian right to act unilaterally but declared its willingness to consent to protective regulations. A *modus vivendi* was reached, retaining the delimitation of the prohibited area while providing for joint enforcement by British and Russian cruisers. The agreement was extended in 1894,[305] and a similar agreement was concluded with the United States that same year.[306] When Japanese sealing threatened the species with extinction, a four-power arrangement was reached on July 7, 1911.[307] This convention avoided any reference to a definite limit of territorial waters but obligated each party to prohibit its nationals from sealing farther than three miles from its own coasts. Each party also was granted enforcement power beyond the "territorial jurisdiction" of the other parties.

Quite apart from sealing, fishery competition between Russia and Japan intensified. Japan had been exploiting Russian coastal fisheries since at least the late eighteenth century with little opposition from the native population. The bulk of the Japanese salmon supply came from waters adjacent to Russia. Under the Russo–Japanese Treaty of May 7, 1875, wherein Russia exchanged the Kurile Islands for Sakhalin, Japan was granted most-favored-nation treatment with regard to coastal fishing.[308] However, since Japanese fishing activity off Kamchatka seemed to portend territorial claims, the Russian government imposed restrictions on foreign fishermen which resulted in numerous conflicts within Russian territorial waters.

Japanese efforts to achieve a more satisfactory arrangement were not realized until after the Russo–Japanese War. The Treaty of Portsmouth, signed in 1905, granted Japan the right to fish off Russian coasts in the Sea of Japan, the Okhotsk Sea, and the Bering Sea, a right subsequently defined by a fishery treaty of July 15,

304. *BFSP*, LXXXVI, 217–21; *SS&D*, VI (1969), 20.
305. *BFSP*, LXXXVI, 232, 267.
306. Malloy, *Treaties, Conventions, International Acts*, II, p. 1531.
307. Charles I. Bevans (ed.), *Treaties and Other International Agreements of the United States of America, 1776–1949* (Washington D.C.: GPO, 1968–), I, p. 804. Japan's formal denunciation of the convention took effect in 1942. *DSB*, V (1941), 336.
308. *BFSP*, LXVI, 218.

1907.[309] The Japanese were permitted to purchase "fishing lots" (the purchaser may catch a specified amount of certain fish in his lot and also use a specified coastal area for factories, for storing equipment, etc.) on an equal basis with Russian subjects whenever lots were offered to the general public.[310]

The various pressures leading to the adoption in 1911 of a decree establishing an exclusive 12-mile fishing zone for the far eastern coast and the energetic protests by Japan and Great Britain have already been discussed. After enacting the decree of 1911, however, Russia conceded in practice that the enactment did not affect Japanese rights under the 1907 treaty. Thus, on the eve of the Bolshevik revolution, Russia had succeeded in obtaining a measure of protection for its coastal seal fisheries; but besides the 1911 decree, which was not enforced, no effective legislative or other actions were taken to arrest the continuing decline of the Russian fishing industry in the face of foreign offshore competition.

Soviet regulation of coastal fisheries: 1917–45. Beseiged from within and without, the Soviet regime was unable to police coastal fisheries in the immediate aftermath of the Russian Revolution. In the decree of May 15, 1918, establishing the border guard, that agency had been empowered to defend the "water resources in our frontier and territorial waters from plunder," but the breadth of neither expanse of water was defined.[311] The constitution of the RSFSR of July 10, 1918, similarly declared that "all . . . minerals, and waters of general state significance . . . are national property" without any additional delimitation.[312]

In the far east the Japanese virtually seized Russian fishing lots and collected the lot fees for themselves, vigorously exploiting the fisheries to the fullest extent, and British, Norwegian, and other fishing fleets frequented the northern coast of Soviet Russia without apparent opposition.

The year 1920, with the end of the civil war and the signing of peace treaties between Soviet Russia and many neighboring countries, marked the emergence of a defined policy toward coastal fisheries. As part of the peace settlement between the RSFSR and Finland, the right to fish in Russian territorial waters along the northern coast was

309. E. A. Adamov (ed.), *Sbornik dogovorov Rossii s drugimi gosudarstvami 1856–1917* (Moscow: Gospolitizdat, 1952), p. 337. In a convention of October 16, 1907, Russia and Rumania established a 10-mile exclusive fishery zone seaward of the delta of the Danube River in the Black Sea. *BFSP*, CI, 569.

310. L. Larry Leonard, *International Regulation of Fisheries* (Washington D.C.: Carnegie Endowment, 1944), p. 29.

311. *SU RSFSR* (1918), no. 44, item 539; *SS&D*, VI (1969), 25.

312. Article 3(b). *SU RSFSR* (1918), no. 51, item 582.

granted to Finnish nationals.[313] The privilege became reciprocal under a Soviet–Finnish fishing convention of October 21, 1922, although the expanse of Russian waters open to Finnish nationals was somewhat reduced.[314]

However, in a Note to Norway of April 15, 1920, Chicherin complained that foreign fishermen were sealing in Russian territorial and internal waters, penetrating even into the mouth of the Dvina River.[315] Responding to a Norwegian request for a clarification of Soviet claims to restrict hunting and fishing along the northern coasts, Chicherin declared that ". . . temporarily and up to and including a general resolution of the question pertaining to the extent of Russian territorial waters," the RSFSR claimed a "zone of three miles" as territorial waters, the White Sea being "an internal sea" whose outward boundary is a line running from Cape Sviatoi Nos to Cape Kanin Nos.[316]

On May 7, 1921, three Norwegian vessels were detained in the White Sea for illegal sealing, the Soviet government citing its Notes of April 15 and May 4, 1920, as authority for the seizures.[317] The British government also was notified on May 13, 1921, of the texts of the Notes to Norway and advised that "foreign nationals and vessels violating this prohibition shall bear legal responsibility in accordance with Russian legislation."[318]

The appearance of foreign fishermen off Soviet coasts in May 1921, at a time when severe famine plagued the country, apparently persuaded the Soviet leadership that greater protection of marine resources was essential. On May 24, 1921, the RSFSR revived the abortive proposal made during the Tsarist regime concerning fisheries off the coast of the Archangel *Guberniia* and excluded foreigners from fishing in the White Sea south of a straight line drawn from Sviatoi Nos to Kanin Nos, in the Cheshskaia Bay south of a line between Mikulin Nos and Sviatoi Nos, and within 12 miles of the coast running from the Finnish border to the northern tip of Novaia Zemlia.[319] These restrictions were confirmed in a decree of May 31, 1921, granting the exclusive right to exploit the northern fisheries to the Chief Administration of the Fishing Industries and Fisheries.[320]

313. Article 7. *SDD*, I, 76–92; *LNTS*, II, 5–79; *SS&D*, VI (1969/70), 129.
314. *SDD*, V, 13–16; *LNTS*, XXIX, 197–209; *SS&D*, VI (1969/70), 132.
315. *Dokumenty*, II, 457.
316. *Dokumenty*, II, 500; translated in Butler, *Soviet Territorial Waters*, p. 169; *SS&D*, VI (1969/70), 208.
317. *Dokumenty*, IV, 111.
318. *Dokumenty*, IV, 125.
319. *SU RSFSR* (1921), no. 49, item 259; *SS&D*, VI (1969), 26.
320. *SU RSFSR* (1921), no. 50, item 265.

The governments of Germany, Great Britain, Japan, and Norway protested the decree.[321] The British government objected to any extension of the boundaries of territorial waters beyond the existing three-mile limit but recognized that marine hunting represented a special case which might be settled through an international agreement.[322]

While efforts were underway to resolve the issue through negotiations, British vessels continued to operate up to within three miles of the Soviet coast. On January 31, 1922, the British trawler *Magneta* was seized by Soviet authorities about nine miles off the Murmansk coast and, while under Soviet detention, was wrecked during a storm with loss of life. A month later the *St. Hubert,* allegedly seized beyond the twelve-mile zone, was confiscated by a Soviet court.[323]

In response to vigorous protests by the British government, the Ministry of Foreign Affairs of the RSFSR submitted a lengthy memorandum outlining the Soviet position, which may be summarized as follows. In the Soviet view neither international legal theory nor practice fixed a definite limit for territorial waters. The absence of general recognition of the three-mile rule was proved by statements of delegates to the 1921 Geneva conference concerning the Aaland Islands and to the 1921 Barcelona conference. The very fact that in 1911 the British government had expressed its willingness to consider the problem of the limits of territorial waters at an international conference negated the statement that Great Britain could not "in any event" recognize a boundary of territorial waters exceeding three miles. In addition to these general propositions, the Soviet government contended that a general twelve-mile limit had not been fixed by the Soviet decree. The decree merely created a zone for the "special purpose of protecting Russian fishery interests." The arrests of the British trawlers had been carried out in complete conformity with the 1921 decree, and all claims for compensation were denied.[324]

The British government curtly rejected the views contained in the memorandum and indicated that warships had been sent to the area to prevent any harassment of British trawlers. Clearly alarmed, the USSR suggested that such action would jeopardize British–Soviet relations and indicated that Soviet naval vessels would reinforce border guard ships in the region. On October 14, 1922, the Soviet government again warned of incidents. Great Britain continued to press its claim for

---

321. Böhmert, "Die russische Fischereigrenze," pp. 483–93.
322. *Dokumenty,* IV, 159; also see *ibid.,* IV, 306.
323. The decision of the Soviet court in the case of the *St. Hubert* is translated in Butler, *Soviet Territorial Waters,* pp. 172–73.
324. *Dokumenty,* V, 163.

damages suffered in the loss of the *Magneta,* and the USSR continued to deny responsibility on the ground of *vis major.*[325] On March 31, 1923, the *James Johnson* was captured off Murmansk, the vessel and catch confiscated, and the master sentenced to hard labor.

These incidents occurred at a time when the Soviet government sought to expand foreign trade and secure diplomatic recognition. When the British government indicated that the Anglo–Soviet trade agreement of March 16, 1921, would be terminated unless satisfaction were forthcoming, the Soviet government in Notes of May 7, and 11, 1923, referred to the absence of universally binding international rules and to the diverse practices of various countries with regard to coastal jurisdiction but indicated its willingness to participate in and accept the findings of any international conference on the subject. Moreover, the Soviet government announced that the decision of the Murmansk People's Court in the case of the *James Johnson* had been vacated by the Supreme Court of the USSR and that all other British trawlers in custody had been released. With respect to British claims arising out of the sinking of the *Magneta,* Russia denied any liability but offered to arbitrate the issue.[326]

The Soviet initiative was nearly subverted by the seizure on May 11, 1923, of the *Lord Astor* for illegally fishing within four miles of shore. However, the People's Commissariat of Foreign Affairs hastened to reassure the British government that there were no obstacles to its release, "in view of the decision of the Supreme Court in the case of the *James Johnson.*"[327]

In a Note of May 23, 1923, the Soviet government followed up these concessions by indicating its readiness to conclude a convention with Britain granting its nationals the right to fish beyond the three-mile limit, pending the ultimate resolution of the issue at an interna-

325. *Dokumenty,* v, 212, 615; *ibid.,* vi, 113.

326. *Correspondence Between His Majesty's Government and the Soviet Government Respecting the Relations between the Two Governments* (London: HMSO, 1923), *Command Paper 1869,* p. 10 (hereinafter cited by number of Command Paper).

327. *Cmd. 1874,* p. 6; *Dokumenty,* vi, 287. Security considerations were also paramount in the Soviet decision to resolve the fishery dispute before the 1923 season was well advanced. In a speech to the Presidium of the Moscow Soviet on May 12, 1923, Chicherin recalled that:

> The security of our shores is one of our primary responsibilities. What kind of threat the warships of the strongest naval power represent is shown at the present moment when an English gunboat has entered our closed White Sea and threatens our vessels and our coasts with the application of force if we guard our fisheries from the plundering penetration of English capitalists.

Dokumenty, vi, 305.

tional conference, and to pay compensation to British nationals for the cases at issue.[328] In its reply of May 29, 1923, the British government suggested a provisional understanding whereby the Soviet Union would issue instructions to its border guard not to impede British fishing operations beyond the three-mile limit and to record the same in an exchange of notes.[329] Reserving its international legal position, the USSR accepted the counter-offer in an exchange of notes on June 4, 1923.[330]

No attempts were made during the latter half of 1923 or early 1924 to convene an international conference treating the issue of territorial waters, so at the insistence of the Soviet delegation the question of fishery jurisdiction was raised at the Anglo–Soviet conference held in London during the spring of 1924. There the USSR sought to justify restrictions upon foreign fishing in its northern waters on grounds of economic necessity and historic rights. Fishery resources along the northern Soviet coast, it was argued, were not inexhaustible, and continued intensive trawling by foreign fleets threatened the existence of certain species. The Soviet government was particularly concerned because fish products were the prime source of nourishment and livelihood for the local populace. Moreover, the coastal population which had traditionally fished off the Murmansk region viewed foreign trawling as a direct threat to their very existence.[331]

On August 8, 1924, Great Britain and the Soviet Union concluded a General Treaty resolving outstanding questions of prerevolutionary treaties, fisheries, claims and loans, and several other issues. Article 5 granted to British subjects or nationals the right to fish within 3 to 12 miles of the northern Soviet coast, established certain seasons and conservation measures, prescribed in detail various procedures to be observed by all trawlers, and provided for an inspection system to ensure compliance with treaty provisions.[332] However, in consequence of the Zinov'ev Letter incident[333] and the Labor Government's fall from power, the treaty was never ratified, and the fishery question remained open until 1930.

The *modus vivendi* reached in 1930, pending the conclusion of a formal convention, permitted British vessels to fish within 3 to 12 miles of the Soviet coast, between 132° and 48° east longitude of the

328. *Cmd. 1890*, p. 3; *Dokumenty*, vi, 325; also see *SS&D*, vi (1969/70), 142.
329. *Cmd. 1890*, p. 5; *Dokumenty*, vi, 327.
330. *Ibid.*
331. *Dokumenty*, vii, 229–30.
332. For the text of the treaty, see *Dokumenty*, vii, 612.
333. William E. Butler, "The Harvard Text of the Zinov'ev Letter," *Harvard Library Bulletin*, xviii (1970), 43–62.

line running from Sviatoi Nos and Kanin Nos, and within 3 to 12 miles of a line drawn across bays whose width did not exceed 10 miles. The agreement was concluded without prejudice to the views of the parties regarding the limits of territorial waters in international law.[334]

Soviet–Norwegian relations were also affected by fishery disputes, although in this case the protagonists were more equal. The three Norwegian vessels detained by Soviet authorities on May 7, 1921, were finally released to their owners in late October of that year. As a diplomatic gesture, the Soviet government indicated that the fines imposed on their masters had been transferred for review by a higher court in Moscow.[335] These arrests, it will be recalled, were made prior to the enactment of the decree of May 24, 1921.

On March 21, 1922, the Norwegian government formally protested the 1921 decree as contravening principles of international law but expressed a willingness to negotiate about reserving the White Sea exclusively for Russian nationals. In its reply of April 21, 1922, the USSR reasserted its right to fix the boundaries of a special fishing zone and declined to negotiate any modifications of the 1921 decree.[336] In May 1922, the Norwegian government sought a clarification of certain provisions of the Soviet fishing restrictions and further time to notify Norwegian vessels thereof; the USSR accordingly suspended enforcement of the decree for a two-week period.[337] However, the Norwegian vessels seized prior to the temporary suspension were still detained in Soviet ports.

In return for the release of all Norwegian vessels held by Soviet authorities, Norway offered to publish a notice recognizing the existence of the Soviet decree on condition that after such publication vessels operating in the disputed zone or having no knowledge of the notice would not be detained nor their cargo confiscated. This offer was accepted by the Soviet government.[338]

334. *SDD*, vi, 43; *LNTS*, cii, 103; *SS&D*, vi (1969), 37.
335. *Dokumenty*, iv, 438.
336. *Dokumenty*, v, 262.
337. *Dokumenty*, v, 435.
338. *Dokumenty*, v, 455. The crucial issue here was formal recognition by Norway of the Soviet decree. The Norwegian "notice" fell considerably short of recognition:

Up to now the Norwegian Government has been unable to come to an agreement with the Russian Government over the disputed question of the boundaries of Russian territorial waters in the White Sea and must suppose that it will not reach such during the coming fishing season. Taking this into consideration, the Norwegian Government considers it neces-

On February 19, 1923, the People's Commissariat for Food of the RSFSR signed a concession contract with a Norwegian firm granting to the latter the exclusive rights for marine trapping and hunting "within the limits of Russian maritime territorial waters to the north of European Russia from the Finnish border up to Novaia Zemlia along the entire coast of the continent and islands except for the waters of the White Sea south of a line between the Orlovskii Lighthouse and Cape Kanushin."[339] Having assumed that the concession contract was a means of avoiding a direct confrontation with Norway over the issue of fishery jurisdiction, the Soviet government was outraged when a Norwegian auxiliary cruiser appeared in the White Sea in April 1923 to protect Norwegian fishermen operating in the disputed zone. Norway stressed that the 1921 decree "had not received international recognition" and suggested that, since the issue of jurisdiction seaward was unresolved, the presence of the cruiser would help avert conflicts or incidents.[340]

Under a treaty of commerce and navigation concluded December 15, 1925, Norwegian fishermen were granted most-favored-nation treatment to fish and hunt in the White Sea and along the northern Soviet coast, provided that with regard to fishing the other most-favored-nation derived the right from a treaty.[341]

Pursuant to a treaty of October 12, 1925, between the USSR and Germany, the Soviet Union agreed to sign a concession contract with a German fishery association on condition that during the contract period the German government would renounce further rights arising from the most-favored-nation clause of the Treaty of Rapallo and "as a consequence of its legal views toward the three-mile zone with respect to fishing."[342] Under the concession contract signed on the same date, the German fishery association received the right to fish up to within three miles of the northern coast of the USSR in waters lying

---

sary to call the attention of all Norwegians concerned in such expeditions to the danger they subject themselves by fishing in the zone which by a decree of May 24, 1921, Russia has declared to be Russian. Hoping that negotiations with Russia will find a solution to this question before the beginning of the fishing season of next year, the Norwegian Government also considers it necessary to suggest that all those concerned refrain from operating in the said zone. For its part, the Russian Government has released the vessels and cargo previously detained.

Dokumenty, v, 456. The Soviet government requested that the last sentence be deleted from the Norwegian notice.

339. *Dokumenty,* vi, 617.
340. *Dokumenty,* vi, 269.
341. *SDD,* iii, 114; *LNTS,* xlvii, 9.
342. *Dokumenty,* viii, 621.

between 67°40′ N. lat., 32° E. long., and 48° E. long. The contract was for a two-year term.[343]

Although the Minister of Foreign Affairs of the Far Eastern Republic, A. Krasnoshchekov, strenuously protested the transfer of the far eastern fishing grounds to the jurisdiction of the Japanese command in a Note of January 18, 1921, the reassertion of Russian control over far eastern coastal fisheries had to be deferred until the final consolidation of Bolshevik authority in that region.[344] The approach adopted by the Soviet regime was modeled on the Russian–Japanese fishing treaty of 1907, suggesting that the Soviet authorities merely wished to re-establish control over the pre-existing system seized by the Japanese. In contrast to the decrees affecting the northern coast, the decree of May 2, 1923, regulating fishing on the far eastern coast, did not exclude aliens from fishing in Soviet waters but did grant Soviet nationals priority in the distribution of fishing lots.[345]

In taking this approach, the Soviet government hoped "to smash the united economic and political front organized by the Anglo-American imperialists against our state;"[346] in other words, the Bolsheviks sought to sharply differentiate British and Japanese fishery interests off Russian coasts and to avert thereby coordinated Anglo–Japanese diplomatic and military pressure.

At first, the Soviet government refused to recognize the validity of the fishing treaty of 1907. While negotiations for diplomatic recognition were in progress, however, a temporary arrangement was achieved on April 6, 1924, restoring the regime of fisheries established in the 1907 fishing treaty.[347] The following year diplomatic relations were re-established, and the parties agreed to continue leasing fisheries to Japanese subjects under the 1924 agreement until the 1907 treaty could be revised.[348]

343. *Dokumenty*, VIII, 804. In a Note to the USSR of September 3, 1926, the German government indicated its adherence to the three-mile limit of territorial waters and suggested that an agreement with the Soviet Union would be difficult if the latter insisted upon a twelve-mile zone. *Dokumenty*, IX, 307.

344. *Dokumenty*, III, 484.

345. *SU RSFSR* (1923), no. 36, item 378; *SS&D*, VI (1969), 27.

346. Uustal', *Mezhdunarodno-pravovoi rezhim territorial'nykh vod*, p. 106.

347. Cited by N. L. Rubinshtein, *Vneshniaia politika sovetskogo soiuza v 1921–1925 godakh* (Moscow: Gospolitizdat, 1953), p. 506; *Dokumenty*, VII, 178. The arrangement was very nearly upset when on September 13, 1924, a Japanese destroyer landed 40 men to free a Japanese cutter being detained by local Soviet authorities for illegal fishing. The Japanese delegation at Peking admitted most of the facts of the incident but denied that 40 persons had disembarked. *Dokumenty*, VII, 451, 716.

348. *SDD*, III, 10–12; *LNTS*, XXXIV, 31–37; *SS&D*, VI (1969/70), 148. In the Soviet view only aliens who had obtained special permission from Soviet authorities, that is, had leased fishery lots, were entitled to fish within 12 miles

The revisions were contained in the fishing treaty of January 23, 1928, which with supplementary agreements served to define Soviet–Japanese fishing relations until 1945.[349] The right of Japanese subjects to exploit Soviet coastal fisheries in the Sea of Japan, the Okhotsk Sea, and the Bering Sea was preserved with a modest increase in the number of inlets from which the Japanese were excluded. The public auction system for leasing fishery lots was retained in its general form, and Japanese rights to use the Soviet coast for landing, preparing, and storing fish, the licensing of boats and crews, questions of taxes and fees, and the export and import of fish caught in territorial waters were set forth with greater precision than in the 1907 treaty.[350] The failure of the parties to include a provision regulating the exchange rate between the ruble and the sen was the source of considerable acrimony throughout the duration of the treaty.

More important for our purposes, however, is the fact that Soviet and Japanese fishing interests in the coastal region were fundamentally incompatible. The Japanese believed they possessed a vested right to fish in Soviet coastal waters based on historical tradition and uninterrupted practice. The Soviet Union regarded the convention of 1928 as a temporary concession to Japanese fishermen to be revised or terminated as the Soviet capability to exploit coastal fisheries increased. In conducting the auctions of fishing lots, the Soviet Union reserved the right to withhold as many lots as Soviet enterprises wished to exploit. Between 1927 and 1933, the Japanese percentage of the total of salmon and trout catches dropped from 87 to 58 percent, while the USSR's share rose from 12 to 42 percent; for crab, the Japanese share went from 89 to 48 percent, whereas that of the Soviet Union increased from 11 to 52 percent.[351]

---

of the coast. Japanese vessels continued to operate within the 12-mile zone, often escorted by Japanese naval vessels. On one occasion a Japanese warship intervened to prevent the arrest of a Japanese fishing vessel for illegal crabbing by the Soviet border guard. The USSR characterized the incident as a "grave violation of international custom." Japan insisted the arrest was attempted on the high seas beyond Soviet jurisdiction. *Dokumenty,* IX, 366. Thus, Soviet-Japanese relations were strained by two distinct, yet interrelated, issues: (1) the annual Japanese participation in the allocation of fishing lots in Soviet coastal waters, regulated by treaty; (2) the validity of Soviet legislation prohibiting Japanese vessels from fishing within up to three miles of the coast in areas not governed by treaty. Disagreement over the second issue resulted in many incidents, with some loss of life on both sides.

349. *SDD,* V, 89–106; *LNTS,* LXXX, 341–99; *SS&D,* VI (1969/70), 148.

350. Barbara Wertheim, "The Russo-Japanese Fisheries Controversy," *Pacific Affairs,* VIII (1935), 187. Because of the 1923 Soviet decree fixing a 12-mile fishing zone on the far eastern coast, the protocol to the 1928 fishery convention, in contrast to the treaty of 1907, avoided any reference to territorial waters, stating merely that the 1928 convention did "not apply to high seas."

351. *Ibid.*

Japanese adherence to the anti-Comintern pact made the negotiation of a new agreement impossible. The old treaty was twice extended in the form of a *modus vivendi;* a temporary agreement reached in 1939, mostly on Soviet terms, was renewed, with some difficulty, annually through 1944. An agreement continuing Japanese fishing activity off the Soviet coast for five years with additional limitations was signed at Moscow on March 30, 1944.[352]

According to one Soviet jurist, the RSFSR decrees of 1921 and 1923 were replaced by a Statute on Fisheries of July 3, 1925 (although those decrees were not expressly repealed in the statute),[353] which in turn was superseded by a fishing decree of October 25, 1935. The 1935 decree expressly fixed 12-mile fishing zones in the Black Sea, along the northern and far eastern coasts, and in the Gulf of Finland (where the zone extended to 4 miles). In addition, the Sea of Azov, the Aral Sea, the White Sea, and the Caspian Sea were each treated as internal seas for fishery purposes. Foreigners were prohibited from fishing within such waters unless special authorization was granted pursuant to international agreements or contracts.[354]

Thus, from the viewpoint of enacting restrictive legislation, the Soviet government assumed a much more protective attitude toward its coastal fisheries than had the Tsarist government. However, what the Soviet regime claimed by legislative fiat had to be given away through treaty concessions.

Soviet regulation of coastal fisheries: 1946–69. It became exceedingly difficult to obtain permission for aliens to fish within the Soviet 12-mile fishing zone after 1945. In 1954,[355] and again in 1958,[356] the Soviet Union enacted fishery legislation absolutely prohibiting foreign fishing within a 12-mile zone unless provided otherwise in an international agreement. The same prohibition is included in the 1960 statute on the state boundary. Articles 163–166 of the 1960 RSFSR Criminal Code contain severe penalties for illegally engaging in fishing or other marine extractive trades, for hunting seals or beavers, for blasting in

352. The text of a supplementary agreement signed August 13, 1932, revising the 1928 convention, became available only in 1969 in *Dokumenty*, xv, 469. Also see *SS&D*, vi (1969/70), 163. On subsequent Protcols through 1939, see Leonard Shapiro (ed.), *Soviet Treaty Series: 1917–1939* (Washington D.C.: Georgetown University Press, 1950–55), ii, pp. 164, 173, 191, 202, and 219. Data on fishery developments in the 1940's, including the text of the agreement of March 30, 1944, is given in Strohl, *International Law of Bays,* p. 347; *SS&D,* vi (1969/70), 164–70.
353. *SZ SSSR* (1925), no. 58, item 440; Uustal', *Mezhdunarodno-pravovoi rezhim territorial'nykh vod,* pp. 106–7.
354. *SZ SSSR* (1935), no. 50, item 420; *SS&D,* vi (1969), 39.
355. Translated in *SS&D,* vi (1969), 41.
356. *SP SSSR* (1958), no. 16, item 127; *SS&D,* vi (1969), 42.

violation of rules for the protection of fishery stocks, and for illegal hunting.[357]

With the incorporation of Latvia, Estonia, and Lithuania into the Soviet Union in 1940, the 12-mile fishing zone was extended to the Baltic coasts. A number of Danish and Swedish fishing vessels were seized by Soviet patrol boats during the early 1950's. Two British trawlers were also captured off the Murmansk coast while allegedly fishing within the 3-mile limit. Fines were levied, and the catch and gear were confiscated.[358] Japanese sources report that more than a thousand Japanese vessels have been detained by Soviet authorities along the far eastern coast in 1948–62.[359]

The temporary fishing agreement of 1930 with Great Britain was denounced by the Soviet Union in 1953 and, after negotiations, renewed provisionally for 1954 and 1955. A new agreement with Britain, concluded for a five-year period and signed May 25, 1956, entered into force on March 12, 1957. British vessels continued to enjoy the right to fish within three to twelve miles of Soviet coasts but in a more restricted area.[360] On March 12, 1961, the Soviet Union announced its unwillingness to continue the arrangement, and the agreement terminated one year from that date.[361]

In 1959 Finnish nationals were allowed to fish within certain portions of Soviet territorial waters in the Gulf of Finland;[362] these rights were extended by a protocol concluded in May 1965,[363] and were expanded in a new agreement of June 13, 1969.[364]

Under the terms of a 1962 agreement between the Soviet Union and Norway, Norwegian fishermen were permitted to fish within 6 to 12 miles of the Soviet coast in the Varangerfjord until October 31, 1970.[365]

The Soviet–Japanese fishing agreement of March 30, 1944, lost force with the Soviet declaration of war on Japan in 1945.[366] Since that time, Japanese fishermen have been excluded from fishing within 12 miles of Soviet coasts. Indeed, in 1956, in order to force the Japanese

357. Berman and Spindler, *Soviet Criminal Law and Procedure*, pp. 208–9.
358. Uustal', *Mezhdunarodno-pravovoi rezhim territorial'nykh vod*, p. 112.
359. Oda, *International Control of Sea Resources*, p. 25.
360. *SDD*, xix, 154; *UNTS*, cclxvi, 209; *SS&D*, vi (1969/70), 144.
361. Barabolia, *Voenno-morskoi spravochnik*, p. 286.
362. *SDD*, xxi, 244; *UNTS*, cccxxxviii, 3; *SS&D*, vi (1969/70), 135.
363. *Vedomosti SSSR* (1966), no. 22, item 388; translated in *ILM*, vi (1967), 729; *SS&D*, vi (1969/70), 139.
364. *ILM*, ix (1970), 507; *SS&D*, vi (1970), 400.
365. *SDD*, xxii, 308; *UNTS*, ccccxxxvii, 175; *SS&D*, vi (1969/70), 175.
366. Uustal', *Mezhdunarodno-pravovoi rezhim territorial'nykh vod*, p. 110.

to agree to reduce their salmon catch beyond the 12-mile limit in the Okhotsk Sea, the USSR unilaterally proclaimed a conservation zone embracing the entire sea and prohibited fishing therein except during specified seasons.[367] The decree was superseded by a Soviet–Japanese Fishery Convention concluded May 14, 1956.[368]

In 1963 the Soviet Union reached an agreement with the Japan Fisheries Association permitting certain fishermen to gather sea kale in Soviet territorial waters near the Island of Kaigara. The number of vessels permitted to do so is limited; an annual fee is paid for each vessel.[369]

Thus, except for very minor concessions to Finland and Japan (it is not expected that Norwegian privileges will be renewed after 1970), the Soviet Union has effectively asserted exclusive fishing jurisdiction within its 12-mile limit.

Regime of Airspace over Territorial Waters

The regime of Soviet airspace is governed by the Air Code of the USSR,[370] instructions issued pursuant thereto by Soviet state agencies,[371] and international air agreements. Article 1 of the code provides:

The Union of Soviet Socialist Republics exercises full and exclusive sovereignty over airspace of the USSR.

Airspace of the USSR shall mean the airspace above the land and water territory of the USSR, including territorial waters, as determined by USSR laws and international agreements concluded by the USSR.

The provisions of the code are binding for all types of civil aviation and civil aeronautics within the limits of the Soviet Union.

The Soviet Union does not recognize a right of innocent passage for foreign aircraft over Soviet territorial waters. Flights of foreign aircraft in Soviet airspace may be performed only in accordance with international air agreements to which the USSR is a party or on the basis of special authorization. In either case, international flights must follow established air lanes.

367. *Pravda,* March 21, 1956, p. 1; *SS&D,* vi (1970), 357.
368. *SDD,* xvii–xviii, 312; *SS&D,* vi (1970), 359.
369. English texts appear in *Japanese Annual of International Law,* viii (1964), 92; *SS&D,* vi (1969/70), 170.
370. *Vedomosti SSSR* (1961), no. 52, item 538; translated in Dennis A. Cooper, *The Air Code of the U.S.S.R.* (Charlottesville, Va.: Michie Company, 1966).
371. See the "Flight Rules for Foreign Civil Aircraft Within the Territory of the USSR," in United States Senate, Committee on Commerce, *Air Laws and Treaties of the World* (Washington D.C.: GPO, 1965), ii, p. 2570.

Prior to the explicit incorporation of a 12-mile breadth of territorial waters into Soviet legislation in 1960, the Soviet Union, as we have previously noted, avoided mention of the expression "territorial waters" in diplomatic correspondence with the United States relating to certain alleged intrusions of Soviet airspace by American aircraft. The single apparent exception to this practice occurred on July 1, 1960, only a month before the 1960 statute on the state boundary was enacted, when an American RB–47 aircraft was shot down, according to the Soviet Note, over Soviet territorial waters. The precise coordinates of the incident and the limit of territorial waters claimed by the Soviet government were not mentioned in the Soviet Notes.[372] A similar pattern was followed on August 30, 1962, when an American U–2 craft flew over Sakhalinsk and "territorial waters." On this occasion, the United States admitted that a violation had unintentionally occurred.[373]

The Legal Regime of the Caspian Sea

The legal regime of the Caspian Sea is unique. Geologically speaking, the Caspian is a landlocked, saltwater lake which historically has been called a sea. The regime of the Caspian is governed by Soviet–Iranian treaties and agreements and by the domestic legislation of each state. General norms of international law relating to the high seas, to vessels and their crews on the high seas, and to research and exploitation of the natural resources of the high seas do not apply to the Caspian.

In a treaty of friendship concluded with Iran on February 26, 1921, the Soviet government abrogated all prior treaties, agreements, and conventions of the Tsarist government and annulled Russian concessions in the Caspian.[374] The treaty provided for each party to have equal rights in sailing the Caspian in vessels under their respective flags. The Iranian government further agreed to exclude subjects of a third government from the Iranian fleet who would use their presence for ends unfriendly to Russia.

The friendship treaty was affirmed by the nonaggression and neutrality pact of 1927, which enjoined the parties from participating in "political alliances or agreements directed against the safety of . . . territorial waters. . . ."[375] Moreover, the Iranian government consented

372. The Soviet Notes are published in *DSB*, XLIII (1960), 164–65, 210–11.
373. *American Foreign Policy 1962: Basic Documents*, pp. 744–45.
374. *SDD*, I, 148–53; *LNTS*, IX, 383; *SS&D*, VI (1969/70), 179.
375. *SDD*, IV, 23–26; *LNTS*, CXII, 275–96.

to exclude non-Iranian subjects, including former subjects of third powers who acquired Iranian nationality, from among the employees, laborers, and contractors at Port Pehlevi for a period of 25 years.

A fisheries agreement contracted in 1927 raised for many observers the spectre of renewed Russian colonialism in the Caspian region. The agreement provided for the organization of a joint Soviet-Iranian company and granted special concession privileges to that firm for a 25-year period.[376] Iran elected not to renew the arrangement in 1953 but is bound not to grant another concession for these fisheries to a third government for an additional 25 years.

Under a Treaty of Commerce and Navigation of March 25, 1940, Soviet and Iranian merchant vessels in the Caspian Sea receive national treatment in each other's ports, including the assessment of port fees. Each party has reserved a 10-mile fishing zone adjacent to its coast for its own flag vessels; beyond the 10-mile zone, fishing may be pursued exclusively by Soviet and Iranian nationals. Other marine trades are restricted to national waters. Seabed resources are reserved to each party within its portion of the sea. The sanitary standards of the 1956 International Quarantine Convention are applicable to vessels while in ports of the other party.[377]

While engaged in cabotage on the Caspian, Soviet vessels are regulated by internal legislation, but these rules are superseded by the 1940 treaty provisions with regard to intercourse between the USSR and Iran. In the latter event, Soviet vessels are governed by the Merchant Shipping Code of the USSR. The provisions of the 1960 statute on the state boundary apply to the Caspian insofar as the statute regulates border lakes. There are no territorial waters in the Caspian, only the 10-mile fishing zone.[378]

The Soviet–Iranian treaties do not contain provisions affecting the navigation of Soviet or Iranian warships on the Caspian or overflights of aircraft. Soviet jurists assume, however, that the "general

---

376. *SDD*, v, 74–84; *LNTS*, cxii, 297; *SS&D*, vi (1969/70), 182.

377. *SDD*, x, 56–71; *BFSP*, cxliv, 419–31.

378. The Bureau of Intelligence and Research of the U.S. Department of State has erroneously asserted that the "margins" of the Caspian Sea are claimed as territorial waters. See U.S. Department of State, *Sovereignty of the Sea* (Washington D.C.: gpo, 1969), p. 18. However, prior to the 1921 RSFSR–Persia treaty of friendship there were references in Soviet diplomatic correspondence to a legal regime in the Caspian other than that of a closed lake. In an "Appeal of the People's Commissariat of Foreign Affairs to the Workers and Peasants of Persia," dated August 28, 1919, it was promised that upon being purged of "piratical vessels of English imperialism," the Caspian "would be declared free for the navigation of vessels under the Persian Flag." *Dokumenty*, ii, 241. In Notes of June 5, and 20, 1920, reference was made to the "territorial waters" of Persia without, however, any indication as to what was meant by that expression. *Ibid.*, ii, 557, 580.

principles" of the treaties and a mutual interest in national security require that warships of one party obtain the authorization of the other party before entering the latter's part of the Caspian.[379]

In an exchange of Notes of September 15, 1962, Iran agreed not to "accord to any foreign state the right to have missile bases of any type on the territory of Iran."[380] Soviet jurists have interpreted the Notes as barring the creation of foreign missile and naval bases on Iranian territory and in the Caspian Sea.[381]

379. Bakhov, *Voenno-morskoi spravochnik*, p. 258; Barabolia, *Voenno-morskoi spravochnik*, p. 375.
380. Translated in Butler, *Soviet Territorial Waters*, p. 168; *SS&D*, VI (1969/70), 195.
381. Barabolia, *Voenno-morskoi spravochnik*, p. 375.

Chapter 3

THE LEGAL REGIME
OF INTERNAL SEA WATERS

Internal waters are considered constituent parts of coastal state terri-tory and subject to its complete sovereign authority; the navigation of foreign vessels in internal waters may be totally prohibited by the coastal state. All foreign vessels, including warships, are obliged to observe local laws and customs while in internal waters.

The great majority of international lawyers, including Russian ju-rists,[1] have generally accepted these principles. Considerable differ-ence of opinion has been expressed by Soviet jurists, however, as to which waters adjacent to Soviet coasts should be classified as internal. (See Map 3.)

The prevailing view among Soviet jurists up to the time of its pub-lication was expressed in the 1947 international law textbook. It de-fined "internal waters" as the waters of ports and of bays and gulfs whose coasts belong to a single state and whose aperture does not ex-ceed 10 nautical miles. This was the definition approved at the 1930 Hague conference, and, in the Soviet view, had been adopted by the great majority of states.[2]

After 1947, the Soviet definition of internal waters was signifi-cantly broadened. The 1951 international law textbook abandoned the previous definition for one formulated in terms of internal seas. These were seas fully encircled by the territory of a single state or seas whose shores were connected with another sea, both of which belong to the same state. Examples mentioned were the Sea of Azov and the White Sea, where navigation and fishing by foreign vessels were prohibited by Soviet law.[3]

Keilin partially restored the 1947 definition and acknowledged certain revisions in its application. He concluded that the waters of

1. F. F. Martens, *Sovremennoe mezhdunarodnoe pravo tsivilizovannykh narodov* (5th ed.; St. Petersburg: Tipo. A. Benke, 1904–05), I, 391.
2. V. N. Durdenevskii and S. B. Krylov (ed.), *Mezhdunarodnoe pravo* (Moscow: Iurizdat, 1947), pp. 246–47. Excluded from this discussion are in-land rivers, lakes, and canals, which are classified as internal or national waters.
3. E. A. Korovin (ed.), *Mezhdunarodnoe pravo* (Moscow: Gosiurizdat, 1951), p. 308.

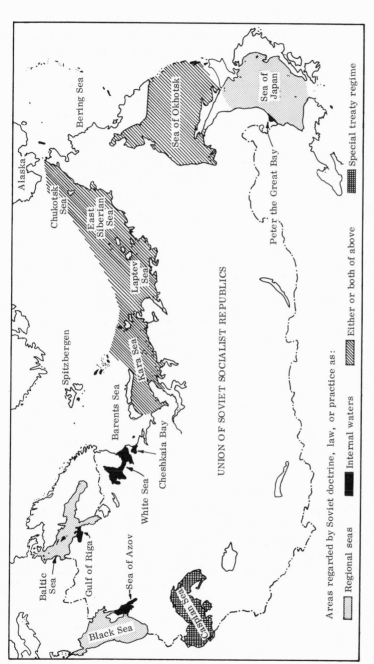

Map 3. *Some Areas Treated in Soviet Doctrine, Law, or Practice as Closed Seas, Historic Bays or Seas, or Internal Waters*

Areas regarded by Soviet doctrine, law, or practice as:

Regional seas

Internal waters

Either or both of above

Special treaty regime

ports, of internal and external roadsteads,[4] of bays, gulfs, and estuaries whose shores belong to a single state, as well as of certain closed seas and border lakes, were internal waters. In addition, Keilin mentioned as internal sea waters the historic bays and "seas of the bay type" which are encircled by the coasts of a single state, although connected with the ocean by a strait or canal.[5] The 10-mile closing line rule for bays was abandoned by the Soviet Union following the judgment of the International Court of Justice in the *Anglo–Norwegian Fisheries* case in 1951.

A more precise classification was offered by Meshera, who subdivided Soviet internal waters into six categories: (1) sea ports; (2) intrastate bays and seas which are under Soviet authority and whose aperture does not exceed 24 miles; (3) historic bays and seas of the USSR as determined by special economic, security, or other vital interests; (4) the Soviet part of the Caspian Sea; (5) water expanses formed by tides along Soviet coasts; (6) water expanses between Soviet shores and straight base lines.[6]

To the second category Meshera attributed the Sea of Azov, the White Sea, and the Gulf of Riga. The Kara, Laptev, and East Siberian Seas were subsumed within the third category. Vereshchetin added the Chukotsk Sea to the third category, and Shmigel'skii mentioned the Aral Sea and Peter the Great Bay.[7]

The 1960 statute on the state boundary defined "Soviet internal waters" as the waters of ports, the waters of bays, gulfs, inlets, and estuaries, whose shore belongs wholly to the USSR up to a straight closing line from shore to shore in a place where one or several apertures, each of which does not exceed 24 nautical miles in breadth, are formed leading into the sea. In addition, the waters of bays, coves, in-

---

4. A. S. Bakhov (ed.), *Voenno-morskoi mezhdunarodno-pravovoi spravochnik* (Moscow: Voengiz, 1956), p. 113. Keilin and Zhudro concurred with this view, but Vereshchetin considered roadsteads to be part of territorial waters, as did the editors of the 1947 and 1951 international law textbooks. Volkov regarded roadsteads "which are commonly used for the loading, unloading, or anchoring of ships" as part of the territorial sea even in those instances in which they are situated beyond the territorial waters of the coastal state. Such roadsteads must be clearly demarcated and appropriately designated on sea charts. A. A. Volkov, *Morskoe pravo* (Moscow: izd-vo Pishchevaia promyshlennost', 1969), p. 101.

5. A. D. Keilin, *Sovetskoe morskoe pravo* (Moscow: izd-vo Morskoi transport, 1954), p. 91.

6. V. F. Meshera, *Morskoe pravo* (Moscow: izd-vo Morskoi transport, 1958–59), III, p. 10.

7. V. S. Vereshchetin, *Svoboda sudokhodstva v otkrytom more* (Moscow: izd-vo IMO, 1958), p. 7; G. L. Shmigel'skii and V. A. Iasinovskii, *Osnovy sovetskogo morskogo prava* (Moscow: izd-vo Morskoi transport, 1959), p. 29.

lets, and estuaries, as well as of seas and straits historically belonging to the Soviet Union, are internal waters.[8]

"Historic" bodies of water were not specifically named in the statute, nor did the statute expressly embrace the latter three categories posited by Meshera. Soviet jurists do not regard the listing of the 1960 statute as exhaustive, for maritime law textbooks published since 1960 include the waters between a straight base line and the coast as part of the internal waters of the coastal state. The omission of that category from the 1960 statute means that the straight base line principle is not applied to Soviet coasts, although the validity of the principle in international law is recognized by the USSR and was incorporated into the Geneva Convention on the Territorial Sea.

Historic Waters

Historic waters are considered to be part of the internal waters of the coastal state and subject to its unlimited sovereignty. Soviet jurists define "historic waters" as those having a special economic or strategic significance for the coastal state or as having been established by historical tradition.[9] To these criteria, the authors of the 1966 naval international law manual added "special geographic conditions" as an independent factor.[10] Although this definition has not received further elaboration, Soviet writers attempt to establish the presence of all factors in defending the designation of a given body of water as historic. The definition, however, is formulated in the alternative, and presumably the presence of any single factor, in the Soviet view, would justify an application of the historic bay or sea principle. It is an exaggeration to conclude, as has one Western observer, that the "unilaterally proclaimed Soviet doctrine [of historic bays] virtually replaces the concept of the territorial sea belt."[11]

Considerable confusion has resulted in Soviet literature from the classification of some bodies of water as both closed seas and historic bays. For example, in 1893 Tsarist Russia looked upon the White Sea as a closed sea; in 1920 the Soviet government referred to it as an "in-

8. Article 4. *Vedomosti SSSR* (1960), no. 34, item 324.
9. F. I. Kozhevnikov (ed.), *International Law,* trans. Dennis Ogden (Moscow: Foreign Languages Publishing House, [1961]), pp. 205–6.
10. P. D. Barabolia *et al., Voenno-morskoi mezhdunarodno-pravovoi spravochnik* (Moscow: Voenizdat, 1966), p. 216.
11. William N. Harben, "Soviet Positions Concerning Maritime Waters," *JAG Journal,* xv (1961), 149–54, 160. Harben wrote that the Soviet coastline is bounded by historic bays and seas, but he confused the closed or regional sea with the historic bay.

ternal Russian sea"; the 1956 international law manual described it as an historic bay;[12] and Meshera concluded that the White Sea can be classified as an historic sea whose closing line is drawn from Cape Sviatoi Nos to Cape Kanin Nos and as an internal sea whose aperture does not exceed 24 nautical miles if the closing line is drawn from Cape Pogoredskii to the opposite shore near Cape Intsii.[13]

The number of bodies of water which Soviet jurists designated as historic increased until the late 1960s. The 1947 international law textbook mentioned the White Sea, the Sea of Azov, and the Gulf of Riga as historic bays.[14] The 1951 international law textbook added "seas of the bay type"—that is, the Kara, Laptev, East Siberian, and Chukotsk Seas.[15] Shmigel'skii concurred in this definition.[16] But the 1956 naval international law manual treated historic bays and historic seas as separate entities, whereas the 1966 naval international law manual preferred the generic term "historic waters."[17]

By 1969, however, there were indications that doctrinal briefs for historic waters were falling into disrepute. A maritime law textbook reverted to a listing of historic waters based solely upon Soviet legislation and treaty practice. The White Sea was cited as the "sea of a bay type" and Peter the Great Bay as an example of historic waters.[18] As the first omission of a broad and ritualistic definition of historic waters in more than two decades, this new formulation suggests that the Soviet legal community may be discarding the earlier concept as inappropriate for a large maritime power.

HISTORIC BAYS

A celebrated application of the historic bay doctrine occurred on July 21, 1957, when the Council of Ministers of the USSR proclaimed Peter the Great Bay, a bay of the Sea of Japan, to be part of the internal waters of the USSR and, except for the shipping lanes to Nakhodka, closed to foreign vessels and aircraft.[19] The closing line established for the bay was 108 miles in length. (See Map 4.) No Soviet

12. Bakhov, *Voenno-morskoi spravochnik*, pp. 114–15.
13. Meshera, *Morskoe pravo*, III, p. 10.
14. Durdenevskii and Krylov, *Mezhdunarodnoe pravo*, p. 248.
15. Korovin, *Mezhdunarodnoe pravo*, p. 296.
16. Shmigel'skii and Iasinovskii, *Osnovy sovetskogo morskogo prava*, p. 35.
17. Bakhov, *Voenno-morskoi spravochnik*, pp. 118–19; Barabolia, *Voenno-morskoi spravochnik*, p. 215.
18. Volkov, *Morskoe pravo*, p. 119.
19. *Izvestia*, July 21, 1957, p. 1; English text in William E. Butler, *The Law of Soviet Territorial Waters* (New York: Frederick A. Praeger, 1967), p. 108; *SS&D*, VI (1969/70), 209.

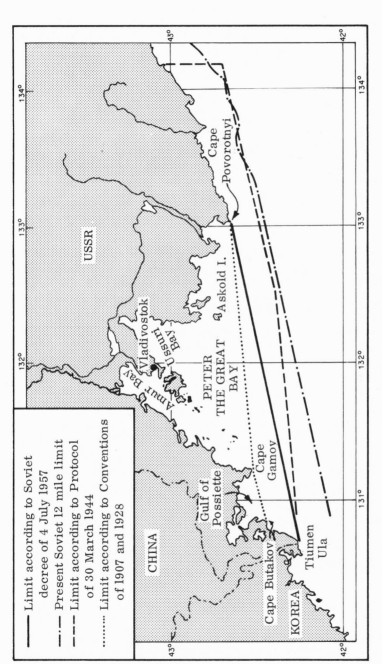

Map 4. *Peter the Great Bay*

jurist had previously mentioned or in any way alluded to Peter the Great Bay as an historic bay.[20]

Many nations entered formal diplomatic protests, Japan being the most immediately aggrieved.[21] The People's Republic of China expressed its approval of the Soviet decree.[22]

Soviet international lawyers, relying heavily upon the Soviet Note to Japan of January 7, 1958, defended the decree as an appropriate application of the historic bay doctrine and on the ground that there was no generally accepted norm governing the length of the closing line for bays. Reference was made to Russian exploration in the region during the 1850–60s and to the founding of Vladivostok along the coast of the bay in 1860. A. N. Nikolaev cited fishing regulations supposedly enacted by the Tsarist government in 1901, in which "the fishing rights in the territorial waters of the Amur General–Governorship are granted only to Russian subjects . . ." with certain exceptions in the "southern part of the Primorye Region from the mouth of the Tiumen-Ula to Cape Povorotny."[23] A source reference to the text of the 1901 regulation was not given, and diligent searches by Western and Japanese scholars have found no trace of such regulations.[24]

20. Leo J. Bouchez, *The Regime of Bays in International Law* (Leyden: Sijthoff, 1964), p. 225; Mitchell P. Strohl, *The International Law of Bays* (The Hague: Nijhoff, 1963), pp. 332–67. On May 7, 1929, the British government entered a protest against those provisions of the 1928 Soviet-Japanese fisheries convention which amounted to a recognition of Soviet jurisdiction over Peter the Great Bay and Possiette Bay. Such jurisdiction was said to be unjustified from the viewpoint of international law, and the United Kingdom reserved all rights with regard to those waters. The Soviet government responded that the fishery convention, in prohibiting fishing in certain bays and gulfs, did not affect those waters enjoying the status of high seas, neatly avoiding the question of whether Peter the Great Bay enjoyed the status of high seas. The Soviet Note also called attention to the broad interpretation of international legal norms governing Hudson Bay, the Bay of Conception, Miramichi Bay, and others in British practice and rejected the protest of Great Britain. The Notes were published from Soviet archival sources in 1967. *Dokumenty,* xii, 327.

21. Bouchez, *Regime of Bays,* p. 225. Diplomatic protests were entered by the Netherlands (October 31, 1957); Japan (July 26, 1957, and January 17, 1958); the United States (August 12, 1957, and August 6, 1958); the United Kingdom (September 10, 1957); France (October 11, 1957); Sweden (December 9, 1957); the Federal Republic of Germany (February 5, 1958). On January 7, 1958, the Soviet government sent Notes of slightly different content simultaneously to Japan, the United States, and the United Kingdom, rejecting the protests. The Note to Japan appears in the *Japanese Annual of International Law,* ii (1958), 215; and in *SS&D,* vi (1969/70), 210.

22. "Peter the Great Bay Has Always Been the Internal Sea of Russia," *People's Daily,* September 23, 1957, p. 6.

23. A. N. Nikolaev, "O zalive Petra Velikogo," *Mezhdunarodnaia zhizn',* no. 2 (1958), 50–57.

24. Strohl, *International Law of Bays,* p. 341. Strohl concluded, however, that the provisions of such a regulation "appear in some greater or lesser degree to have been enforced." *Ibid.*

Nikolaev further denied that a claim to an historic bay must be recognized by all states in order to be valid; this would be impossible and was not the general practice.[25] Damage to Japanese fishing rights in the bay, Soviet sources predicted, would be minimal because in recent years the Japanese had been excluded from the bay. While economic and strategic factors were alluded to in justification of the decree, they were not elaborated. Romanov argued that the Soviet decree merely synthesized prior (unspecified) legislation and fixed a precise boundary in a place where it had been the subject of doubt.[26]

The true reasons for the sudden "nationalization" of Peter the Great Bay remain unclear. There may have been concern that the impending 1958 Geneva Conference on the Law of the Sea would adopt a binding rule with regard to historic bays that would prejudice Soviet claims. A more probable explanation is that strategic considerations were paramount. Missile bases were under construction in the region,[27] and Vladivostok, the major Soviet naval base in the Pacific theater and only 10 miles from the Chinese frontier, is situated on the bay.

Soviet jurists have compared the action of the Soviet government with regard to Peter the Great Bay to the practice of other states: England (Bristol Bay); Canada (Hudson Bay, the Bay of Fundy); and the United States (Chesapeake Bay).[28]

The government of the USSR has taken no legislative action with respect to the Gulf of Riga, which both Tsarist and Soviet jurists cited as an example of historic waters. Martens included both the Gulf of Riga and the Gulf of Finland in the category of internal sea waters,[29] although Ul'ianitskii regarded the Gulf of Finland as too large to be so considered.[30] Soviet jurists cite the Treaty of Nystad of 1721 as the basis of such a claim.

HISTORIC SEAS

The status of the seas adjacent to the northern coast of Russia has been the subject of considerable discussion and controversy among

25. This view was also taken by Barabolia:

Recognition on the part of other states of one or another bay as a "historic bay" belonging to the littoral state does not have, from the viewpoint of international law, decisive significance.

Barabolia, *Voenno-morskoi spravochnik*, p. 216.

26. V. Romanov, "Zaliv Petra Velikogo—vnutrennie vody sovetskogo soiuza," *SGIP*, no. 5 (1958), 53.

27. Z. Ohira, "Fishery Problems Between Soviet Russia and Japan," *Japanese Annual of International Law*, II (1958), 19.

28. Barabolia, *Voenno-morskoi spravochnik*, p. 217.

29. Martens, *Sovremennoe mezhdunarodnoe pravo*, I, p. 391.

30. V. A. Ul'ianitskii, *Lektsii po mezhdunarodnomu pravu* (Moscow: Obshchestvo rasprostraneniia poleznykh knig, 1900), p. 146.

Tsarist and Soviet jurists. During the Tsarist period, the government received various recommendations that certain of the polar seas be closed; the more influential Russian jurists, however, were not enthusiastic about the legal validity of such a policy.[31] When in 1926 the USSR laid claim to territory "already discovered or discovered in the future" in the Soviet Arctic, some Soviet jurists criticized the decree for restricting itself only to "lands and islands."[32] E. A. Korovin urged that the intent of the decree was to include ice blocks and waters washing the lands and islands, but his view was not widely accepted.[33]

Another Soviet jurist, V. L. Lakhtin, subdivided the Arctic seas which were free of ice into categories: (1) the mouths of rivers, bays, and landlocked seas whose aperture did not exceed twice the breadth of the marginal sea, such as the White Sea and the Kara Sea, which would be regarded as national waters; (2) territorial waters lying between the islands of archipelagoes; (3) remaining waters, which were analogous to territorial waters. In waters of the latter two categories, sovereignty of the coastal state would be limited by the right of innocent passage, but police, customs, and sanitary control would be exercised by the Soviet Union.[34]

Lakhtin considered the Kara Sea to be a closed sea, landlocked by ice. However, as the ice pack shifted, so would the boundary of territorial waters. Vessels sailing in the area could pass in and out of Soviet jurisdiction several times a day without altering course. Apart from this difficulty, Lakhtin's theory did not provide the requisite degree of Soviet sovereignty in the zone established by the 1926 decree, and it was not generally accepted by other Soviet jurists.

After World War II, the legal status of the polar seas took on greater urgency for the Soviet Union. The strategic value of the northern sea route for the clandestine transfer of warships from west to east was demonstrated vividly in 1940 when a German auxiliary cruiser, under exceptionally favorable ice conditions and with Soviet assistance, made the eastward voyage in 14 days actual running time. As the Cold War intensified, Soviet jurists developed theories to support Soviet claims to exclusive sovereignty over the Arctic seas.

The "historic waters" approach to the legal status of the polar seas, as developed in Soviet literature, is an amalgam of arguments based upon historical discovery, geographical and geological data, and

31. *Ibid.*, p. 138; Martens, *Sovremennoe mezhdunarodnoe pravo,* I, p. 372.
32. English text in Butler, *Soviet Territorial Waters,* p. 97; *SS&D,* III, no. 4 (1967), 9.
33. E. A. Korovin, "SSSR i poliarnye zemli," *Sovetskoe pravo,* no. 3 (1926), 46.
34. V. L. Lakhtin, "Rights Over the Arctic," *AJIL,* XXIV (1930), 703–17.

economic development and utilization of the area. As the authors of the 1951 international law textbook pointed out, from a geographical and geological point of view the polar seas are in reality bays of the Arctic Ocean.[35] The juridical notion of "seas of the bay type" is based upon this geological peculiarity. Moreover, it has been argued that the polar seas are not truly seas because navigation, in the customary sense of the word, was impossible. Vessels sailing in the region required the assistance of special icebreakers and other services of the coastal state—that is, vessels must be *led* through these seas.[36]

Historically speaking, it was contended that the northern sea route has been a national route since the sixteenth century. Russia granted exclusive trading privileges in the mouths of certain northern rivers to English merchants in 1582. From 1616 to 1620, the tsar promulgated four edicts prohibiting commercial navigation in the Kara Sea, which Ivan IV regarded as lying "in our land." Vyshnepol'skii stressed that the Russian regime of the Kara Sea was not protested by foreign states for more than three hundred years.[37]

The strongest argument pressed by Soviet jurists emphasized the coastal nature of the northern sea route, its development and utilization by the USSR, and its subordination to Soviet authority. The coastal nature of a particular route, wrote Vyshnepol'skii, was not to be determined merely by the oceans and basins through which it passed. The decisive criteria were the nature of its usage, the destination of cargo, and the initial and final ports of destination of the vessels navigating the route. On the basis of these criteria, the route from Leningrad to Vladivostok via the polar seas was a coastal route.[38] Vyshnepol'skii included the entire area serviced by the northern sea route, even though the route "is bounded on the west by the passages between the Kara and Barents Seas and on the east by the Bering Strait."[39] Nevertheless, he acknowledged that the Bering and Barents Seas are open seas by virtue of long established fishing operations by many states.

Other jurists have attributed the sovereign rights of the Soviet Union in the polar seas to the economic, administrative, and scientific activities carried on by the USSR in the northern Polar Basin, to the opening of the northern sea route, to the explorations and discoveries

35. Korovin, *Mezhdunarodnoe pravo,* p. 296.
36. S. A. Vyshnepol'skii, "K probleme pravovogo rezhima arkticheskoi oblasti," *SGIP,* no. 7 (1952), 36–45.
37. *Ibid.*
38. S. A. Vyshnepol'skii, *Mirovye morskie puti i sudokhodstvo* (Moscow: Geografgiz, 1953), pp. 52–53.
39. Constantine Krypton, *The Northern Sea Route and the Economy of the Soviet North* (New York: Frederick A. Praeger, 1956), p. 22.

in polar seas by Russian navigators and explorers, and to the historical traditions based on these factors.[40]

Zhudro asserted that the Soviet regime over the polar seas acquired international recognition and acceptance when foreign vessels under contract to Soviet foreign trade organizations agreed to follow all instructions transmitted to them during a voyage by Soviet state agencies responsible for administering Arctic maritime operations. These included a report upon arrival in the Kara Sea and a daily report of position thereafter. Zhudro believed that a generally recognized international custom had thereby been established.[41]

As recently as 1967, Soviet authorities tried to accentuate the sovereign authority of the USSR over the northern sea route by encouraging foreign vessels to use that route instead of the longer Suez Canal or South African route, paying special fees for the use of Soviet facilities en route.[42]

HISTORIC STRAITS

Most straits in the northeast passage are less than 24 miles wide and therefore are overlapped by Soviet territorial waters. Two other wider straits, the Laptev Strait and the Sannikov Strait, in the opinion of some Soviet jurists, belong to the USSR by historical prescription. These have "never been used for international navigation, and in view of specific natural conditions and frequent ice jams, the legal status of these straits is sharply distinguished from all other straits being used for international navigation."[43]

The Soviet Union reportedly first made this claim in an exchange of diplomatic correspondence with the United States concerning a prospective oceanographic research voyage sponsored by the latter through the northeast passage.[44]

Notwithstanding Soviet theories about "seas of the bay type" and announcements of the "opening" of the northern sea route, the legal regime of the polar seas along the Soviet Arctic coast is comprised of

40. Shmigel'skii and Iasinovskii, *Osnovy sovetskogo morskogo prava* (2d ed.; 1963), p. 42.
41. A. K. Zhudro (ed.), *Morskoe pravo* (Moscow: izd-vo Transport, 1964), p. 100.
42. *New York Times,* March 29, 1967, p. 1.
43. Barabolia, *Voenno-morskoi spravochnik,* p. 289.
44. *Boston Globe,* August 29, 1965, p. 22. The legislative basis for the claim appears to be Article 4(c) of the 1960 statute on the state boundary of the USSR. The inclusion in the statute of ". . . straits, historically belonging to the USSR" appears to have gone unnoticed at the time; other governments apparently did not protest or seek clarification of that language. The statute did not specifically name any historic straits nor, prior to the Soviet Note of 1965, had the subject been discussed in Soviet legal media.

the general rules regulating Soviet territorial waters supplemented by rules necessitated by the unusual climatic conditions and geographical configuration of the region. The voyages of American icebreakers into these seas since 1964 have confirmed that as a matter of state practice the USSR treats the polar seas as open seas. Although Soviet international lawyers would assimilate the region into the regime of historic internal waters, this has not been accomplished in either international law or Soviet legislation. It would now appear that Soviet jurists may be significantly revising their doctrines of historic waters to bring them into accord with existing legislation.

Chapter 4

THE CLOSED SEA

Expansive claims to dominion or *imperium* over the seas have always been asserted by littoral states. John Selden's celebrated defense of *mare clausum* in the seventeenth century purported to find precedents not only in antiquity but in legend and mythology as well. Grotius' concept of freedom of the seas, however, was more responsive to the tempo of expanding merchant navigation and naval power. The concept of the closed sea was eventually reduced to that of a completely landlocked body of water and received but passing notice from Western jurists in the nineteenth and twentieth centuries.

This was not the case in Russia. Throughout modern history, Russia has been exceptionally vulnerable to sea blockade or attack and, as a neutral, has suffered dislocation of commerce and shipping. All of the seas bordering the Russian empire (and this is equally true of the Soviet Union today) had comparatively narrow entrances which have been and can be commanded easily by hostile foreign powers. At the same time, the states sharing coastal seas with Russia have usually been weaker powers. This combination of geographic configuration and geopolitical circumstance inspired Russian and Soviet publicists to resuscitate and reformulate the closed sea doctrine whenever Russian dominion over certain coastal seas seemed either attainable or advisable. Thus, the doctrine of the closed sea figured in diplomatic correspondence and was accorded special attention in Russian textbooks and treatises on international law.

Tsarist Doctrine and Practice

Although international law developed comparatively late in Russia as a systematic body of scholarship, the principle of the closed sea had been invoked by Russia with regard to the Baltic Sea in the late eighteenth century and had been rejected with respect to the Black Sea.

The political history of the Baltic is that of the rise and demise of the notion that the littoral states could by agreement treat the Baltic as their own closed sea and restrict the activities of nonlittoral powers thereon during wartime. Such an arrangement would imply the creation of some type of alliance or a policy of mutually benevolent neutrality among the littoral states. Although there were early attempts in the seventeenth century, the idea of closing the Baltic reached fruition in the Russian-initiated treaties of armed neutrality of 1780–81, concluded among Russia and Sweden, Denmark, Norway, and Prussia. The parties contracted to maintain the Baltic "perpetually" as a closed sea "in which all nations may navigate in peace and enjoy the advantages of perfect tranquility; in consequence they will take all measures to guarantee that sea and its coasts against all hostilities, piracy and violence."[1]

A similar arrangement was reached among Denmark, Norway, and Russia in 1800.[2] In each instance, however, the major maritime powers (England, France, the Netherlands) refused to accept the permanent neutrality of the Baltic, and England so replied to a complaint of the tsar in 1807 against the bombardment of Copenhagen. Russia subsequently found itself subjected to naval blockade in the Baltic during the Crimean War (1854–56), World War I, the Russian civil war, and World War II.

The consent of Denmark, registered in a Convention and Protocol of 1857, "not to subject any ship, on any pretext, to any detention or hindrance in the passage of the Sound or the Belts" appeared to erase any vestiges of a claim to close the Baltic Sea.[3] Russian publicists treated the Baltic as an open sea. The "attempts of Russia, Sweden, and Denmark to declare it closed in general during wartime have not been successful. . . . The treaties of Armed Neutrality of 1780 and 1800 . . . had only a temporary character."[4]

The closed sea doctrine was alluded to in 1822 by the Russian ambassador to the United States, the Chevalier de Poletica, in a Note to Secretary of State John Quincy Adams justifying the well-known 1821 edict of Tsar Alexander by which Russia claimed exclusive fishing and sealing rights within 100 Italian miles of the coast of eastern

---

1. John Westlake, *International Law* (2d ed.; Cambridge: The University Press, 1910), I, 201; also see *SS&D*, VI (1969/70), 227. The Netherlands accepted this provision in an Act of December 24, 1780. Other governments associated themselves with the principles of armed neutrality but not necessarily with the closed status of the Baltic Sea.
2. James Brown Scott (ed.), *The Armed Neutralities of 1780 and 1800* (New York: Oxford University Press, 1918), pp. 305, 537; *SS&D,* VI (1969/70), 228. Similar conventions signed with Sweden and Prussia that same year did not contain secret articles nor refer to the closed status of the Baltic Sea.
3. Convention for the Redemption of the Sound Dues, *BFSP,* XLVII, 24, 35.
4. N. A. Zakharov, *Kurs obshchago mezhdunarodnogo prava* (Petrograd: Veisbrut, 1917), p. 178; V. A. Ul'ianitskii, *Lektsii po mezhdunarodnomu pravu* (Moscow: Obshchestvo rasprostraneniia poleznykh knig, 1900), p. 138.

Siberia and northwest America. Poletica argued that the edict embodied restraint by asserting only limited rights to those seas, despite the fact that the Bering Sea and the northern Pacific comprehended "all the conditions which are ordinarily attached to closed seas (mers fermees)." The Russian government, Poletica hinted, might judge itself authorized to extend the right of sovereignty over the seas in question.[5]

In the face of vigorous protests by the United States and Great Britain, Russia implicitly abandoned any pretension of extending the closed sea doctrine to these seas. When the Russian–America Company requested its government to exclude American whalers from the Sea of Okhotsk in 1842, the Foreign Ministry replied: "The claim to a *mare clausum,* if we wished to advance such a claim in respect to the northern part of the Pacific Ocean, could not be theoretically justified."[6]

The status of the Black Sea has a history and literature of its own that is beyond the scope of the present study. For centuries the Ottoman Empire held the lands surrounding the Bosporus and the Black Sea. Until 1774, when Russia gained a foothold on the Black Sea coast, that body of water was considered to be an Ottoman lake. Navigation through the Bosporus was prohibited to foreign merchant ships and warships alike. Thereafter, the regime of the sea and the straits was a shifting compromise of Russian efforts to acquire a permanent warm-water access to world commercial routes and of primarily Anglo–French opposition to Russian imperial ambitions in the near east. For the most part, Russia was unsuccessful in limiting the access of foreign warships to the sea during wartime or in building up its own naval strength to a significant degree in the Black Sea theater.[7] Al-

5. See Walter Lowrie and Walter S. Franklin (ed.), *American State Papers: Foreign Relations* (Washington D.C.: Giles & Seaton, 1834), IV, p. 861; *SS&D,* VI (1969/70), 233.

6. P. A. Tikhmenev, *Istoricheskoe obozr'nie obrazovaniia Rossisko-amerikanskoi kompanii i d'istvii eia do nastoiashchago vremeni* (St. Petersburg: E. Veimar, 1861–63), II, pp. 130–39.

7. See, in general, S. Goriainov', *Bosfor' i Dardanelly* (St. Petersburg: Tipo. Skorokhodov, 1907); Coleman Phillipson and Noel Buxton, *The Question of the Bosporus and Dardanelles* (London: Stevens & Haynes, 1917); James T. Shotwell and Francis Déak, *Turkey at the Straits* (New York: Macmillan Co., 1940). The legal history of the straits is shrouded to this day in lost texts, secret protocols, linguistic divergencies, factual discrepancies, and deliberate falsifications of evidence. Goriainov', in particular, is suspected of taking great liberties with Russian archives in writing what many scholars regard as a brief for the Russian Ministry of Foreign Affairs. A recent attempt, severely critical of Russian scholarship, to reconstruct the pattern of Russian-Ottoman treaty relations is J. C. Hurewitz, "Russia and the Turkish Straits: A Reevaluation of the Origins of the Problem," *World Politics,* XIV (1962), 605–32. Also see *SS&D,* VI (1969/70), 234.

though Russian diplomacy labored to remove these burdens, Russian textbooks of international law were content to describe the Black Sea as an open sea whose straits were subject to a special regime. There was no effort to manipulate geographic criteria in order to reach a different result.[8]

The definition of the closed sea found in Russian textbooks and treatises was a narrow one. The closed sea was a body of water completely landlocked by the territory of a single state, not being joined with the open sea but constituting a sea and not a lake, or a body of water joined to the open sea by a strait whose narrowest point does not exceed six miles in width.[9] The Aral Sea clearly met the first criterion; most Russian jurists believed the Sea of Azov also qualified. The Caspian Sea was assimilated to the status of closed sea because under the Treaties of Gulistan (1813) and Turkmenchai (1828), Persia had ceded exclusive rights of dominion over the Caspian to Russia.[10]

The status of the seas bordering Russia's northern coasts posed a much more difficult problem. Considerable sentiment existed to eliminate any military or economic threat to Russian interests by declaring the White Sea and the Kara Sea closed to foreign vessels. Such a recommendation received official support from the special interdepartmental commission chaired by Vice Admiral Hildebrandt in 1906–07, but the proposal was never acted upon. However, Russia accentuated the territorial character of the Kara Sea at this time by granting a request of the Norwegian government to send a scientific and industrial mission through the Kara Strait.[11]

F. F. Martens and V. A. Ul'ianitskii were among those Russian international lawyers who derided characterizations of the Kara Sea as closed. Martens wrote that

one glance at a map shows that the Kara Sea is immediately adjacent to the Arctic Ocean and is completely open to the ingress of vessels. If one then says that the Kara Sea is closed by ice for nine months of the year, the ice

8. Ul'ianitskii, *Lektsii po mezhdunarodnomu pravu*, p. 138.

9. V. A. Ul'ianitskii, *Mezhdunarodnoe pravo* (Tomsk: Tipo. Sibir. t-va. pechatnogo dela, 1911), p. 84. In discussing bodies of water similarly situated, Westlake also regarded the width of the strait as dispositive so long as there was only one littoral state; Westlake, *International Law*, I, p. 197.

10. Ul'ianitskii, *Mezhdunarodnoe pravo*, p. 84; Martens, *Sovremennoe mezhdunarodnoe pravo*, I, pp. 372–73; Zakharov, *Kurs obshchago mezhdunarodnogo prava*, p. 156.

11. René Waultrin, "La Question de la Souveraineté des Terres Arctiques," *Revue Générale de Droit International Public*, xv (1908), 78–125, 185–209, 401–23. Westlake, emphasizing the character of the mission, believed the Norwegian request was proper, since "no kind of action in such waters by a foreign government or its agents is allowable without permission." Westlake, *International Law*, I, p. 204.

constituting a prolongation of Russian territory, it must be objected that ice has yet to be equated with dry land and, furthermore, freedom of navigation in the Kara Sea may interest other states when the sea is free of ice. As far as the Edict of Tsar Mikhail Fedorovich promulgated in 1620 on fishing in the Kara Sea is concerned, it not having been objected to by Western powers, one forgets that neither Russia nor the Western powers were interested in the Kara Sea even had they known about the existence of the Moscow edict.[12]

Martens did point out, though, that the question of who owned the Kara Sea had not preoccupied European states and that instructions relating to the Kara Sea promulgated by the Russian government in 1833 and 1869 had not been protested by other powers. Only on the basis of these instructions, Martens declared, "can one assert that the Kara Sea up to now actually belongs to Russia, but from the legal point of view it is an open and free sea."[13] Although Martens did not further describe the instructions, a search of the *Collected Laws of the Russian Empire* suggests that Martens was referring to normative acts of March 16, 1833, and March 10, 1869, pursuant to which certain Russian citizens were granted exclusive privileges to fish, hunt, construct factories, and develop a trade route in the Kara Sea, the Siberian Sea, the mouth of the Enisei River, and the coasts of Novaia Zemlia and Siberia for 25 and 20 years respectively.[14]

Neither instruction described the Kara Sea or other coastal Arctic seas as Russian territory. In the nineteenth century it might have been inferred that the tsar believed he owned what he granted, and Martens seems to suggest that an explicit affirmation to that effect would lay the groundwork for a legal claim to full sovereignty over the Kara Sea. In the absence of such an affirmation the better view would be that the Russian government merely granted an exclusive license to the persons concerned, which license would protect against competition from other Russian nationals. Foreign nationals would retain the right to pursue whatever interests they had beyond the limits of Russian territorial waters in the Kara Sea. Perhaps this also explains why no Soviet jurist has mentioned either the 1833 or 1869 decrees in adducing arguments to support the modern closed sea doctrine.

12. Martens, *Sovremennoe mezhdunarodnoe pravo,* I, p. 372; Ul'ianitskii, *Lektsii po mezhdunarodnomu pravu,* p. 138. However, ice was equated with dry land in the 1911 decree regulating fishing on the far eastern coast. The decree provided that the extent of territorial waters was to be measured from the low water mark or "from the edge of ice along the coast." *Polnoe sobranie,* XXXI (3d ser.), 449–52.

13. Martens, *Sovremennoe mezhdunarodnoe pravo,* I, p. 372.

14. *Polnoe sobranie,* VIII (2d ser.), 151–52; XLIV (2d ser.), 219–20; *SS&D,* VI (1969/70), 252.

Soviet Doctrine and Practice

Soviet jurists exhibited no propensity to discuss or reformulate the principle of the closed sea until 1948. Pashukanis' treatise on international law, for example, did not even mention the doctrine.[15] The 1947 international law textbook introduced the closed sea concept in its narrowest possible form by defining it as a landlocked body of water. The Caspian and Aral Seas were offered as examples, and they were described as large lakes whose regime was that of national or frontier waters.[16] (See Map 3.)

The 1947 textbook was the last major Soviet international legal publication of the pre-Cold War era. Although a distinctively Soviet interpretation of public international law, it was not dominated by the vitriolic, xenophobic characterizations of legal principles and state practice that distinguished its successor volume of 1951. Indeed, it is surprising that the 1947 volume was published at all, given the direction of Soviet foreign and domestic policy at that time.

The closed sea doctrine appeared in Soviet diplomatic correspondence in connection with the question of revising the regime of the Black Sea Straits: the Montreux Convention of 1936. This was not the first time that the Soviet Union had asserted a closed status for the Black Sea. During the Lausanne Conference of 1922–23, the Soviet delegation objected to Lord Curzon's argument that all straits, according to international law, between seas are open to all states and to all vessels of whatever type:

. . . the parallel drawn by Lord Curzon between the Bosporus and Dardanelles regime and that of other Straits is not justified since the former are not, properly speaking, a passage between two open seas, but the entry and outlet of a sea which many authors . . . regard as *mare clausum*.[17]

At the abortive Rome Conference on Naval Disarmament in February 1924, the Soviet representative demanded that both the Black

15. E. B. Pashukanis, *Ocherki po mezhdunarodnomu pravu* (Moscow: izd-vo Sovetskoe zakonodatel'stvo, 1935).

16. V. N. Durdenevskii and S. B. Krylov (eds.), *Mezhdunarodnoe pravo* (Moscow: Iurizdat, 1947), pp. 237–38.

17. *Lausanne Conference on Near Eastern Affairs, 1922–23, Record of Proceedings* (London: HMSO, 1923), p. 160; *SS&D,* VI (1969/70), 236. Article 21 of the Russian draft of the straits convention provided that the parties would agree to sign a special international act recognizing the Black Sea as *mare clausum* of the littoral powers within three months after the Lausanne convention was adopted. *Ibid.,* p. 253. The final text of the convention placed the straits under international control, and warships of nonlittoral states were admitted only under certain circumstances. The Soviet government refused to ratify the convention. *BFSP,* CXVII, 592.

and Baltic Seas be made inaccessible to warships of nonlittoral states.[18]

In 1945 at the Yalta Conference the United States and Great Britain agreed to entertain Soviet proposals for revision of the straits regime and to take up the straits question at the next meeting of the three foreign ministers. Thereafter, Soviet policy was notably more hostile toward Turkey, and it was clear that pressure was being applied to reach a bilateral Soviet–Turkish accord in which the United States and Britain would presumably have to acquiesce. In a Note of August 7, 1946, the Soviet government outlined the principles on which a new straits regime should be established: (1) merchant vessels of all states should have a right of free passage; (2) warships of Black Sea powers should also enjoy free passage at all times; (3) warships of nonlittoral powers should be permitted passage only in special circumstances; (4) establishment of the straits regime should be solely within the competence of the Black Sea powers; (5) Turkey and the Soviet Union should organize joint means of defense to prevent use of the straits by other states whose aims are hostile to the Black Sea powers.[19]

The assumption underlying the fourth principle, as was clarified in a Note to Turkey of September 24, 1946, was the closed sea doctrine:

. . . the Soviet Government desires before all to invite the attention of the Turkish Government to the special situation of the Black Sea as a closed sea. Such a situation means that the Straits of the Black Sea represent a seaway leading only to the shores of a limited number of powers, namely, to the shores of several Black Sea powers. Therefore, it is entirely natural that the Soviet Union and the other Black Sea powers are the most interested in the regulation of the regime of the Straits of the Black Sea and accordingly their situation in this matter cannot be compared with that of other powers. . . . With regard to the Straits of the Black Sea leading into the Black Sea, which is a closed sea, it seems proper in this case to establish such a regime of the Straits which above all would meet the special situation and the security of Turkey, the U.S.S.R., and the other Black Sea powers.[20]

It was further suggested that Turkey had accepted the principle of exclusive jurisdiction of the littoral states over the Black Sea and the straits regime as early as 1774 in treaties with Tsarist Russia and again in its early treaties with the Bolshevik regime.

This latter observation foreshadowed a rewriting of Russian and

18. *Dokumenty*, VII, 124; *SS&D*, VI (1969/70), 232. Also see Kazimierz Grzybowski, "The Soviet Doctrine of Mare Clausum and Politics in Black and Baltic Seas," *Journal of Central European Affairs*, XIV (1955), 344.

19. Harry N. Howard, *The Problem of the Turkish Straits* (Washington D.C.: GPO, 1947), pp. 47–49; *SS&D*, VI (1969/70), 238.

20. Howard, *Problem of the Turkish Straits*, pp. 56–57; *SS&D*, VI (1969/70), 241.

Soviet accounts of the legal status of the Black Sea. Most Russian and Soviet legal scholars had been quite straightforward in their histories of the straits and their interpretations of the international agreements governing them at various times: Turkey held complete sovereignty over the straits until 1833. Pursuant to an agreement of that year, Russian warships were permitted access until 1840, when Turkey regained control under the London Protocol; thereafter, the straits were an object of concern for the international community at large.[21]

The task of revising history fell to B. A. Dranov, who revived earlier tendentious interpretations of the straits question in 1948. The Treaty of Kuchuk Kainardzhii (1774) was said to have transformed the Black Sea from an "internal lake" of the Ottoman Empire into a Russo–Turkish internal lake. Even though that treaty granted certain privileges only to Russian merchant ships, Dranov argued that these automatically extended to Russian warships without a special treaty provision by virtue of Russia's new status as a Black Sea power. He concluded:

Beginning with the Treaty of Kuchuk–Kainardzhii of 1774, all treaties . . . have recognized the special position of littoral states in the Black Sea and to a greater or lesser degree have restricted the access of warships of non-Black Sea powers to the Black Sea. . . . Thus, the basic source of international law—international treaties and agreements—recognizes the Black Sea as a closed sea.[22]

The closed character of the Black Sea, in Dranov's view, also was determined by the legal nature of the straits. Dranov distinguished among three categories of straits: (1) those leading into internal seas whose shores belong to one state—for example, the Kerchensk Strait leading into the Sea of Azov; (2) those leading into a closed sea—for example, the Bosporus and Dardanelles leading into the closed Black Sea; (3) those joining high seas and oceans—for example, Gibralter. The regime of the second category must be regulated by those states most interested in freedom of commercial navigation and security of the sea—the coastal states.[23]

21. Durdenevskii and Krylov, *Mezhdunarodnoe pravo,* pp. 265–68.
22. B. A. Dranov, *Chernomorskie prolivy: mezhdunarodno-pravovoi rezhim* (Moscow: Iurizdat, 1948), pp. 52–53, 227. A more strident defense of the views expressed in the Soviet Notes to Turkey of 1946 is to be found in K. V. Bazilevich, *O chernomorskikh prolivakh* (Moscow: izd-vo Pravda, 1946).
23. Dranov was not unaware of the problems this classification scheme could create if applied worldwide:

The proposed classification . . . does not exhaust the complex and multifarious international legal relations connected with the problem of the legal nature of the straits.

Dranov, *Chernomorskie prolivy,* p. 228.

The closed sea doctrine was extended to the Baltic Sea by Soviet jurists in a rather novel way. Resurrecting the Soviet proposal to the Rome Disarmament Conference of 1924, a Soviet doctoral candidate, S. V. Molodtsov, suggested that there were ample legal and historical grounds for the littoral states to declare the Baltic closed to warships of nonlittoral states. In particular, German operations in the Baltic during World War II showed the regime of the sea and straits to be completely satisfactory in protecting vital Soviet interests. The doctoral dissertation was accepted, and an interesting insight into the affair was provided by a remark of Professor Korovin, who was present during the defense of the dissertation. One of the great merits of the thesis, he said, was that the author evidenced "creative daring," since for the preceding quarter century there had been no official documentation which could serve as the basis for research. Nevertheless, the author of the dissertation

. . . not only formulated the correct Soviet conception on this question . . . but also reinforced its fundamental legal and historical documentation, which may serve as a solid confirmation of our viewpoint on this question.[24]

The theses of both Dranov and Molodtsov were incorporated into the 1951 international law textbook, which referred to the Caspian, Black, and Baltic Seas as closed, despite "minor" differences in their regimes. In the case of the latter two seas, only the littoral states were said to enjoy freedom of navigation and the right to engage in fishing and other maritime trades. Commercial navigation by vessels of non-littoral states "may be permitted" in the interests of international trade.[25]

Since the early 1950's, the Soviet Union has urged non-Communist Baltic states to join in an agreement to make the Baltic a "sea of peace" by excluding the warships of nonlittoral powers. In this way the doctrine of the closed sea has served Soviet foreign policy by suggesting a legal basis for a regional administration of the Baltic. The idea of furthering Baltic unity has also been expressed in Soviet proposals to denuclearize the sea, to cooperate in fishing and oceanographic research, to explore jointly the water resources of northern Europe, and to coordinate methods of rescue at sea. The Soviet gov-

24. "Mezhdunarodno-pravovoi rezhim baltiiskikh prolivov (Dissertatsiia S. V. Molodtsova)," *SGIP*, no. 5 (1950), 62–63.

25. E. A. Korovin (ed.), *Mezhdunarodnoe pravo* (Moscow: Gosiurizdat, 1951), p. 309. Also see A. D. Keilin, *Sovetskoe morskoe pravo* (Moscow: izd-vo Vodnyi transport, 1954), p. 61.

ernment regularly protests against naval training exercises conducted by NATO forces in the Baltic.[26]

Molodtsov's interpretation of the legal history of the Baltic recently was defended by I. V. Ivanov, another Soviet doctoral candidate. Molodtsov had argued that the 1857 Treaty of Copenhagen, under which Denmark agreed to abolish all charges on merchant vessels passing through the sound and belts, was wholly compatible with the principles set forth in the treaties of Armed Neutrality of 1780–81 and 1800; that is, the Baltic states had retained the right to establish the general regime for the Baltic straits and to close the sea to warships of nonlittoral states.

Molodtsov's thesis was disputed by H. Reinkemeyer, a West German jurist. He pointed out that the Treaty of Copenhagen did not contain provisions affecting the passage of warships through the straits, that the right to close the straits to warships of nonlittoral states provided for in prior treaties had therefore been superseded, and that since 1857 the Baltic straits have remained open in peacetime to all vessels of all nations.[27]

Ivanov replied that the 1857 treaty in no way affected the regime of warships in the Baltic, which in any event had never been subjected to tolls by Denmark. The treaty was aimed at eliminating the last obstacle to the freedom of merchant shipping in the Baltic, a freedom expressly affirmed in prior treaties; earlier restrictions on warships remained in effect. Alternatively, Ivanov argued that since there exists no objective necessity for warships of nonlittoral states to pass through the straits, such passage is a violation of the sovereignty of the littoral states. The principle of freedom of navigation cannot apply, he contended, to warships of nonlittoral states in a regional sea.[28]

The closed sea doctrine has experienced a variety of refinements. Initially, these were made in the geographic determinants of the closed sea. The authors of the 1956 naval international law manual, for example, differentiated among three types of closed seas (in contrast to Dranov, who stressed the legal nature of the straits leading into the sea as being dispositive): (1) a sea completely enclosed by the territory of two or several states which has no outlet to another sea—the Caspian; (2) a sea enclosed by the territory of a limited (but unspecified) number of states that is joined with other seas by one or several narrow

26. Klaus Törnudd, *Soviet Attitudes Towards Non-Military Regional Cooperation* (Helsinki: Centraltryckeriet, 1961), p. 81.
27. H. A. Reinkemeyer, *Die sowjetische Zwölfmeilenzone in der Ostsee und die Freiheit des Meeres* (Köln: Heymann, 1955), p. 122.
28. I. V. Ivanov, "Mezhdunarodnye soglasheniia v oblasti regulirovaniia pravovogo rezhima regional'nogo moria," *Pravovedenie*, no. 1 (1966), 112–13.

straits, whose regime is governed by an international convention—the Black and Baltic Seas; (3) a sea enclosed by the territory of two or several states whose regime is *not* regulated by an international convention—the Sea of Japan and the Okhotsk Sea. Adding the stipulation that "basic maritime routes of international significance" should not pass through the sea, the authors concluded:

States not contiguous to these seas can not and do not have any legal grounds for claiming [the right to] participate in deciding questions concerning the regime of navigation in closed seas or in the straits leading to such seas.[29]

Nonetheless, merchant vessels of nonlittoral states would have the same rights, including access to a closed sea, as those of littoral states. Except in time of war, the regime for merchant vessels in the closed sea would be identical to that of the high seas, apart from whatever straits regulation may be necessary. The warships of littoral states would enjoy a right of free and unrestricted navigation in closed seas beyond the territorial waters of other littoral states, but the warships of nonlittoral powers would have no right of access to closed seas.

At the 1958 Geneva Conference on the Law of the Sea, the closed sea principle was introduced in the form of an amendment sponsored by the Ukrainian SSR and Rumania to Article 26 (definition of the high seas) of the draft articles on the regime of the high seas. The proposed amendment would have added the following sentence to Article 26(1) of the draft: "For certain seas a special regime of navigation may be established for historical reasons or by virtue of international agreements."[30] It was prompted by the last sentence of the International Law Commission's commentary on Article 26 which stated: "These rules [defining the high seas] may, however, be modified for historical reasons or by international arrangement." The sentence apparently originated in a remark by S. B. Krylov, then the Soviet representative on the International Law Commission, concerning "certain waters such as land-locked seas" which had "special characteristics." Krylov added that he was not "proposing to amend [the] Article [26], but merely to insert in the commentary a reference to the fact that certain waters had special characteristics."[31]

29. A. S. Bakhov (ed.), *Voenno-morskoi mezhdunarodno-pravovoi spravochnik* (Moscow: Voengiz, 1956), pp. 53–54.
30. Doc. A/CONF.13/C.2/L.26. United Nations Conference on the Law of the Sea, Geneva, 1958, *Official Records* (London: United Nations, 1958), IV, 123; *SS&D,* VI (1969/70), 226.
31. *Yearbook of the International Law Commission 1956* (New York: United Nations, 1956), I, paras. 7 and 14.

The Ukrainian and Rumanian representatives made it clear that their amendment comprehended at least the Black Sea and the waters surrounding archipelagoes. The United States viewed the two-power proposal—quite correctly—as an attempt to win recognition in international law for the doctrine of the closed sea. Rather than risk a formal recording of what clearly would have been a lopsided vote against the closed sea amendment, the Rumanian and Ukrainian delegates withdrew their amendment just before it was to be voted upon.[32]

Several Soviet jurists have called attention to the inconsistent and sometimes incorrect applications of the closed sea doctrine by their colleagues. Vereshchetin has pointed out that in Western literature the expression "closed sea" has frequently been used as the antonym of "high seas"—that is, it has been applied to all expanses of sea to which the regime of the high seas does not extend.[33] According to some Western and prerevolutionary Russian jurists, the closed sea was permanently closed to vessels of nonlittoral states at all times. Molodtsov urged that a more precise legal concept would deprive Western jurists and politicians of the opportunity to juggle the word "closed" and to "create the legend of a renaissance in contemporary conditions of the ancient doctrine of closed seas."[34]

Either interpretation would go far beyond the closed sea doctrine posited by Soviet jurists, who have been anxious to graft on rather than substitute the category of closed sea for the traditional categories of jurisdiction over the seas and who also do not wish to undermine the principle of freedom of navigation for merchant shipping.

In order to minimize semantic confusion deriving from the various historical interpretations and applications of the closed sea principle, S. A. Malinin suggested that the term "regional sea" replace "closed sea" in Soviet international legal writing. Malinin proposed to define regional seas as expanses of water enclosed by the territory of two or several states, the seas being joined to the high seas by a strait or canal and also having importance as a maritime route only for the littoral states. In Malinin's view, therefore, a body of water classified as a closed or regional sea must fulfill four independent legal requirements: (1) a particular geographic configuration of the coastline; (2) a limited number of states whose territory completely encloses the body of water; (3) restricted possibilities of access or comparatively

---

32. *1958 Official Records,* IV, 36–39, 52.

33. V. S. Vereshchetin, *Svoboda sudokhodstva v otkrytom more* (Moscow: izd-vo IMO, 1958), p. 11.

34. S. V. Molodtsov, *Mezhdunarodno-pravovoi rezhim otkrytogo moria i kontinental'nogo shel'fa* (Moscow: izd-vo AN SSSR, 1960), p. 49.

narrow entrances to the sea; (4) absence of international (as opposed to regional) maritime routes.[35]

Malinin's classification scheme presumably would relegate the totally landlocked sea, such as the Caspian or Aral Seas, to a separate category; moreover, Malinin attached no theoretical significance to the presence or absence of existing international conventions appertaining to the Black and Baltic Straits. In this he departed from other Soviet jurists. He stressed that the regime of a regional sea must take into account the vital interests, primarily the security, of the littoral states, and that the specific norms of the regime would depend upon the content of an agreement to be concluded by the coastal powers. Military maneuvers and navigation by warships of nonlittoral powers, however, could be proscribed, but freedom of merchant navigation for all states would have to be safeguarded.[36]

Malinin's conceptual and terminological contribution has been adopted by Siling,[37] Ivanov,[38] and East European international lawyers.[39] Siling included the Black, Baltic, and Okhotsk Seas, and the Sea of Japan, among regional seas.[40] Shmigel'skii noted that the regime of the latter three seas "is subject to establishment."[41]

The 1966 naval international law manual and various editions of Soviet international law textbooks have continued to adhere to the expression "closed sea." The 1966 manual, while accepting the differentiation of three types of closed sea found in the 1956 edition, did place considerably greater emphasis upon historical and legal precedents relating to the regime of the closed sea. This would appear to be a modification of no little significance. The predominantly geographic orientation of previous formulations of the closed sea doctrine have been reduced to a descriptive classification scheme. Soviet jurists have probably recognized that geography alone cannot predetermine a given legal regime for a sea.

The authors of the 1966 manual, therefore, maintained that in diplomatic and treaty practice closed seas are those for which, because

35. S. A. Malinin, "K voprosu o pravovoi klassifikatsii vodnykh prostranstv," *Morskoe pravo i praktika,* XLVI (1960), 13–19.

36. *Ibid.*

37. A. N. Siling, *Morskoe pravo* (Moscow: izd-vo Transport, 1964), p. 63.

38. I. V. Ivanov, "Mezhdunarodnye soglasheniia," p. 111.

39. See, for example, S. Stefanova, *Mezhdunarodnopraven rezhim na otkritoto more* (Sofia: Nauka i izkustvo, 1965), p. 3.

40. Siling also applied the regional sea concept to Lake Geneva in Switzerland and to the Great Lakes in North America—all of which are fresh water lakes. Siling, *Morskoe pravo,* p. 63.

41. G. L. Shmigel'skii and V. A. Iasinovskii, *Osnovy sovetskogo morskogo prava* (2d ed.; Moscow: izd-vo Morskoi transport, 1963), p. 55.

of historical reasons or by virtue of international agreements, a special regime has been established closing the sea or restricting the regime of navigation of warships and military aircraft of nonlittoral powers. Areas of water beyond the territorial waters of a coastal state in a closed sea would be available for the common enjoyment of all littoral states on equal basis, giving due consideration to the interests of each state. One littoral state should not disregard the economic and security interests of another littoral power. The authors concurred in the view that closed seas should be open in peacetime to the merchant shipping of all countries. But the reference to excluding military aircraft of nonlittoral states had not been made in earlier works.[42]

Included in the 1966 manual is a reference to a Note of the RSFSR to Great Britain "demanding" the removal from the Black and Baltic Seas of "warships of all those nations which do not have possessions on their shores." The Note had never been cited in previous Soviet writings on the closed sea, and for good reason. It was sent in 1920 to protest an order given by the British government authorizing British vessels to attack Russian submarines without warning in the Black and Baltic Seas. The full text of the paragraph partially quoted in the Soviet manual read:

The Soviet Government would consider withdrawal from these waters of warships of all those nations which have no possessions on their shores as the best means of preventing any armed skirmishes both in the Black and in the Baltic Seas.[43]

The Note did not "demand," did not refer to the closed sea doctrine, nor make any claim relating to exclusive jurisdiction of the littoral states over these waters, nor assert the illegality of the British presence in that area.

Soviet jurists have been unable to produce much in the way of historical or legal precedent with regard to the closed status of the Sea of Japan or the Okhotsk Sea. At the San Francisco Conference convened in September 1951 to work out a peace treaty with Japan, the Soviet Union submitted a proposal on regulating the regime of the Sea of Japan.[44] Since that time, the USSR has repeatedly expressed its will-

---

42. P. D. Barabolia, *et. al., Voenno-morskoi mezhdunarodno-pravovoi spravochnik* (Moscow: Voenizdat, 1966), p. 129.

43. *Dokumenty,* III, 285–87; *SS&D,* VI (1969/70), 229.

44. *Pravda,* September 7, 1951, p. 1. In laying claim to the Kurile Islands in 1945, Stalin remarked that never again would they serve as a means of blocking ingress and egress to Soviet ports on the Pacific. See *Pravda,* September 3, 1945, p. 1. Japan had demonstrated the strategic significance of the straits between the Kuriles by blocking lend-lease shipments to Soviet ports in Siberia with relative ease.

ingness to reach agreement with other littoral states to exclude warships and military aircraft of nonlittoral states from both the Okhotsk Sea and the Sea of Japan. These proposals, as the 1966 manual conceded, "have not been accepted."[45] The closed status of either sea lacks historical and legal precedent.

The Closed Sea Doctrine and Soviet Foreign Policy

The closed sea doctrine is not merely a manipulation of international legal theory in the interest of Soviet foreign and strategic policy; it represents an attempt to *create* a principle of international law for transparently political and military purposes, irrespective of the implications that principle may have for the public order of the oceans.

The military component of the doctrine has been alluded to above. During World War I, the Baltic and Black Sea Straits were closed to all shipping because minefields, the German fleet, and Turkish artillery denied passage to and from the two seas. The Allied victory opened both seas and created a foreboding naval presence to the new Soviet government. Indeed, it was command of the seas which made possible the much-exaggerated and maligned Allied intervention in regions of Siberia, the Murmansk coast, and the Black Sea in 1917–20.[46] The Soviet campaign against Poland in 1920–21 was influenced in part by the ability of French vessels to supply essential munitions to Polish armies.

In World War II, the situation was much the same. Germany controlled the Baltic, and the Allies convoyed supplies by sea to the Soviet Union via Murmansk at an appallingly high cost of human life and shipping. Although Turkey remained officially neutral throughout much of the war, there is incontestable evidence that the Turkish government was involved in violations of the 1936 Montreux Convention by permitting the clandestine passage of German vessels through the straits.[47] With the Allied victory and the later development of the Cold War, the USSR was confronted by superior American naval power off its coasts.

It has been fashionable to portray the closed sea doctrine during

45. Barabolia, *Voenno-morskoi spravochnik*, p. 133.
46. Protests against activities of foreign navies off Soviet coasts figured prominently in Soviet diplomatic correspondence of this period. See, for example, *Dokumenty*, I, items 46, 49, 135, 221, 222; II, 124; III, 224; IV, 173, 176; V, 32, 155; VI, 70, 96, 290; VII, 28, 167, and others.
47. See I. Vasil'ev, *O turetskom "neitralitete" vo vremia vtoroi mirovoi voiny* (Moscow: Gospolitizdat, 1951).

the Cold War era as a potential legal rationalization for aggressive Soviet designs toward a regional domination of its immediate non-Communist neighbors. A more accurate characterization must stress the doctrine's origins as a defensive response grounded in the profound naval weakness of the Soviet Union. The doctrine purported to secure the Baltic and Black Sea flanks from Western military influence by excluding, in cooperation with other littoral states, the warships of nonlittoral powers; it would establish a line over which a nonlittoral power could not send its warships without subjecting itself to the charge that it had committed a violation of international law. The stipulation of regional regulation of the regime of a closed sea is an important qualification, for the Soviet Union has been careful not to assume the transparently unlawful right to determine or police such a regime unilaterally.

Although the closed sea principle has exceedingly significant military aspects, the doctrine did not originate as a Soviet legal theory applied in practice but rather as a doctrinal elaboration and canonization of a position first mentioned in the Soviet Note to Turkey of September 24, 1946. Soviet jurists developed the closed sea doctrine in response to Soviet foreign policy—prepared a *post hoc* rationalization for a legal position of dubious validity. One may presume (though this cannot be proved) that high government and party authorities instructed that this rationalization be developed. Dranov's exposition of the categories of closed sea was heavily indebted to the language of the 1946 Note.

Postwar Soviet theories of the closed sea, it may be observed, have no precedent in either Russian or prewar Soviet international law. Soviet foreign policy, supported by a legal rationale, is suggestive of tsarist policy of the late eighteenth and early nineteenth centuries, when Russia also was a weak naval power. In an almost whimsical way, the Soviet Union seems to have attempted to revive and extend the concept of the League of Armed Neutrality to at least 5 of the 14 seas washing its coasts.

The closed or regional sea doctrine has found little favor in international law. The 1958 Geneva Conference on the Law of the Sea flatly refused to discuss the subject, although in its commentary to Article 26 of the Draft Convention on the High Seas, the International Law Commission recognized that some seas required a special regime. States bordering seas considered by the USSR to be subject to closure have, so far as the public record reveals, ignored Soviet overtures to reach a mutually acceptable arrangement. It is tempting to assume this will continue to be the case unless the Soviet Union achieves military and political preponderance in the far east, the Baltic, and the near east regions.

There are inconclusive indications, however, that the closed sea doctrine may have outlived its usefulness. Since the closed sea principle was formulated some 20-odd years ago, the Soviet Union has become a maritime power of the first rank. The coastal or regional maritime interests of the Soviet Union are rapidly being transformed into global interests. Soviet policy-makers will soon have to decide whether the closed sea principle does not represent a greater threat than advantage to their marine policy. Although Soviet jurists have generally refrained from specifying bodies of water other than those immediately adjacent to Soviet territory to which the closed sea principle might be applied, and also have refrained from passing judgment on the claims asserted by other states to closed seas, events in 1967 involving the Gulf of Aqaba (which Arab jurists have claimed to be a closed body of water) testified to the explosive and disruptive potential of the theory. In a world of constantly increasing national claims to exclusive jurisdiction over adjacent sea expanses, the Soviet Union may find its own high seas fishing and merchant fleets, and its naval vessels, excluded from areas historically part of the high seas.[48]

In this regard it is noteworthy that the Soviet government has been reluctant to espouse the closed sea principle in state practice since the 1946 Note to Turkey. Soviet jurists cite no other examples. Moreover, they have, by formulating the regional sea principle, moved away from the geographic particularism of the early closed sea doctrine, which invited application to other bodies of water by other states. The regional sea theory stresses a regional, that is, a multinational instead of a unilateral approach based on subjective criteria susceptible to easy manipulation. By unilaterally characterizing the "objective" conditions leading to the formation of a regional regime, the Soviet Union may be in a position not to recognize regional arrangements inimical to Soviet interests.

It is highly significant in this connection that the author of a recent work on maritime law referred to closed seas (Black Sea, Baltic Sea, Sea of Japan) solely in a geographical sense and not as a legal classification of seas. While he indicated that the issue with regard to the regime of the Baltic Sea is still "unresolved," the casual and low-key treatment of the closed sea question was in marked contrast to

48. The deployment of American and Soviet fleets in the Mediterranean Sea prompted Yugoslavia to propose to other littoral states that a conference be convened to agree upon the exclusion of naval vessels of nonlittoral countries from that sea. *Der Spiegel,* no. 8 (1968), p. 126.

earlier Soviet legal writings. This would suggest that the closed sea may be accorded much lower priority in Soviet legal doctrine than it has been in the past.[49]

Whatever the fate of the closed sea principle in Soviet international legal doctrine, one must concur with Hartingh's observation: "It is incontestable that this theory of 'closed seas' constitutes a menacing danger to the freedom of the seas."[50] To paraphrase the observations of Lord Curzon on the Russian proposal to close the Black Sea, it is apparent that the Soviet doctrine of the closed sea would place other littoral states at the mercy of the littoral power possessing the strongest land and naval forces—in other words, the Soviet Union. The Soviet doctrine would transform the contiguous closed seas into Soviet lakes, giving the USSR an exceptional and unjustifiable military and political suzerainty over the regions affected.

49. A. A. Volkov, *Morskoe pravo* (Moscow: izd-vo Pishchevaia promyshlennost', 1969), pp. 124, 129.
50. France de Hartingh, *Les Conceptions Soviétiques du Droit de la Mer* (Paris: Pichon, 1960), p. 30.

Chapter 5

THE LEGAL REGIME
OF THE CONTINENTAL SHELF

The continental shelf is a submerged natural geological extension of the adjacent territory projecting seaward in a gentle gradient until it descends rather abruptly to much greater depths. The features of the shelves vary throughout the world, but they have been described as having an average width of about 42 miles and an average depth of approximately 70 meters.[1]

The breadth of the shelf off Soviet coasts varies from sea to sea. Along the Arctic coast of the USSR, the edge of the continental shelf is taken to be the outer boundary between the Barents, White, Kara, Laptev, East Siberian, and Chukotsk Seas, respectively, and the Arctic Ocean.[2] Consequently, the entire seabed of these six seas is considered to be part of the Soviet continental shelf. The shelf of the Baltic Sea recently has been declared to be "continuous" and therefore subject to delimitation among the respective Baltic states.[3] All of these seas are comparatively shallow, and their seabeds are pockmarked by depressions and troughs.[4]

The Black Sea has exceedingly steep shores. Except for the Karakinitsk Bay in the northwestern part of the sea, the 200 meter isobath approaches the coast nearly everywhere. (See Map 5.) The angle of the floor dip is usually 4 to 6 degrees, but often reaches 12 to 14 degrees.[5] A small shelf and great depths are equally characteristic of the far eastern seas. The shelf zone is quite narrow in the Okhotsk Sea and narrower still in the Sea of Japan, where it comprises about 20 percent of the area of the sea. However, the northern and northeastern part of

1. R. Cowen, *Frontiers of the Sea* (Garden City, N.Y.: Random House, 1961), p. 71.
2. L. Zenkevitch, *Biology of the Seas of the U.S.S.R.*, trans. S. Botcharskaya (New York: Interscience Publishers, 1963), p. 28.
3. Declaration on the Continental Shelf of the Baltic Sea, signed at Moscow, October 12, 1968. *Izvestia*, October 24, 1968, p. 3; English text in *ILM*, VII (1968), 1393; *SS&D*, VI (1970), 261.
4. The Chukotsk Sea for the most part is less than 50 meters deep, and the Baltic, except for depressions, does not exceed 100 meters. The Laptev, Barents, and Kara Seas are somewhat deeper. Zenkevitch, *Biology of the Seas*, pp. 77, 261, 270.
5. *Ibid.*, p. 382.

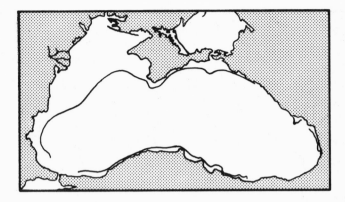

Map 5. Black Sea, Showing the 200 Meter Isobath

the Bering Sea is occupied by vast shallows, the basin being divided almost in half by the 200 meter isobath.[6] (See Map 6.)

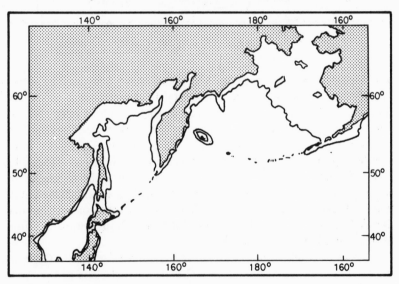

Map 6. Chart of the 200 Meter Line of the Continental Shelf in the Seas of Japan and Okhotsk and the Bering Sea

The Caspian, Aral, and Azov Seas are unusual cases. The Sea of Azov is essentially a broad, very shallow inlet of the Don River. (See Map 7.) Although its greatest depth is only 13½ meters, it is considered to be one of the world's most productive seas in terms of marine

6. *Ibid.*, p. 675.

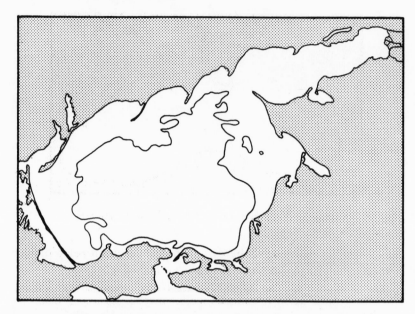

Map 7. Sea of Azov, Showing the Ten Meter Isobath

life. Geologically speaking, the Aral and Caspian Seas may be viewed merely as depressions in the continental land mass—that is, as large salt water lakes. The Aral Sea has an average depth of only 16.2 meters. The Caspian, with an average depth of 180 meters, ranges from an average of 6.2 meters in the northern portion to 325 meters in the southern portion. The greatest depth is about 1000 meters.[7] (See Map 8.) Although the Soviet–Iranian treaties governing the regime of the Caspian do not refer to the continental shelf, a recent Soviet international law manual has observed that "the resources of the continental shelf also belong to each Party [USSR and Iran] within the limits of its respective area of the sea."[8]

Soviet exploitation of the shelf is comparatively recent. This must be partly attributed to the adverse climate characteristic of the Arctic coastal basin and the Bering Sea, where most of the Soviet shelf lies. However, offshore oil production is extensive in the Caspian Sea. The first offshore oil field discovered there in 1949 now produces more than one-half of the crude oil of the Azerbaidzhan SSR, and a second offshore field discovered in 1963 has begun to produce. Offshore Caspian wells have higher production rates than the onshore wells in the

7. *Ibid.*, pp. 465, 539.
8. P. D. Barabolia, *et al.*, *Voenno-morskoi mezhdunarodno-pravovoi spravochnik* (Moscow: Voenizdat, 1966), p. 373.

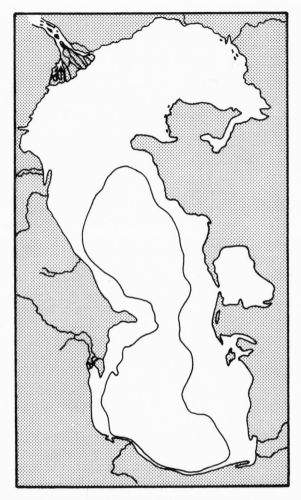

Map 8. Caspian Sea, Showing the 100 Meter Isobath

Azerbaidzhan Republic.[9] Using structurally strengthened platforms in 130 feet of water, slant-drilling techniques now reach formations below a water depth of 200 feet.[10] Soviet achievements in off-shore oil extraction, however, remain considerably behind those of Western oil companies.

Soviet oil drilling has materially contributed to the polluting of the Caspian Sea. Experience in the southern Caspian is said to dem-

---

9. *Oil and Gas Journal,* LXVI, no. 4 (1968), 56.
10. *Ibid.,* no. 24 (1968), 68–69.

onstrate that up to 10 percent of offshore drilling production escapes into the sea, killing the organic life on the bottom, in the mid-water, and on the surface. Seismic exploration techniques also have been credited with destroying large quantities of fish in the Caspian.[11] In October 1968, the USSR Council of Ministers adopted a decree on measures for the prevention of pollution of the Caspian Sea which, *inter alia,* instructed the USSR Ministry of the Oil Refining Industry to prohibit new wells from producing unless effective measures are taken to prevent pollution, to eliminate the collection of deposits that produce chemical reagents in Caspian wells, and to abstain from using explosives for any type of work in the Caspian.[12]

It remains to be seen how effective the October decree will be and whether it will become necessary to curtail oil production on the Caspian shelf. However, the threat of polluting the unique Caspian basin may encourage exploitation of oil reserves believed to underlie the Soviet continental shelf of the Kara and Baltic Seas. A prominent Soviet oil geologist declared in 1967: "The time is not far off when we will go out into our northern seas and extract oil and gas from beneath the ice."[13] Soviet seismic ships have been active in the Baltic for several years. The offshore shelf from above Ventspils in northern Latvia to the Soviet–Polish border has also been described as promising.[14]

Indications of other types of mineral wealth in the Soviet shelf are beginning to appear. Iron and manganese nodules have been discovered in the Baltic Sea; in the Gulf of Riga they are said to contain 24 percent iron and 7 percent manganese. In many portions of the shelf, the quantity of such nodules is believed to exceed 3500 tons per square kilometer.[15] Heavy mineral sands containing titanium ore are present in Baltic coastal waters at depths of 3 to 8 meters. A preliminary survey reveals them to be of commercial grade,[16] and an enterprise has been organized to mine them. Deposits of rutile and zircon have been located in the Baltic and Black Seas and the Sea of Japan; iron ore, in

11. See the reports of S. V. Mikhailov, a prominent marine economist, in *Priroda,* no. 6 (1968), 24–31.

12. English text in *SS&D,* VI (1969/70), 197; summarized in *Izvestia,* October 3, 1968, p. 3.

13. N. P. Budnikov, interviewed in *Komsomol'skaia pravda,* August 16, 1967, p. 1. By 1970, gas had actually been extracted from the Kara seabed. Soviet geologists compared the geological structure of the shelf to that of the Gulf of Mexico and predicted that vast oil fields may exist in the Arctic Ocean out as far as the 85th parallel. See *Soviet News,* February 3, 1970, p. 58.

14. *Sovetskaia latviia,* November 24, 1968, p. 4.

15. *Ibid.*

16. *Ocean Science News,* X, no. 49 (1968), 4.

the Black Sea and Sea of Azov; and tin ore, in the Laptev and East Siberian Seas.[17]

The living organisms of the continental shelf have economic importance to the Soviet Union in the far eastern seas, particularly in the Okhotsk Sea off the Kamchatka coast where crabbing has become a major undertaking in competition with the Japanese. Advanced underwater laboratory craft are being constructed in the Soviet Union to study the rich flora and fisheries on the continental shelf of the far east and elsewhere.[18]

Soviet military utilization of the continental shelf is not as yet a matter of public record. Making due allowance for harsh climatic conditions, it must be assumed that the Soviet shelf could be used for approximately the same purposes as the continental shelf of advanced Western military powers. This would include the installation of underwater detection devices for antisubmarine warfare, the possible emplacement of missiles, and the construction of other monitoring, communication, service, and research facilities. More than 30 Soviet aquanauts are participating in experiments in a Black Sea submerged laboratory to test man's ability to adapt to an underwater existence.[19]

Interest in the continental shelf is a comparatively new development dating from the early 1940's. Russia, however, deserves some credit for originating the legal theory of the continental shelf. In 1916 a Russian declaration communicated to the other Allied powers used the term "plateforme continentale de la Sibérie" in justifying a claim to certain islands north of Siberia. In confirming that claim on November 4, 1924, the Soviet government referred to the "plateforme continentale sibérien."[20] However, the Soviet decree of April 16, 1926, claiming that lands and islands located in the northern Arctic Ocean were Soviet territory did not employ either term or otherwise refer to the continental shelf.[21] Moreover, Soviet jurists have not cited either the Russian or Soviet Notes when writing about the shelf; this may be an indication that the Notes of 1916 and 1924 embraced only lands and islands and were in no way intended to refer to the modern notion of the continental shelf.

17. *Izvestia,* September 6, 1969, p. 5.
18. *Commercial Fisheries Review,* xxix, no. 1 (1967), 31.
19. *Izvestia,* September 29, 1968, p. 6; October 14, 1970, p. 4.
20. The Notes are published in French by V. L. Lakhtin, *Prava na severnye poliarnye prostranstva* (Moscow: Litizdat NKID, 1928); English text in *SS&D,* VI (1970), 255. Also see M. A. Mouton, *The Continental Shelf* (The Hague: Nijhoff, 1952), pp. 240–41.
21. *SZ SSSR* (1926), no. 32, item 203; translated in William E. Butler, *The Law of Soviet Territorial Waters* (New York: Frederick A. Praeger, 1967), p. 97; *SS&D,* III, no. 4 (1967), 9.

International attention was attracted to the continental shelf in 1945, when the United States proclaimed that the "natural resources of the subsoil and sea bed of the continental shelf beneath the high seas but contiguous to the coasts of the United States, as appertaining to the United States, are subject to its jurisdiction and control."[22] The United States action was almost immediately followed by decrees and declarations of other states, especially those of South America, claiming similar adjacent submarine areas but asserting varying degrees of sovereignty over the shelf and superjacent waters.

The Soviet legal community observed these far-reaching claims without undue alarm until 1950, when V. M. Koretskii, a leading jurist whose term as the Soviet judge on the International Court of Justice expired in 1970, published the first article on the continental shelf. Koretskii surveyed postwar claims to the shelf in considerable detail. The claims of Saudi Arabia, Argentina, and Peru, he noted, were examples in which "sea spaces are usurped and are transformed into 'national waters.' " In making its 1945 proclamation, the United States "simply dictated its will to international law, proclaiming *its* 'policy' with respect to the continental shelf . . ."[23] in response to pressures from oil monopolies and to its aspirations for world domination. Thereafter, the subject was ignored in Soviet legal media except for brief reference to the deliberations of the International Law Commission.[24]

The question of the continental shelf was taken up in 1950 by the International Law Commission of the United Nations as part of its consideration of the regime of the high seas. Given the general con-

22. Presidential Proclamation No. 2667, September 28, 1945. *Federal Register*, x (1945), 12303. The proclamation did not define the continental shelf, but the accompanying White House Press Release of the same date said that it was the area seaward to the 600 foot depth line. *DSB*, XIII (1945), 484. The text of the Truman proclamation was used in informal consultations prior to its formal issuance with representatives of several countries, including the Soviet Union. None of the governments consulted expressed opposition to the proposal. See Zdenek J. Slouka, *International Custom and the Continental Shelf* (The Hague: Nijhoff, 1968), p. 43n.

23. V. M. Koretskii, "Novoe v razdele 'otkrytogo moria' (Vopros o kontinental'nogo shel'fa)," *SGIP*, no. 8 (1950), 54–61; also see V. N. Durdenevskii and S. B. Krylov (eds.), *Mezhdunarodnoe pravo* (Moscow: Iurizdat, 1947), p. 259. Commenting on the avalanche of claims following the United States proclamation, Koretskii described the process of norm-formulation: "Americans declare, satellites 'follow,' 'science' recognizes—and a norm has been born."

24. F. Ivanov and S. Volodin, "Piataia sessiia Komissii mezhdunarodnogo prava ООN," *SGIP*, no. 7 (1953), 88–100; S. Serbov, "Shestaia i sedmaia sessii Komissii mezhdunarodnogo prava," *SGIP*, no. 8 (1955), 108–12. Also see A. D. Keilin, *Sovetskoe morskoe pravo* (Moscow: izd-vo Vodnyi transport, 1954), pp. 59–60; A. S. Bakhov (ed.), *Voenno-morskoi mezhdunarodno-pravovoi spravochnik* (Moscow: Voengiz, 1956), pp. 37–39.

sensus that coastal states should exercise exclusive competence over their adjacent seabed, the major issue was whether coastal state control should be limited by reference to a specific depth or should be determined by a flexible criterion of exploitability. The Soviet representative on the commission, F. I. Kozhevnikov, later succeeded by S. B. Krylov, generally took a moderate attitude toward most of the issues —a somewhat surprising posture when one recalls the international political climate of the early 1950's. One reason may have been foreshadowed in Koretskii's 1950 article, where it was observed that offers of states to negotiate continental shelf claims would be "futile in the face of United States power."[25] The Soviet Union may have concluded that the International Law Commission afforded the best opportunity to reach a solution compatible with her interests.

In any event, Kozhevnikov vigorously opposed proposals submitted to the International Law Commission to create an international organ empowered to investigate methods of exploring or exploiting the continental shelf or to ascertain that such exploration or exploitation does not interfere with freedom of the high seas. Such a concept, he said, was fundamentally "a faulty one. Its advocates started from a false premise, namely, that no trust could be placed in the good will of States."[26] He objected as well to any scheme for compulsory arbitration of disputes.

In a more positive vein, Kozhevnikov expressed concern that the structures erected on the shelf and the security zones encircling them not be situated "in narrow straits and commonly used sea lanes essential to international navigation." He further recommended that use of the median line to delimit the shelf between adjoining states would be "unrealistic given the great variations in specific configurations of the shelf."[27] On the whole, Soviet jurists were guardedly optimistic about the success of the International Law Commission draft articles on the continental shelf and, without prejudging the issues, expressed hope for their success.

The 1958 Geneva Conference on the Law of the Sea

At the Geneva conference, the Soviet Union found the draft articles prepared by the International Law Commission "largely satisfactory," for

25. Koretskii, "Novoe v razdele," p. 61.
26. United Nations, *Yearbook of the International Law Commission 1953* (New York: United Nations, 1954), I, p. 116.
27. Ivanov and Volodin, "Piataia sessiia," p. 96.

the International Law Commission text guaranteed the exclusive right of the coastal state to utilize the wealth of the continental shelf while limiting that right to a definite purpose, thus making any claim of the coastal state to superjacent waters or air space juridically untenable.[28]

In taking this carefully developed, moderate position, Soviet jurists were and continue to be highly critical of those states which advocate either a more or less restrictive regime for the shelf. Proposals by some states (Japan and the Federal Republic of Germany) to disregard "the interests of the coastal state" in exploring, exploiting, and protecting the natural resources of the shelf by establishing for all states the right to exploit shelf resources—"considering that any other regime would conflict with the freedom of the high seas"—were unacceptable, since a "struggle by states for appropriation of submerged areas of the high seas" would lead to the strongest capitalist powers acquiring the continental shelf. Moreover, such an application of the high seas regime would be unjust, "since the shelf is not, as are most seas and all oceans, a means of communication between peoples of the world."[29]

Various theories and proposals set forth by some Latin American states to extend full coastal state sovereignty over the shelf and superjacent waters were opposed by the Soviet delegation at the conference on the basis of their incompatibility with the interests of noncontiguous states in fishing and freedom of navigation[30] and have been subjected to vigorous criticism in Soviet legal media. "The necessary recognition of the right of the coastal state to explore and exploit the natural resources of the continental shelf," declared Molodtsov, "should not result in the abolition of the principles of the freedom of the high seas."[31] Many of the unilateral Latin American declarations asserting an extensive claim to the continental shelf were, in the Soviet view, "altogether doubtful, as the claims affected the high seas, in whose use other states were interested."[32] Even the fact that some Latin American states stipulated that their claims to the shelf in no way affected freedom of navigation was considered insufficient "to remove the con-

28. United Nations Conference on the Law of the Sea, Geneva, 1958, *Official Records* (London: United Nations, 1958), VI, 66.

29. S. V. Molodtsov, "Kodifikatsiia i dalneishee razvitie mezhdunarodnogo morskogo prava (K itogam Zhenevskoi diplomaticheskoi konferentsii po morskomu pravu)," *Sovetskii ezhegodnik mezhdunarodnogo prava 1958* (Moscow: izd-vo AN SSSR, 1959), p. 341.

30. A. N. Nikolaev, "Zhenevskaia konferentsiia po morskomu pravu," *SGIP*, no. 9 (1958), 51–60.

31. *1958 Official Records*, VI, 20.

32. S. V. Molodtsov, "Problema kontinental'nogo shel'fa," *Morskoi flot*, no. 10 (1958), 28.

tradiction" between the exclusive rights asserted by the coastal states and the freedom of the seas.[33]

Soviet jurists also rejected the theory espoused by some Latin American publicists that the unilateral claims to the shelf made prior to 1958 constituted new customary norms of general or regional international law. In this case (contrary to the theory in the case of Peter the Great Bay), Soviet international lawyers required that the new customary norm be universal, uniform, and of long duration. None of these conditions is said to have been met with regard to the continental shelf. In support of this contention (and in contrast to normal practice in Soviet legal media), a diplomatic protest entered in July 1948 by the United States against an extension of sovereignty to the continental shelf and superjacent waters was cited in a Soviet treatise.[34]

The so-called theory of "compensation" advanced by jurists from Chile, Ecuador, Peru, and Costa Rica, which would allow states with little or no continental shelf by virtue of "geological accident" to claim offshore expanses of seabed, is regarded by Soviet jurists as just another variant of the "eco-system" or "bioma" theories. The latter both emphasize the inherent biological and ecological similarities or identities of particular expanses of sea, especially those off Latin America. Volkov, an international lawyer in the Ministry of Fisheries of the USSR, has rejected all three theories as "artificial" means of demarcating the seabed or shelf and as granting to certain states an unwarranted monopoly to exploit enormously productive areas of the ocean.[35]

The posture of restraint which the USSR assumed toward unilateral claims to the continental shelf is particularly noteworthy in light of the Soviet attitude toward the breadth of territorial waters throughout this period. Whereas the Soviet Union would encourage states to determine the breadth of their territorial waters in accordance with their needs and interests, the opposite was true with regard to the shelf. During the conference deliberations on the territorial sea, the Soviet delegation was in the vanguard of those pressing for recognition of expansive claims. In the negotiations on the shelf, the Soviet Union played the role of conciliator among, on the one hand, the "high seas" approach advocated by Japan or the "exclusive" rights approach urged by the United States, and on the other side, the "full sovereignty" over the shelf and superjacent waters doctrine supported by Latin American

33. V. M. Chkhikvadze *et al.* (eds.), *Kurs mezhdunarodnogo prava v shesti tomakh* (Moscow: izd-vo Nauka, 1967), III, p. 288.

34. *Ibid.*

35. A. A. Volkov, "Mezhdunarodnopravovye voprosy ekspluatatsii zhivykh resursov kontinental'nogo shel'fa," *Sovetskii ezhegodnik mezhdunarodnogo prava 1964–1965* (Moscow: izd-vo Nauka, 1966), p. 224.

countries. The ultimate decision of the conference to recognize the "sovereign rights" of coastal states over the shelf was a compromise for which Soviet diplomacy claims partial credit.[36]

Post-Geneva Developments: 1958–70

The Soviet Union ratified the Convention on the Continental Shelf on October 20, 1960.[37] Since that time, Soviet diplomatic practice, legislation, treaties, and writings of international lawyers have provided a reasonably composite picture of Soviet policy regarding the continental shelf.

DEFINITION OF THE CONTINENTAL SHELF

The continental shelf of the USSR is defined in the 1968 edict on the continental shelf as:

... the seabed and subsoil of the submarine areas adjacent to the coast or to islands of the USSR, but outside the area of the territorial sea, to a depth of 200 meters or, beyond that limit, to where the depth of the superjacent waters admits of the exploitation of the natural resources of these areas.
The seabed and subsoil of depressions situated in the continuous mass of the continental shelf of the USSR, irrespective of their depth, shall be part of the continental shelf of the USSR.[38]

The first paragraph of the above definition incorporates verbatim the provisions of the Geneva Convention on the Continental Shelf. The second paragraph resolves an ambiguity in the 1958 convention as to whether huge depressions or trenches constituted the outward boundary of the shelf or whether the shelf-mass beyond the depression also should be considered part of the shelf. In resolving the question as it did, the USSR undoubtedly had in mind the existence of several sizable troughs intersecting portions of the polar seas off Soviet coasts.

DELIMITATION OF THE CONTINENTAL SHELF

The Soviet definition of the shelf included the so-called exploitability clause of the continental shelf convention with regard to the outward boundary of the shelf—that is, the shelf extends to a depth of 200 meters or, beyond that limit, to the depth which technology permits to be exploited. Soviet jurists interpret this provision to mean that the most technologically advanced state in the world determines the outward boundary of the shelf for all states as it develops its own shelf

---

36. Molodtsov, "Kodifikatsiia i dalneishee razvitie," p. 343.
37. *Vedomosti SSSR* (1960), no. 42, item 390; *UNTS*, cccxcix, 311.
38. Article 1. *Vedomosti SSSR* (1968), no. 6, item 40; *ILM*, vii (1968), 392; *SS&D*, vi (1970), 258.

at ever-greater depths. To do otherwise, Soviet jurists suggest, would enable highly developed states to explore the seabed and subsoil off the coasts of other countries at a depth exceeding their own continental shelf. This would "contravene the spirit of the Convention on the Continental Shelf, which leaves to each state the right of exploration and exploitation of areas of its seabed and subsoil. . . ."[39]

However, the application of this principle would not extend, in the Soviet view, to the deep ocean bed beyond the geological continental shelf. Even though the Convention on the Continental Shelf does not contain any provision expressly prohibiting coastal states from extending their sovereign rights to explore and exploit the shelf to the deep seabed, Soviet jurists have concluded that there is no basis for interpreting Article 1 of the convention in such a manner. These jurists also find nothing in the proceedings of the International Law Commission to justify such an interpretation; throughout its discussions, the commission is said to have assumed that there existed a natural, geological limit to the shelf beyond which sovereign rights to explore and exploit the seabed are not granted.[40]

The problem of delimiting the boundary of a continental shelf shared by two or more states came before the International Court of Justice in the *North Sea Continental Shelf* cases of 1969, wherein the court was requested to decide what the applicable "principles and rules of international law" are in respect to delimitation of certain portions of the continental shelf boundary between the Netherlands and the Federal Republic of Germany and between Denmark and Germany.[41] The court found, by 11 votes to 6, that Article 6(2) of the Convention on the Continental Shelf (providing that in the absence of agreement and of special circumstances the principle of equidistance is to be used in determining the shelf boundary of adjacent states) was not obligatory between the parties to the dispute since Germany had not ratified the convention. The court prescribed certain "equitable principles" which the parties should take into account when delimiting the shelf.[42] The language of Article 6 of the convention had been incorporated without modification as Article 2 of the 1968 edict on the continental shelf of the USSR.

In his dissenting opinion, the Soviet judge, V. M. Koretskii, urged that the principles and rules embodied in Article 6 of the convention

39. Chkhikvadze, *Kurs mezhdunarodnogo prava*, III, p. 288.
40. A. D. Keilin and V. F. Tsarev, "Kontinental'nyi shel'f i ego granitsy," *SGIP*, no. 1 (1970), 98–102.
41. International Court of Justice, *Reports of Judgments, Advisory Opinions and Orders, The North Sea Continental Shelf Cases, Judgment of February 20, 1969* (Netherlands, 1969), p. 6.
42. *Ibid.*, p. 54.

qualified both as principles of general international law and of customary international law binding for all states. Koretskii interpreted Article 6 as creating a "triad" of inter-connected delimitation alternatives. The principal and most appropriate method is the agreement of states. The second element of the triad, "special circumstances," concerns an unusual geographical configuration of the coastline of either side, and a justiciable dispute would exist in the event of disagreement over whether a certain situation could be regarded as constituting a special circumstance. Only if these two elements fail should the principle of equidistance be used, "offering a way out of the impasse in a geometrical construction which introduces a mathematical definitude and a certainty of maritime boundaries."[43] The triad view was further said to incorporate common principles for the general delimitation of maritime spaces, including the territorial sea.

The majority of the court, however, rejected the triad concept and treated the principle of equidistance as a *method* to be accorded no special priority over other methods unless the state had specifically agreed to this particular method in an international treaty.

Agreements concluded between the USSR and Finland to delimit their continental shelf have applied two methods. In an agreement of May 20, 1965, concerning the continental shelf in the Gulf of Finland, the parties made the shelf boundary coterminus with the boundary of their respective territorial waters.[44] The boundary of their shelf in the northeastern part of the Baltic Sea, under an agreement of May 5, 1967, is a median line.[45] (See Map 9.) The equidistance method was used to demarcate the shelf boundary in the Gulf of Gdansk in a Soviet–Polish agreement of August 28, 1969, and negotiations are reportedly in progress with Norway.[46] The Soviet Union has thus utilized all three of the methods for delimitation of the shelf stipulated in Article 6 of the Convention on the Continental Shelf.

On October 23, 1968, surely by no coincidence the same day on which the International Court of Justice began to hear oral arguments in the *North Sea Continental Shelf* cases,[47] the Soviet Union, Poland,

43. *Ibid.*, pp. 155–56.
44. *UNTS*, DLXVI, 31; *ILM*, VI (1967), 727; *SS&D*, VI (1970), 264. Pursuant to Article 5 of this agreement, the Joint Finnish-Soviet Commission for Designating the Sea Boundary Between Finland and the USSR in the Gulf of Finland to the Northeast of Gogland (Suursaari) Island placed the necessary boundary markers. For an English text of the Protocol-Description of the sea boundary, see *SS&D*, VI (1970), 265. The protocol was signed April 5, 1967.
45. *ILM*, VII (1968), 560; *SS&D*, VI (1970), 268.
46. The text of the Soviet-Polish Agreement is translated in *ILM*, IX (1970), 697; *SS&D*, VI (1970), 407. Negotiations with Norway were reported in *Ocean Industry*, IV, no. 9 (1969), 52.
47. *Izvestia*, October 18, 1968, p. 2.

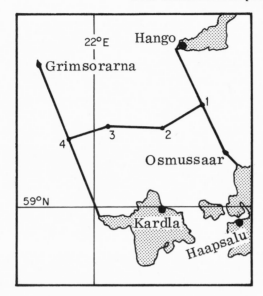

Map 9. Soviet-Finnish Continental Shelf
Boundary in the Northeastern Baltic Sea

and East Germany signed a joint Declaration on the Continental Shelf of the Baltic Sea.[48] The declaration provided that the "surface and subsoil of the bed of the Baltic . . . are a continuous continental shelf" whose delimitation must be carried out in conformity with the "principles set forth in the 1958 Geneva Convention on the Continental Shelf and, in particular, Article 6. . . ."[49] The base lines used to compute the breadth of the territorial sea in conformity with the 1958 Convention on the Territorial Sea were reciprocally recognized and considered to be the base lines for delimiting the shelf, whose precise coordinates are to be determined in bilateral or multilateral agreements among the states concerned.[50] In this manner the Soviet government communicated its attitude toward the pending cases before the Inter-

48. *Izvestia*, October 24, 1968, p. 3; English text in *ILM*, vii (1968), 1393; *SS&D*, vi (1970), 261.
49. *Ibid.*, Articles 1 and 4.
50. *Ibid.*, Articles 5 and 6. A Polish jurist has concluded:

. . . l'analyse des dispositions de la Déclaration de Moscou de 1968 a permis de constater qu'elle est conforme aux principes des conventions de Genève de 1958 sur le droit de la mer et en particulier à la Convention sur le plateau continental et qu'elle est de nature à satisfaire la pratique des Etats en matière de délimitation du plateau continental.

Franciszek Przetacznik, "La Déclaration sur le Plateau Continental de la Mer Baltique et le Droit International," *Revue belge de droit international*, vi (1970), 483.

national Court of Justice, and, as it turned out, the substance of the position defended by Koretskii.

NATURAL RESOURCES OF THE CONTINENTAL SHELF

In the Convention on the Continental Shelf and in the 1968 edict, the natural resources of the continental shelf are defined as the "mineral and other non-living resources of the seabed and subsoil, as well as living organisms belonging to sedentary species. . . ." In the USSR these resources are state property, and their exploration and exploitation must be carried out in conformity with Soviet law.

On October 29, 1968, the Ministry of Fisheries of the USSR confirmed a List of Living Organisms Which are Natural Resources of the Continental Shelf of the USSR.[51] The List contained 52 species of marine life. Reflecting its insistence at the 1958 Geneva Conference on the Law of the Sea that crustacea must be included in the concept of shelf resources, the Soviet list specified Tanner and Alaska King Crabs, as well as other crab species on the USSR continental shelf, "except species which swim when mature." This formulation leaves some negotiating room to the Japanese, for whom the Alaska King Crab gathered off the Kamchatka coast has been an important product.

Scallops were placed on the Soviet list because they move about the seabed with the same "swimming-jumping" motion as lobsters, which in the French–Brazilian dispute were ultimately treated as creatures of the shelf.[52] Other species that may be commercially exploited in the future, or that may be described as a new species of the fauna (or flora) of the USSR, or that may be acclimatized or artificially cultured on the Soviet continental shelf (assuming that they are sedentary species), are included as well.

Under the Northwest Pacific Fisheries Convention of May 14, 1956, the annual Japanese king crab catch is to be negotiated within the Northwest Pacific Fisheries Commission established by the convention.[53] Since the Convention on the Continental Shelf came into force, the question of whether crabs are a sedentary species or whether they swim has been hotly disputed in the Soviet–Japanese negotiations. In the Soviet view, king crabs "crawl, their feet rest on the surface of the sea bottom . . . ," whereas the Japanese assert that the king crab uses a kicking motion to leap to great heights.[54] If the Soviet opinion pre-

51. *Rybnoe khoziaistvo*, no. 2 (1969), 4–5; English text in *SS&D*, vɪ (1970), 282.

52. L. G. Vinogradov and A. A. Neiman, "Organizmy kontinental'nogo shel'fa, sostavliaiushchie gosudarstvennym sobstvennost' SSSR," *Rybnoe khoziaistvo*, no. 3 (1969), 6.

53. Article 3. *SDD*, xvɪɪɪ, 312; *SS&D*, vɪ (1970), 359.

54. *New York Times*, April 12, 1969, p. 10.

vails, the crab is a creature of the shelf and not available for exploitation by Japan. The general pattern of the negotiations has been to argue the issue without reaching any consensus and to reduce the annual quotas of the Japanese catch.[55]

RESEARCH, EXPLORATION, AND EXPLOITATION
OF THE CONTINENTAL SHELF

The 1968 edict (Article 5) prohibits foreign individuals and companies from engaging in research, exploration, and exploitation of natural resources and in other work on the continental shelf of the USSR unless permission has been expressly granted in an international agreement to which the USSR is a party, or unless competent Soviet authorities issue a special permit. In the Declaration on the Continental Shelf of the Baltic Sea, the parties agreed not to give over parcels of that shelf for exploration, exploitation, or other use to non-Baltic states, citizens, or firms.

The scope of this prohibition, in light of Soviet commentary on an apparent inconsistency between Article 5(1) and (8) of the continental shelf convention, are somewhat ambiguous. The Soviet Union opposed Article 5(8) in the plenary session of the 1958 Conference on the Law of the Sea, asserting that

if no kind of scientific research into the continental shelf could be undertaken there without the consent of the coastal state, much valuable purely scientific work would be stopped.[56]

Molodtsov, Koretskii, Tunkin, and others have noted that all natural processes taking place in sea waters interact with processes occurring in submarine areas of the sea. "Physical and biological phenomena occurring in waters superjacent to the continental shelf may not be correctly understood and analyzed without simultaneously researching these phenomena on the seabed."[57] Hence, "oceanographic research is connected with the seabed; *i. e.,* the continental shelf."[58]

Nevertheless, the Soviet government gave an outright refusal in 1967 to a request made by the United States to conduct research on the

---

55. In the 1965 United States-Soviet Agreement Relating to Fishing for King Crab, the parties agreed that the king crab is a natural resource of the continental shelf within the terms of Article 2 of the Convention on the Continental Shelf. *T.I.A.S.*, no. 5752; *ILM*, iv (1965), 359.

56. *1958 Official Records*, ii, 15.

57. S. V. Molodtsov, *Mezhdunarodno-pravovoi rezhim otkrytogo moria i kontinental'nogo shel'fa* (Moscow: izd-vo Akademiia nauk, 1960), p. 317.

58. V. M. Koretskii and G. I. Tunkin (eds.), *Ocherki mezhdunarodnogo morskogo prava* (Moscow: Gosiurizdat, 1962), p. 285.

continental shelf beneath the polar seas off the Soviet coast.[59] In 1965 the Soviet government filed a formal protest with the United States, claiming that sea-bottom coring operations carried out by the United States Coast Guard icebreaker *Northwind* in the Kara Sea violated the Convention on the Continental Shelf.[60]

Pursuant to a decree adopted by the Council of Ministers of the USSR on July 18, 1969, "On the Procedure for Conducting Work on the Continental Shelf of the USSR and the Protection of its Natural Resources," any research, exploration, and exploitation of natural resources of the shelf is permitted only after registration in the established procedure. Organizations and persons conducting work on the shelf must use the natural resources of the shelf rationally, prevent pollution of the shelf and superjacent waters by industrial and other economic wastes, sewage, radioactive substances, and take measures to conserve marine life.[61] Installations erected on the shelf in conformity with a proper permit and safety zones around such installations must not interfere with the use of recognized sea lanes essential to international navigation. Foreign vessels may enter such safety zones only with the special authorization of competent Soviet authorities.[62]

Violations of the 1968 edict by individuals are punishable by a court with a fine of up to 10,000 rubles or with deprivation of freedom up to one year. Foreign vessels operating in violation of the edict, as well as all implements, instruments, and everything illegally extracted from the shelf, are subject to confiscation (Articles 6 and 7).

The task of enforcing the edict with respect to the protection of natural resources has been entrusted to the Ministry of Fisheries of the USSR with assistance, when necessary, from the border guard. Control over the propriety of exploiting the mineral and other nonliving resources of the Soviet continental shelf is delegated to the State Mining–Technical Inspection Agencies of the USSR (Articles 8 and 9).

PEACEFUL USES OF THE CONTINENTAL SHELF

Article 3 of the Declaration on the Continental Shelf of the Baltic Sea stipulated that the shelf "must be used by all states exclusively for peaceful purposes." At the Geneva Conference on the Law of the Sea,

---

59. William T. Burke, *International Legal Problems of Scientific Research in the Oceans* (Washington D.C.: National Council on Marine Resources and Engineering Development, 1967), p. 53.

60. Richard Petrow, *Across the Top of Russia* (New York: McKay, 1967), p. 351.

61. Reported in *Izvestia*, August 2, 1969, p. 2; English text in *ILM*, IX (1970), 975; *SS&D*, VI (1970), 409.

62. Article 4, Edict on the Continental Shelf of the USSR. *Vedomosti SSSR* (1968), no. 6, item 40; *ILM*, VII (1968), 392; *SS&D*, VI (1970), 258.

the Soviet Union had unsuccessfully sought to insert an identical restriction into the Convention on the Continental Shelf.[63] Similarly, Soviet jurists emphasize that Article 5(1) of the continental shelf convention can apply solely to peaceful research, since "military research is not published for general information."[64] One Soviet jurist has contended that "peaceful use" has acquired a general meaning in international law that would preclude "any military activity" in an area reserved exclusively for such uses.[65]

63. *1958 Official Records,* VI, 137.
64. Molodtsov, *Mezhdunarodno-pravovoi rezhim otkrytogo moria,* p. 316.
65. G. F. Kalinkin, "Ob ispol'zovanii morskogo dna iskliuchitel'no v mirnykh tseliakh," *SGIP,* no. 10 (1969), 122.

Chapter 6

THE LEGAL REGIME
OF THE DEEP SEABED

In geophysical terms, the submerged portion of the earth's surface may be broadly divided into the continental shelf, the continental slope, and the deep seabed or ocean floor. As noted previously, the shelf is a natural geological extension of the adjacent land mass extending seaward. At an average depth of about 600 feet, the gradient of the shelf begins to increase sharply, marking the continental slope. At the base of the slope, the seabed is a rolling plain interrupted by deep gorges, ridges, or sea mounts.[1]

Although the ocean bed received systematic attention when transatlantic cables began to be laid nearly a century ago, it is only within the past decade or less that the seabed proper became an object of serious scientific, economic, and political concern. Much of what passed for seabed activity (pearl fishing, offshore oil drilling, mining of iron and coal through shafts sunk in adjacent land territory) was in fact exploitation of the continental shelf. The drafters of the 1958 Geneva Convention on the Continental Shelf defined the outward boundary of the shelf as the "depth of 200 meters . . . or, beyond that limit, to where the depth of superjacent waters admits of the exploitation of natural resources of the said areas" in the belief that exploitation beyond a 200-meter depth was not technologically feasible in the near future.

Extraordinary technological advances have transformed the seemingly judicious prudence of 1958 into undue conservatism. Submarine vessels of revolutionary design and materials now enable states to probe the deepest abysses of the seabed. Studies of man's physiological adaptability to great water depths are permitting ever deeper dives

---

1. Some observers describe the "continental margin" as consisting of the continental shelf, continental slope, and continental rise, conceding that there are places where the slope and shelf cannot be differentiated or where there is no continental rise. See for example, National Petroleum Council, *Petroleum Resources Under the Ocean Floor* (Washington D.C.: National Petroleum Council, 1969), p. 23. Soviet scientists consider the continental rise to be an oceanic rather than a continental formation, and in Soviet usage the rise is called the "sloping oceanic plain." See U.N. Doc. A/AC.135/WG.2/SR.11, July 3, 1968.

and open up the possibility of his living and working for prolonged periods beneath the seas. These advances have immediate economic and military implications.

The President's Science Advisory Committee reported that the deep ocean floor is ". . . paved in many places with nodules containing manganese, iron, cobalt, copper, and nickel in concentrations which approach the mineable levels on land. . . ."[2] Oil geologists believe the deep seabed may contain petroleum reserves far greater than the continental shelf. Although the economically mineable or extractable portion of these resources remains to be determined, scientists are optimistic that exploitation will be possible within one to two decades and, in the case of oil, much sooner.[3]

The military potential of the deep ocean has even more significance. One possible use would be to install guided missiles in the seabed, using either mobile or immobile systems.[4] A second use, presently being developed, is an underwater detection system to monitor submarine and other submersible movements. Another possibility would be to place manned installations under the sea to perform military functions. Both the United States and the Soviet Union are experimenting to learn whether and how man can adapt to living and working for extended periods at great depths.[5] Such installations "could be used for research, as monitoring and communications centers, and as hiding places for special military equipment and supplies, perhaps even to service submarines."[6]

The "exploitability" clause of the Convention on the Continental Shelf left unresolved the question of the legal status of the seabed beyond the shelf. Under one interpretation of the convention, coastal states could be entitled to claim the adjacent seabed ". . . out to the

---

2. *Effective Use of the Sea: Report of the Panel on Oceanography of the President's Science Advisory Committee* (Washington D.C.: GPO, 1966), p. 29. The literature on the resources of the oceans is already immense. See Albert W. Koers, *The Debate on the Legal Regime for the Exploration and Exploitation of Ocean Resources: A Bibliography for the First Decade, 1960–1970* (Kingston: Law of the Sea Institute, 1970).

3. Soviet oil extraction from the seabed is presently confined to the Caspian Sea, where wells have been sunk at depths of 190 feet. Soviet geologists believe that portions of the Sea of Azov, the Black Sea, the Pechorskaia Trench in the Bering Sea, and the northern and other far eastern seas contain rich oil deposits. See S. V. Mikhailov, *Mirovoi okean i chelovechestvo* (Moscow: izd-vo Ekonomika, 1969), p. 137. Most of these deposits seem to be located in the shallow areas of the continental shelf.

4. *Effective Use of the Sea*, p. 33.

5. *Izvestia*, September 28, 1968, p. 6.

6. D. Michael, "Avoiding the Militarization of the Seas," *New Dimensions for the United Nations* (New York: Commission to Study the Organization of Peace, 1966), p. 170.

maximum depth for exploitation reached anywhere in the world, regardless of its own capabilities or of local conditions."[7] This would mean that beyond the 200-meter depth the exploitation of the seabed is already reserved to the coastal state, and the submarine areas of the world would have been theoretically divided among the coastal states by the Geneva convention. Labeled the "national lake" approach, this interpretation would favor states with island possessions (Portugal and Great Britain), but would seriously disadvantage the United States, the Soviet Union, and landlocked nations.[8]

Other proposals to regulate seabed development include the "flag state" approach and the "international regime" approach. Under the former, each coastal state would be permitted to appropriate and exploit any area over which it could claim jurisdiction. Some analysts would limit a claim of jurisdiction to a specific purpose, such as mining or oil extraction.[9] When exploitation is sufficiently intense to create conflicting claims, under the flag state approach states would submit disputes to some type of international diplomatic or judicial settlement that would take into account special circumstances of seabed development which now can only be postulated. This proposal would favor the most technologically advanced states, but it seems least likely to promote the coordinated, conflict-free exploitation of the seas.

Various types of international regimes have been suggested. They range from a very modest "presence" in the form of an international registry office to carry out evidentiary and recording functions for claims made under the flag state approach[10] to a full-fledged international authority that would administer the rights to mine or otherwise exploit the seabed.[11] Some have recommended that incomes and royalties derived by any international authority be used to defray expenses of general international organizations, such as the United Nations.[12]

Publicists have been divided over the present status of customary international law with respect to the deep seabed. The majority reject the view that the seabed has the same legal status as the surface (the

7. Richard Young, "The Geneva Convention on the Continental Shelf: A First Impression," *AJIL*, LII (1958), 735.

8. Francis T. Christy, "A Social Scientist Writes on Economic Criteria for Rules Governing Exploitation of Deep Sea Minerals," *The International Lawyer*, II (1968), 244.

9. Northcutt Ely, "American Policy Options in the Development of Undersea Mineral Resources," *International Lawyer*, II (1968), 215.

10. L. F. E. Goldie, in Lewis M. Alexander (ed.), *The Law of the Sea: Offshore Boundaries and Zones* (Columbus, Ohio: Ohio State University Press, 1967), p. 273.

11. Christy, "Deep Sea Minerals," pp. 239–40.

12. See, in general, *New Dimensions for the United Nations*.

high seas) and therefore is not susceptible to exclusive claim by any state.[13]

By late 1966, the issue of the resources of the deep ocean had become the object of international concern. The United Nations General Assembly on December 6, 1966, requested the secretary-general to prepare a comprehensive survey of activities in marine science technology and to formulate proposals for ensuring the most effective arrangements for an expanded program of international cooperation to improve our understanding of the marine environment and to exploit and develop marine resources, with due regard to conservation of fish stocks.[14]

The issue was confronted directly on August 17, 1967, when the Permanent Mission of Malta to the United Nations proposed that the agenda of the 22d UN General Assembly include an item, entitled in its revised form: "Examination of the Question of the Reservation Exclusively for Peaceful Purposes of the Sea-bed and the Ocean Floor, and the Subsoil Thereof, Underlying the High Seas Beyond the Limits of Present National Jurisdiction, and the Use of the Resources in the Interests of Mankind."[15] In an explanatory memorandum, Malta suggested that the seabed and ocean floor be reserved exclusively for peaceful purposes, that an international framework be created for the use and economic exploitation of the seabed and ocean floor, and that the net financial benefits derived from such activities be used primarily to promote the development of poor countries.

The Maltese proposal was debated extensively in the First Committee (Political), and on December 18, 1967, the General Assembly adopted a resolution creating an Ad Hoc Committee to Study the Peaceful Uses of the Sea-bed and the Ocean Floor Beyond the Limits of National Jurisdiction. The committee, comprised of 35 members, including the USSR, was requested to prepare for consideration at the 23d session a study which would encompass:[16]

(a) a survey of the past and present activities of the U.N., the specialized agencies, the International Atomic Energy Agency, and other intergovernmental bodies with regard to the seabed and ocean floor;
(b) a survey of existing international agreements concerning the seabeds;
(c) an account of the scientific, technical, economic, legal, and other aspects of the seabeds; and

13. See, for example, C. J. Colombos, *The International Law of the Sea* (6th ed.; London: Longmans, 1967), p. 67.
14. G. A. Res. 2172 (xxi), December 6, 1966.
15. Doc. No. A/6695 (xxii), August 18, 1967.
16. G. A. Res. 2340 (xxii), December 18, 1967.

(d) an indication regarding practical means to promote international cooperation in the exploitation, conservation, and use of the seabed and
the ocean floor, and the subsoil thereof.

The emergence of the deep seabed issue found the Soviet Union
without an established legal position. Insofar as the public record is
concerned, no Soviet jurist or government official appears to have discussed or even remarked on the legal status of the deep seabed. It is
scarcely surprising that in submitting its thematic plan for 1968–70,
the leading Soviet legal periodical invited authors to prepare articles on
the subjects of "demilitarization of the seabed and use of its resources"
and "the principle of freedom of the seas in contemporary international
law."[17]

The absence of a legal position did not mean there was a lack of
Soviet interest in the deep seabed. In April 1967, the Soviet Union had
proposed that the Intergovernmental Oceanographic Commission, created in 1960 by UNESCO to coordinate oceanographic research at the
intergovernmental level, set up a special working group on legal aspects of the studies of the ocean and utilization of oceanic resources in
order to

. . . prepare drafts of: (a) a convention on the basic principles of conducting scientific research on the high seas, and (b) a convention on the international norms of exploration and exploitation of the mineral resources of
the high seas.[18]

In addition, the working group was to provide the IOC Secretariat with
advice on legal aspects of scientific studies of the ocean. An international conference was envisaged to discuss and adopt the draft conventions.

The Soviet initiative in the IOC foreshadowed what thereafter
seems to have been a consistently held view that the issue of the deep
seabed should be dealt with in specialized technical bodies—in a relatively depoliticized environment less susceptible to the vagaries of politics than the General Assembly. In debating the Maltese proposal in
the First Committee, the Soviet representative pointed out that a great
deal of preparatory work was needed to identify and then to agree
upon the most appropriate ways of studying matters.[19] This theme was
reiterated during the sessions of the ad hoc committee. The USSR favored steps aimed at a speedy exploration and study of the ocean floor,

17. *SGIP,* no. 7 (1968), p. 147.
18. AVS/9/89, April 3, 1967. The secretary-general of the Intergovernmental Oceanographic Commission, N. Fedorov, is a Soviet national.
19. *United Nations Monthly Chronicle,* v, no. 1 (1968), 30–31.

while at the same time expressing a desire to forestall premature decisions which would jeopardize scientific research, freedom of navigation, and other legitimate uses of the seas and seabeds.

Although Soviet attitudes toward the seabed are still in the formative stage, certain preferences are beginning to emerge. Undoubtedly, many of these will be modified or eliminated by time, technology, or politics, but even at this early date it is apparent that Soviet attitudes will be guided fundamentally by its newly acquired status as a major maritime power. One may also expect many traditional Soviet attitudes, grounded in its previous position as a coastally oriented power, to be modified.

Economic Potential of the Seabed

The Soviet government has been a major sponsor of scientific investigation of the ocean bed through national and international organizations. Soviet scientists have been among those calling attention to the fact that

deposits of iron and manganese nodules, as well as phosphates, have been discovered in enormous areas on the ocean beds, numerous oil and gas deposits already are being exploited on the oceanic shelf, successful searches for oil are being conducted on the continental slope, [and] deposits of sulphur, coal, and other valuable, useful minerals are being worked.[20]

Soviet oceanographers are optimistic in projecting the potentials for manganese, copper, cobalt, and nickel from seabed ore formations. Their metallurgical tests reportedly have demonstrated the effectiveness of processing nodules and "possibly" obtaining an "almost complete extraction of manganese" and other metals.[21] Soviet "experts," however, are said to have advised the Permanent Representative of the USSR to the United Nations that scientific knowledge of the seabed and its mineral resources is very limited and that present technology does not allow large-scale exploitation at great depths. This counsel was invoked by Malik to justify a cautious approach to the regime of the deep seabed.

Military Potential of the Seabed

We have already alluded to some potential uses the deep seabed may have for the nuclear powers; man's fertile imagination will devise

20. A. P. Lisitsyn and G. B. Udintsev, "Sostoianie i zadachi geologii Mirovogo okeana," *Vestnik akademii nauk SSSR,* no. 7 (1963), 30.
21. *Pravda,* November 14, 1968, p. 3.

others. American policy-makers have assumed that the Soviet Union, as the world's second ranking military power, would have roughly the same capability and incentive to use the deep seabed for military purposes as would the United States.[22]

While the incentive might be the same, there is some reason to question whether Soviet and American capabilities to develop the seabed for military purposes are equivalent. It will be recalled that at the 1958 Geneva Conference on the Law of the Sea, the Soviet Union strongly urged that the continental shelf be used for "exclusively peaceful" purposes. At that time, the Soviet proposal constituted part of a larger campaign to curtail all nuclear testing and thereby to redress a serious comparative disadvantage in weapons technology vis-à-vis the United States. In advocating denuclearization of the deep seabed in the 1970's, Soviet commentators emphasize that the conclusion of an appropriate treaty would thwart the plans of "American militarists . . . to grab these areas in violation of generally-recognized principles of freedom of the high seas" for the purpose of emplacing nuclear missiles.[23]

Disparity in seabed capability notwithstanding, the Soviet government appears to have a genuine interest in avoiding a nuclear arms race in "inner space," just as in outer space and the Antarctica. The reference in the Maltese proposal to reserving the seabed for peaceful purposes was pursued by the Soviet government in a Memorandum Concerning Urgent Measures to Stop the Arms Race and Achieve Disarmament, issued on the occasion of signing the nuclear nonproliferation treaty. It was proposed in the memorandum not only to prohibit the construction of fixed installations for military purposes on the seabed but also "any other activities of a military character." The Soviet government further suggested an agreement to terminate patrols by nuclear-armed submarines within range of the contracting parties.[24] In a draft resolution submitted on June 20, 1968, to the Ad Hoc Committee on the Seabed, the USSR had requested the Eighteen Nation Disarmament Committee to consider, as an urgent matter, the "ques-

---

22. See United States Senate, Committee on Foreign Relations, Subcommittee on Ocean Space, *Activities of Nations in Ocean Space, Hearings* (Washington D.C.: GPO, 1969), p. 35.

23. I. I. Vanin, "Morskoe dno i pentagon," *SShA: ekonomika, politika, ideologiia,* I, no. 1 (1970), 68. Soviet diplomats also stressed that an arms race on the seabed would obstruct peaceful exploitation and create a danger of radioactive, chemical, or bacteriological pollution. See the remarks of Roshchin in the First Committee of the General Assembly. Doc. No. A/C.1/PV. 1691, November 17, 1969.

24. *Izvestia,* July 2, 1968, p. 2; *SS&D,* VI (1970), 287.

tion of prohibiting the use for military purposes of the sea-bed and ocean floor. . . ."[25]

Despite some dissent from smaller powers, the United States and the Soviet Union agreed in March 1969 to give first priority to drafting a treaty that would preserve the seabed as a nuclear-free area. The Soviet government introduced a draft treaty on the seabed at the Geneva disarmament conference on March 18, 1969, which included the essential points raised in its memorandum of the preceding July. Under Article 1 of the draft treaty, the use of the seabed for "military purposes" beyond a 12-mile zone would be prohibited, and the emplacement of nuclear weapons, or other weapons of mass destruction, military bases, structures, installations, fortifications, "and other objects of a military nature" was proscribed.[26]

The concept of "use for military purposes" as set forth in the Soviet draft excluded both the installations of offensive and defensive weapons systems and the emplacement of monitoring or other devices to detect the movement of underwater craft. The test of "peaceful purposes" was, in the Soviet view, an objective and all-inclusive one: permitting military activities "with peaceful aims or in fulfillment of peaceful intentions" would depart from the generally recognized interpretation of peaceful uses that had evolved in post-World War II treaty practice. Citing such diverse sources as disarmament *proposals* of the Western powers, documents of the International Atomic Energy Agency, and, more appropriately, the nonproliferation, outer space, and Antarctica treaties, one Soviet representative concluded that in United Nations practice the use of a given environment for exclusively peaceful purposes had meant its complete demilitarization. All military activities, for whatever purpose, were banned.[27]

At the Conference of the Eighteen Nation Committee on Disarmament, the head of the Soviet delegation offered a somewhat more explicit explanation of what demilitarization would entail. Referring to the case of the Aaland Islands, he pointed out that demilitarization did not presuppose limitations on the establishment of means of communication, beacons, or other elements of a communications infrastructure. In addition, the use of military personnel to conduct scientific research has been compatible with demilitarization under the Antarctic Treaty.

25. Doc. No. A/AC.135/20, August 21, 1968.
26. *SS&D*, VI (1970), 288.
27. Kalinkin, in Doc. No. A/AC.138/SC.1/SR.9, March 26, 1969. For a more extensive development of this interpretation, see G. F. Kalinkin, "Ob ispol'zovanii morskogo dna iskliuchitel'no v mirnykh tseliakh," *SGIP,* no. 10 (1969), 117–22.

Submarine tracing stations, however, would in the Soviet view have been barred from the demilitarized zone.[28]

The draft treaty submitted by the United States on May 22, 1969, prohibited only the emplacement of fixed nuclear weapons or other weapons of mass destruction, as well as associated fixed launching platforms beyond a three-mile maritime band.[29]

After intensive bilateral negotiations, a joint Soviet–American draft was presented to the Committee of the Conference on Disarmament on October 7, 1969, and resubmitted in a revised form on October 30, 1969.[30]

The joint draft represented a compromise by both powers. Nuclear weapons, other weapons of mass destruction, and structures, launching installations, or other facilities specifically designed for testing, storing, or using such weapons would be banned from the seabed. For example, the treaty would prohibit mines anchored to or emplaced on the seabed; however, the navigation of submersible craft would not be affected, nor would peaceful research or commercial exploitation. Thus, the Soviet Union accepted a draft proscribing considerably less than "all military activity" on the seabed in return for a promise to continue negotiations on further measures tending to complete demilitarization of the seabed.

The United States in turn agreed to a 12-mile offshore zone as the area beyond which the treaty would apply. In the early stages of discussion, it was envisioned that the treaty would extend to areas lying either beyond the territorial waters or the national jurisdiction of coastal states; however, in view of conflicting claims to territorial waters and to the ambiguity of the concept of national jurisdiction, it was decided to create a special zone only for the operation of the treaty. The 12-mile limit was regarded as most compatible with the territorial limits or contiguous zones claimed by most states.[31]

A number of states expressed dissatisfaction with the verification provisions of the first joint draft. As a consequence, the draft was revised to permit parties to verify compliance either through their own facilities or those of any other participating state in order to ensure equal opportunities for all signatories. To strengthen the requirement of consultation and cooperation between signatories in the event of

28. Roshchin, Doc. No. ENDC/PV.400, April 3, 1969.

29. *ILM*, VIII (1969), 667.

30. *SS&D*, VI (1970), 290.

31. American acceptance of the zone also signified how close Soviet and American views had become on the issue of coastal jurisdiction seaward. In February 1970, the United States announced its support for an international convention fixing the territorial waters of all countries at 12 miles if certain other rights were guaranteed. *ILM,* IX (1970), 434.

doubts about compliance, the draft was modified to allow parties recourse to the United Nations Security Council if consultation and cooperation proved to be inadequate to resolve a dispute.[32]

The revised joint draft of October 30, 1969, was placed before the 24th General Assembly. Following discussion in the First Committee, in which further questions concerning verification and the definition of the maritime zone were raised, a resolution was unanimously adopted welcoming the revised draft and returning it to the Conference of the Committee on Disarmament so that proposals and suggestions made during the session of the assembly could be considered.[33]

International Law and the Future Regime of the Seabed

In general, international law has been invoked by Soviet diplomats for two purposes with respect to the regime of the deep seabed. The first is to "proclaim principles of international law that would prevent imperialist Powers from monopolizing the wealth of the sea."[34] The second and more important purpose of international law is to serve as the basis for the development of a future regime for the seabed and its subsoil.

International law, Malik declared to the ad hoc committee, does not provide all the answers to the "complex questions posed by the progress made in oceanography and the present unprecedented revolution in technology and industry . . . ;" however, the "USSR believed a solution to international legal problems regulating activities with regard to the sea-bed and ocean floor might provide a sound basis for a further expansion of coordination and cooperation between states. . . ."[35] This theme was echoed by the Soviet representatives in sessions of the Legal Working Group of the Ad Hoc Committee:

It would be incorrect and unwise to regard the seabed and ocean floor as a legal vacuum. The solution of any international legal problem could be effective only if it were based on existing international law and principles.[36]

32. For a Soviet interpretation of these events see Iu. Tomilin, "Keeping the Sea-Bed Out of the Arms Race," *International Affairs* [Moscow], no. 1 (1970), 41–45.
33. G. A. Res. 2602 (xxiv), December 13, 1969. *ILM,* ix (1970), 417. The draft was approved, with further minor revisions to accommodate the views of smaller powers, by the 25th General Assembly in December 1970 and opened for signature.
34. Ambassador Malik of the Soviet Union. Doc. No. a/ac.135/sr. 10–12, August 29, 1968.
35. Malik, Doc. No. a/ac.135/sr. 1–9, May 10, 1968.
36. Mendelevich, Doc. No. a/ac.135/wg.1/sr. 1–3, 6–14.

Soviet concepts of "existing international law and principles" applicable to the deep seabed are the most important indicators available at this point as to how the Soviet Union envisages an acceptable future regime of the deep seabed. As is so often the case at this stage of development, it is easier to determine which types of regime are *not* acceptable than those which may be.

Extension of Continental Shelf Boundaries Seaward. We have already noticed that the Convention on the Continental Shelf did not fix a precise outer boundary for the continental shelf. Soviet jurists were among those who, in interpreting the flexible "exploitability" provision of the convention, concluded that the technological capabilities of the most advanced state should determine the outer shelf boundary for all states, irrespective of their individual levels of technological achievement.[37] On its face, the Soviet interpretation was wholly open-ended; that is, the shelf boundary moved seaward to whatever depth exploitation became possible. Under this approach it would be superfluous to distinguish any area of seabed beyond the shelf, for the entire bed of the oceans could be divided among states merely by extending the base points of the continental shelf seaward to meet those of the opposite state.

One Soviet jurist has made it clear that the flexible exploitability criterion can apply only to the continental shelf proper, and perhaps to the continental slope. Labeling "absurd" the opinion that the Convention on the Continental Shelf could sanction unrestricted claims to the ocean bed, he wrote:

Seizures of the seabed may lead to clashes among states and a sharpening of international tension. Division of the world ocean itself is fraught with the danger of constraining the freedom of the high seas. Geologically, the shelf is connected . . . with the continent and is sharply distinguished from the ocean bed, which has a different structure. . . . Finally, allocating . . . exclusive rights with regard to the seabed is premature, since it is still unclear how it will be used in the future.[38]

Making the same point, other Soviet jurists have stressed the importance of affirming that there exists an area of the seabed and ocean floor which lies beyond the limits of national jurisdiction.[39] Soviet representatives at the United Nations have supported the convening of a conference or other appropriate steps to delimit once and for all the extent of national jurisdiction over the continental shelf.

37. V. M. Chkhikvadze *et al.* (eds.), *Kurs mezhdunarodnogo prava v shesti tomakh* (Moscow: izd-vo Nauka, 1967), III, p. 288.
38. I. I. Cheprov, "Mezhdunarodno-pravovoi rezhim morskogo dna," *SGIP,* no. 10 (1968), 81–82.
39. See A. K. Zhudro and A. L. Kolodkin, *Some Legal Aspects of Using the Sea-Bed* (Rome: Instituto Affari Internazionali, 1969), p. 17.

Common, Joint, or International Ownership. In rejecting a division of the seabed by coastal states, Soviet publicists and diplomats also object to the opposite approach: treating the seabed as the joint or common property of the international community or vesting title to the seabed and subsoil in an international organization or authority.

The principle of *res communis* is wholly inappropriate for the seabed, it is argued, because if the seabed were subject to the authority of all states, nothing could be done thereon without the consent of each.[40] The notion of the seabed as the "common heritage of mankind," which in Soviet media is equated with either or both common and joint ownership, is not considered by Soviet jurists to be a principle of international law. To create a special legal status for the seabed on the basis of this principle would be tantamount to acknowledging that a legal lacuna exists, whereas in the Soviet view the contrary is true.

The concept of the "common heritage of mankind" and the principle of common or joint ownership have also been linked by Soviet commentators to the creation of an "international mechanism." Soviet opposition to supranational authorities dates back to the earliest days of the Soviet regime and its suspicion of the League of Nations. With regard to the seabed, the Soviet delegate to the ad hoc committee declared that a supranational authority would be "inadvisable," "incompatible with the freedom of the seas," and "would impair state cooperation in ocean exploration."[41] In the United Nations General Assembly, the Soviet representative declared that "our views are a matter of principle" in opposing a study by the secretary-general of possible forms of international machinery to administer a seabed regime. The implementation of such machinery, it was insisted, would "serve exclusively the interests of capitalist monopolies."[42]

Even more modest proposals for the creation of an international registry or licensing authority or analogous international arrangement with limited, specifically defined functions have been attacked in the Soviet press as "nothing more than attempts to bring to inter-state relations the capitalist principle of selling rights to exploit mineral resources by auction to monopolies."[43] However, such statements may not necessarily preclude an international body with limited authority

40. Smirnov, in Doc. No. A/AC.138/SC.1/SR. 8, March 26, 1969. However, the denial of property interests in the seabed or subsoil would not necessarily preclude recognizing the jurisdiction of a state over particular structures or installations which it emplaces on the seabed to exploit resources. See Zhudro and Kolodkin, *Legal Aspects of Using the Sea-Bed*, p. 21.

41. Malik, Doc. No. A/AC.135/SR. 10–12, August 29, 1968.

42. Mendelevich, Doc. No. A/PV.1752, December 21, 1968.

43. S. Smirnov, "The Ocean and Law," *Izvestia,* January 8, 1970, p. 3; *SS&D,* VI (1970), 294.

under the control of its sovereign member states. Soviet jurists have commented favorably on the special fishery commissions created by multilateral and bilateral agreements and empowered to recommend appropriate measures, supervise their implementation, and enforce rules to conserve resources.

Res Nullius. While acknowledging that many publicists have considered the seabed and/or subsoil thereof to be *res nullius* and subject to ownership if effectively occupied, Soviet jurists point out that this notion originated in a period when exploitation of the seabed or its subsoil occurred close to shore on what is now the continental shelf. Such exploitation was quite exceptional and in no way interfered with the traditional uses of the seas for commerce and trade. Now that the seabed and subsoil can be exploited at great depths by all nations and congestion has become a serious threat to high seas fishing and merchant shipping, Soviet jurists believe it is no longer reasonable or feasible to differentiate between the regime of the high seas and a regime for the seabed and the subsoil thereof.[44] Consequently, the principle of *res nullius* historically applied only to the continental shelf and functionally, in the Soviet view, would be incompatible with the freedom of the seas.

The Theory of Common Use. Many Soviet jurists have concluded that the seabed and its subsoil beyond whatever may be the outer limits of the continental shelf have the same status in international law as the high seas. It follows that the seabed and subsoil thereof are open for the common use of all nations and may not be the object of a sovereign claim by any state. These jurists suggest that the question of ownership of the deep seabed and its subsoil need not be answered at the present time; just as the Geneva Conference on the Law of the Sea defined the legal status of the high seas without specifying under whose ownership or authority they were, so too should the same approach be applied to the seabed. The recognition of limited sovereign rights over the continental shelf, these jurists believe, merely constituted a specific exception to the principle of common use. Except for the right of the coastal state to explore and exploit the natural resources of the shelf, all others appertain to the entire community of states to be exercised as other freedoms of the seas.[45]

In certain respects the regime of the high seas has already been

44. Zhudro and Kolodkin, *Legal Aspects of Using the Sea-Bed,* pp. 10, 12, 17.

45. Soviet jurists also reject the distinction drawn by some publicists between the surface of the seabed, which cannot be an object of ownership, and the subsoil, which many consider to be *res nullius* and subject to occupation. See, in general, *ibid.*

extended to the seabed and its subsoil. Soviet representatives and publicists have variously mentioned in this connection the right of all states to lay submarine cables and pipelines on the bed of the high seas and the obligation of the coastal states not to impede the laying or maintenance of such cables or pipelines on its continental shelf; the right to engage in fisheries conducted by equipment embedded in the floor of the sea under circumstances specified in the Convention on Fishing and Conservation of the Living Resources of the High Seas; the right to perform scientific research on the high seas, including the deep seabed and its resources; the obligation not to pollute the high seas; and the duty to respect the generally recognized freedoms of the high seas.[46]

In August 1969, the Soviet representative on the legal subcommittee of the 42-member Committee on Peaceful Uses of the Sea-Bed and the Ocean Floor Beyond the Limits of National Jurisdiction (formerly the ad hoc committee) listed five principles which may be regarded as embodying the essence of the common use approach as conceived by the Soviet Union: (1) there is an area of seabed and ocean floor which lies beyond national jurisdiction, for which a more precise boundary is to be fixed; (2) this area is not subject to national appropriation and no state may claim or exercise sovereignty or sovereign rights over any part of the seabed or acquire property rights over any part by use, occupation, or other measures; (3) actions of states on the seabed shall be in accordance with international law, including the United Nations Charter; (4) exploration and use of the seabed shall be for the benefit and in the interests of mankind as a whole, irrespective of the geographical location of states; (5) states must bear international responsibility for their national activities on the seabed, whether carried on by the government, nongovernmental organizations, or private individuals.[47]

At this relatively early stage in the discussion of the legal status of the deep seabed and subsoil thereof, the Soviet approach is a cautious one that seeks to reconcile competing interests with minimal international regulation and favors the interests of the more developed

46. Malik, Doc. No. A/AC.135/SR. 10–12, August 29, 1968.
47. Kulazhenkov, A/AC.138/SC.1/SR. 15, August 19, 1969. In opposing the national appropriation of or claims to sovereign or property rights in the seabed, the USSR does not preclude exploitation of seabed resources. The Soviet Union, Byelorussia, and the Ukraine joined the major Western powers in voting against a General Assembly Resolution declaring that, pending the establishment of an international regime, states and juridical or physical persons must refrain from all activities of exploitation of deep seabed resources. The resolution was adopted by a vote of 62 to 28, with 28 abstentions. G. A. Res. 2574 (XXIV), January 15, 1970. *ILM,* IX (1970), 422.

countries. Yet there is a sense of national mission. Soviet international lawyers have been advised to assume the task of making a "maximal contribution to working out the regime of the seabed [and] in shaping it in accordance with the progressive legal principles of the Soviet state."[48]

48. Cheprov, "Mezhdunarodno-pravovoi rezhim morskogo dna," p. 86. Also see G. F. Kalinkin and Ia. A. Ostrovskii, *Morskoe dno: komu ono prinadlezhit?* (Moscow: izd-vo Mezhdunarodnye otnosheniia, 1970).

Chapter 7

THE LEGAL REGIME
OF THE HIGH SEAS

In most respects, the Russian approach to the legal regime of the high seas has been a corollary of its attitude toward coastal jurisdiction at sea. As a minor naval and maritime power throughout most of its history, Tsarist and Soviet Russia have been preoccupied, as we have seen, with considerations of coastal defense and with the protection of economic resources in developing a regime for territorial waters. For essentially the same reasons, Tsarist and Soviet practice and legal doctrine have emphasized the freedom of navigation as the essential principle underlying the freedom of the seas. Being heavily dependent upon foreign shipping to carry her seaborne commerce, it has been important from the Russian point of view that all states be assured equal access to and usage of the international sea lanes and that major naval powers should have minimal rights to place restraints upon or otherwise hamper the ordinary flow of international maritime commerce. The recent expansion of the merchant marine and the high seas fishery fleet has intensified Soviet opposition both to expansive coastal claims over the high seas and to practices tending to favor the right of large navies to "police" the high seas.

Soviet jurists trace Russian endorsement of the principle of freedom of the seas to 1587, when Tsar Ivan Fedorovich rejected Queen Elizabeth's request to close the White Sea to all foreign vessels but English: "The ocean-sea is God's domain; how is it possible to seize, to tame, or to close it."[1] With Peter the Great's success in securing a "window to the West" and in creating the semblance of a Russian navy, the principle of freedom of the seas became an important means of expanding the fur trade and weakening English hegemony at sea.[2]

The Russian government was among those opposed to the "right of salute," a symbol of the inequality of states with regard to the use

1. F. F. Martens (ed.), *Sobranie traktatov' i konventsii, zakliuchennykh' Rossieiu s' inostrannymi derzhavami* (St. Petersburg: Tipo. A. Benke, 1892), IX, p. lvi; *SS&D*, VI (1970), 298.
2. S. V. Molodtsov, *Mezhdunarodno-pravovoi rezhim otkrytogo moria i kontinental'nogo shel'fa* (Moscow: izd-vo Akademii nauk SSSR, 1960), p. 10.

of the sea which originated in English practice during the sixteenth century. In the Russian–Swedish Treaty of Nystad of 1721, ending the Northern War, a special clause provided that vessels of both parties should mutually salute each other and observe full equality.[3] A Russian–French treaty of 1786 abolished the salute on the high seas;[4] treaties with the Two Sicilies in 1787[5] and with Portugal in 1798[6] required their respective warships to salute a warship of the other party commanded by an officer with a higher rank. Treaties of 1801[7] and 1809[8] with Sweden provided for salutes by warships on the high seas on the basis of full equality; and a Danish–Russian Declaration on the Salute at Sea of 1829 eliminated the salute on the high seas between vessels of their respective flags.[9]

The best-known Russian effort to protect freedom of navigation on the high seas took the form of the Armed Neutralities of 1780 and 1800, which declared the right of all neutral vessels freely to navigate from port to port and along the coasts of belligerent nations without being stopped, unless there were just cause and clear evidence. All effects belonging to the subjects of the belligerent nations were free on board with the exception of contraband merchandise.[10] Seven states acceded to the declaration of 1780, while the United States, France, and Spain formally recognized its principles. When Russia became allied with England in 1793 and accepted the British prohibition on all neutral trade with French ports, the Armed Neutrality was substantially undermined. A Second Armed Neutrality declared in 1800 foundered on the defeat of the Danish fleet a year later by Lord Nelson; nevertheless, Russia had contributed to the formation of a vigorous precedent in defense of neutral rights which was destined to be strengthened throughout the nineteenth century.[11]

3. Article 19. A. A. Pazukhin (ed.), *Sbornik gramot' i dogovorov' o prisoedinenii tsarstv' i oblastei k' gosudarstvu rossiiskomu v XVII–XIX v'kakh* (Petersburg: Gosizdat, 1921), pp. 237–38; *SS&D*, VI (1970), 299.

4. Article 20. G. F. von Martens, *Recueil*, IV, 196, 207; *SS&D*, VI (1970), 302.

5. Article 10. Martens, *Recueil*, IV, 229, 234.

6. Article 16. Martens, *Recueil*, VI, 537, 547.

7. Article 22. Martens, *Recueil*, VII, 315, 327; *SS&D*, VI (1970), 302.

8. Martens, *N.R.*, I, 19, 29.

9. Martens, *Recueil N.S.*, I, 688; *SS&D*, VI (1970), 303.

10. James Brown Scott (ed.), *The Armed Neutralities of 1780 and 1800* (New York: Oxford University Press, 1918), pp. 273–74; *SS&D*, VI (1970), 299.

11. D. I. Katchenovsky, *Prize Law: Particularly With Reference to the Duties and Obligations of Belligerents and Neutrals*, trans. Frederic T. Pratt (London: Stevens & Sons, 1867), p. 74; C. John Colombos, *The International Law of the Sea* (6th ed.; London: Longmans, 1967), pp. 633–34.

The Concept of the High Seas

Until the end of the eighteenth century, all of the seas surrounding Europe were in some measure the object of proprietary rights claimed by individual states.[12] As maritime commerce expanded in the nineteenth century, the larger claims were abandoned, and it became a principle of international law that no sovereign has any territorial right over the high seas. While virtually all jurists would concur with this formulation of the principle, there continues to be disagreement with respect to defining the legal concept of the high seas.

Several theories have been advanced. Some writers, drawing upon Roman law, have suggested that the high seas belong to no one *(res nullius)*. Soviet jurists reject this notion since "a thing belonging to no one may become the property of he who seizes it, and this expressly contravenes the principle of freedom of the seas."[13] The opposite view, that the high sea is *res communis,* or the property of the community of states, was endorsed by Lisovskii[14] but rejected by other Soviet jurists because "in recognizing the sea as an object of common ownership each state would be an owner and that in itself would entail the division of common ownership and the acquisition of an individual right of ownership."[15] One consequence of *res communis* would be that any acts of state authority relating to the sea "could be exercised only with the consent of all states as a whole."[16]

Some jurists, concluding that a proprietary rationale is not appropriate to define the nature of the high seas, have stressed the spatial dimension. Westlake observed that the true foundation of the rule that the high seas is not the subject of sovereignty "is the fact that it is not capable of occupation."[17] Russian jurists found that observation unconvincing. Martens wrote in 1905 that

. . . with the modern development of naval forces and defense technology there is no doubt that broad parts of the sea and even the oceans may ac-

12. Colombos, *International Law of the Sea,* p. 48.

13. A. D. Keilin, *Sovetskoe morskoe pravo* (Moscow: izd-vo Vodnyi transport, 1954), p. 48; Molodtsov, *Mezhdunarodno-pravovoi rezhim otkrytogo moria,* pp. 83–106; A. L. Kolodkin, *Pravovoi rezhim territorial'nykh vod i otkrytogo moria* (Moscow: izd-vo Morskoi transport, 1961), p. 59.

14. V. I. Lisovskii, *Mezhdunarodnoe pravo* (Kiev: Kievskii universitet, 1955), p. 130. Lisovskii, *Mezhdunarodnoe pravo* (Moscow: izd-vo Vysshaia shkola, 1970), p. 158.

15. Keilin, *Sovetskoe morskoe pravo,* p. 48; Kolodkin, *Pravovoi rezhim territorial'nykh vod,* p. 59.

16. Keilin, *Sovetskoe morskoe pravo,* p. 48.

17. John Westlake, *International Law* (2d ed.; Cambridge: The University Press, 1910), I, p. 164.

tually be occupied by states . . . the single legal basis of freedom of the seas
. . . is the necessity to develop international trade.[18]

However, in modern Soviet jurisprudence economic necessity is said to be merely a *reason* for making the high seas available for the use of states and in itself is not the legal basis for such use.[19]

Kolodkin has distinguished between two distinct components in the concept of the high seas: (1) the location of the high seas; (2) the legal status of the high seas. In his view, the expression "high seas" is a legal category signifying that a given portion of sea expanse has not been subordinated to the sovereign authority of any state whatsoever. Consequently, the given expanse of sea is open to all "states and peoples."

On the basis of this approach, Kolodkin has criticized other theories formulated by Soviet jurists to define the legal basis of the concept of the high seas. Molodtsov, for example, is accused of confusing the spatial and legal factors in the high seas concept when he notes that the high seas are located beyond the limits of the territorial sea. The location of the high seas merely *conditions* the nature of the legal status of the high seas and is not in itself a decisive factor in determining the content of the concept. On the other hand, Keilin's conclusion that the legal regime of the high seas is determined by the "indisputable situation on the high seas of vessels being subordinate to the laws of that state whose flag the vessel flies" is said by Kolodkin, to be a *consequence* of the freedom of the seas.[20] Vereshchetin's contention that "the specific nature of the high seas eliminates the need of a legal basis for its freedom" is categorically denied.[21]

Kolodkin suggested that the concept of common and equal use should serve as the legal basis for the regime of the high seas. This concept would provide a basis for the use of the high seas by each state without discrimination or deprecation of the rights of other states, would afford a legal basis for joint international regulation of navigation and for cooperation in exploiting the resources of sea expanses, the seabed, and the subsoil, and would offer a legal basis for the joint cooperation of all states and for the categorical rejection of aggressive claims purporting to assert control over individual areas of sea.[22]

18. F. F. Martens, *Sovremennoe mezhdunarodnoe pravo tsivilizovannykh narodov'* (5th ed.; St. Petersburg: Tipo. A. Benke, 1904–5), I, p. 382; L. A. Kamarovskii and V. A. Ul'ianitskii, *Mezhdunarodnoe pravo po lektsiiam* (Moscow: Universitetskaia tipo., 1908), p. 79.

19. Kolodkin, *Pravovoi rezhim territorial'nykh vod*, p. 61.

20. *Ibid.*, pp. 58–59; also see Keilin, *Sovetskoe morskoe pravo*, p. 48.

21. V. S. Vereshchetin, *Svoboda sudokhodstva v otkrytom more* (Moscow: izd-vo IMO, 1958), pp. 20–21.

22. Kolodkin, *Pravovoi rezhim territorial'nykh vod*, p. 62.

The spatial aspect of the concept of the high seas has been a source of concern to Soviet international lawyers in a highly practical respect as well. The 1958 Geneva Convention on the High Seas defined "high seas" as all parts of the sea that are not included in the territorial sea or in the internal waters of a state. During the deliberations at the Geneva Conference on the Law of the Sea, Soviet delegates urged that this definition should contain some reference to the fact that special regulations governing navigation could be established for certain seas and straits pursuant to generally accepted international norms and specific multilateral agreements.[23] The "special regulations" to which Koretskii referred related to the closed sea doctrine, particularly to the Baltic and Black Seas.[24]

Soviet jurists interpret Article 1 of the high seas convention as *not* embracing both general principles and special norms but as being only "generally declaratory of established principles of international law," citing the phrase in the preamble of the convention:

Thus, the effect of special norms of international law or special international treaties relating to the definition of the status of specific parts of the sea are not affected by the provision of the Geneva Convention, and the establishment of a general principle or a general norm does not exclude the possibility of creating specific norms in definite specific instances when this is required by the legal needs of the state concerned.[25]

Despite the Soviet inclination to reserve the right to expand the exceptions to the regime of the high seas, the definitions of the high seas found in Soviet international legal textbooks are not uniform, and many are not even as inclusive as the definition given in the Geneva convention. The 1947 and 1951 international law textbooks contained no reference whatsoever to the spatial aspect of the high seas, defined as "expanses of oceans and seas in the common use of all states."[26] Lisovskii defined the high seas as "seas and oceans in the use of all states and not subordinate to the authority of any of them."[27] N. I. Petrenko wrote: "All water expanses beyond the limits of territorial

23. V. M. Koretskii, in United Nations Conference on the Law of the Sea, Geneva, 1958, *Official Records* (London: United Nations, 1958), IV, 32.

24. Molodtsov, *Mezhdunarodno-pravovoi rezhim otkrytogo moria*, p. 56.

25. *Ibid.*, pp. 75–76; V. M. Chkhikvadze *et al.* (eds.), *Kurs mezhdunarodnogo prava v shesti tomakh* (Moscow: izd-vo Nauka, 1967), III, 230; P. D. Barabolia *et al.*, *Voenno-morskoi mezhdunarodno-pravovoi spravochnik* (Moscow: Voenizdat, 1966), p. 89.

26. V. N. Durdenevskii and S. B. Krylov (eds.), *Mezhdunarodnoe pravo* (Moscow: Iurizdat, 1947), p. 236; E. A. Korovin (ed.), *Mezhdunarodnoe pravo* (Moscow: Gosiurizdat, 1951), p. 289.

27. V. I. Lisovskii, *Mezhdunarodnoe pravo* (2d ed.; Kiev: izd-vo Kievskii universitet, 1961), p. 159.

waters and in the common use of all states have the regime of the high seas."[28] The 1957 and 1966 international law textbooks contained an identical formulation—"The sea expanse beyond the limits of territorial waters is the high seas"—which omitted the category of internal waters.[29] Possibly the most restrictive definition is offered in the 1966 international law manual, which stated that high seas are expanses "which do not comprise either the territorial sea or the internal waters of any state."[30]

Examples of high seas mentioned in both Tsarist and Soviet international legal literature are the Atlantic, Pacific, and Indian Oceans, and the Mediterranean, North, and Caribbean Seas.[31] Conspicuously absent from these examples are any of the seas washing the coasts of the Soviet Union.

Principle of Freedom of the Seas

"The principle of freedom of the seas," wrote Vereshchetin, "is the basis of and comprises the essence of the legal regime of expanses of sea which are called the high seas."[32] Although the principle of freedom of the high seas has played a prominent role in international legal doctrine and maritime practice for centuries, it was only in 1958 that a definition of the principle was reduced to conventional form. Under Article 2 of the Convention on the High Seas, the freedom of the high seas embraces, *inter alia:* (1) freedom of navigation; (2) freedom of fishing; (3) freedom to lay submarine cables and pipelines; and (4) freedom to fly over the high seas.

Without exception, Soviet jurists endorse this statement of the principle, cautioning, however, that this list is not exhaustive and that states must refrain from actions on the high seas that would unfavorably reflect on the use of these seas by nationals of other states.[33] The latter element has been fundamental to Soviet characterizations of the freedom of the seas, particularly in the post-World War II period.

Although Soviet jurists have staunchly defended the freedom of the seas as a legal principle, they have been suspicious of its invocation

28. D. B. Levin and G. P. Kaliuzhnaia (eds.), *Mezhdunarodnoe pravo* (2d ed.; Moscow: Gosiurizdat, 1964), p. 197.

29. F. I. Kozhevnikov (ed.), *Mezhdunarodnoe pravo* (Moscow: Gosiurizdat, 1957), p. 213; F. I. Kozhevnikov, *Kurs mezhdunarodnogo prava* (2d ed.; Moscow: izd-vo IMO, 1966), p. 226.

30. Barabolia, *Voenno-morskoi spravochnik,* p. 89.

31. *Ibid.,* p. 90; N. A. Zakharov, *Kurs obshchago mezhdunarodnogo prava* (Petrograd: Veisbrut, 1917), pp. 170–71.

32. Vereshchetin, *Svoboda sudokhodstva v otkrytom more,* p. 14.

33. Kolodkin, *Pravovoi rezhim territorial'nykh vod,* p. 64. However, Soviet jurists often mention the right to conduct scientific research on the high seas.

and application by major naval powers. Keilin depicted the United States as espousing the principle of freedom of the seas at the end of World War I and again at the outbreak of World War II for the purpose "of creating favorable conditions for facilitating U.S. expansion and strengthening . . . the U.S. position in the Anglo-American maritime rivalry."[34]

Soviet treatments of freedom of the seas in the post-1945 period consist primarily of a lengthy list of "willful and coercive" actions allegedly perpetrated by vessels of the United States and other Western powers against international shipping.[35] Prominent among the incidents mentioned are: the surveillance of Soviet merchant ships by American aircraft in the Yellow Sea and the Sea of Japan in 1948;[36] the creation in 1952 of a "maritime defense zone" encompassing Korean territorial waters and portions of the high seas around Korea in which foreign vessels were subject to search;[37] the shelling of Polish merchant ships by Chinese Nationalist forces;[38] the imposition of the Cuban quarantine by the United States in 1962.[39] In this same connection, Soviet international lawyers recall Soviet participation in the Nyon Arrangement of September 14, 1937, and the Supplementary Agreement of September 17, 1937, whereby several powers cooperated to protect their merchant vessels from submarine, surface, or air attack in the Mediterranean Sea while conveying goods or passengers to Spain during the Spanish Civil War.[40] Somewhat surprisingly, but perhaps to suggest their objectivity on this issue, Soviet jurists still cite a protest made by the Soviet government to Great Britain in a Note of October 25, 1939, against British inspection of neutral merchant vessels.[41] Some publicists have gone so far as to call "any infringement on freedom of navigation . . . a very grave crime against humanity."[42]

Thus, the principle of freedom of the seas in its broadest aspect has been treated in Soviet legal media and in Soviet diplomacy as a politico-legal principle to be characterized and applied so that the

34. Keilin, *Sovetskoe morskoe pravo*, p. 49.
35. *Ibid.;* also see, in general, the works of Kolodkin, Siling, Molodtsov, and Vereshchetin.
36. Notes of protest were published in *Pravda,* February 2 and March 5, 1948; English text in *SS&D*, VI (1970), 306–7.
37. *Izvestia,* November 6, 1952, p. 1; *SS&D,* VI (1970), 308.
38. *Pravda,* October 15 and 24, 1953, p. 1.
39. A. N. Siling, *Narusheniia imperialisticheskimi gosudarstvami svobody moreplavaniia i rybolovstva v otkrytom more* (Moscow: Gosiurizdat, 1963), p. 24; *SS&D,* VI (1970), 309.
40. *SZ SSSR* (1938), no. 16, item 109; *LNTS,* CLXXXI, 135 and 149.
41. *Pravda,* October 26, 1939; English text in *SS&D,* VI (1970), 304. Keilin, *Sovetskoe morskoe pravo,* p. 55.
42. Iu. A. Andreev and I. N. Astrakhanskii, "Amerikanskie piraty na morskikh i okeanskikh putiiakh," *Morskoi sbornik,* no. 1 (1961), 10.

rights of smaller maritime powers receive maximum protection and the undue exercise of naval predominance by adversary powers is tainted by its allegedly inherent unlawfulness.

Legal Status of Vessels on the High Seas

NATIONALITY OF VESSELS

Each state prescribes the conditions and procedure for the granting of its nationality, for the right to sail under its flag, and for the registration of vessels on its territory. According to Article 5(1) of the Convention on the High Seas, a genuine link (in Russian, literally a "real connection" [*real'naia sviaz'*]) must exist between the state and the vessel. In particular, the state must effectively exercise jurisdiction and control in administrative, technical, and social matters over vessels flying its flag.

Neither Tsarist Russia nor the Soviet regime appears to have resorted to "flags of convenience," although during the American Revolutionary War the Russian government was requested by Prussia to allow the latter's merchant ships to fly a Russian flag.[43] Both Tsarist and Soviet legislation have required a substantial link for a vessel to acquire Russian nationality. Under Tsarist law, a Russian vessel had to be owned exclusively by Russian nationals, all officers had to hold Russian citizenship, and not more than 25 percent of the crew could be aliens.[44]

Under Soviet law, the right to sail under the state flag of the USSR is granted to vessels which are owned by the Soviet state, by collective farms or other Soviet cooperative and social organizations, or by Soviet nationals on condition of their respective registration in the State Ship Register or in a ship directory. Upon registration, the vessel is issued a ship's patent or card attesting to its right to sail under the state flag of the USSR. In addition, the vessel must have the other certificates specified in Soviet law or in international agreements to which the USSR is a party. Only Soviet nationals may be members of the crew of a Soviet vessel, except for certain unimportant situations.[45] The illegal display of the state flag of the USSR or of a union republic on a merchant vessel is punishable under the 1960 Criminal Code of

43. Martens, *Sovremennoe mezhdunarodnoe pravo*, II, p. 252.
44. Zakharov, *Kurs obshchago mezhdunarodnogo prava*, p. 163.
45. See Articles 22, 23, 26, 30–33, 41 of the Merchant Shipping Code of the USSR. *Vedomosti SSSR* (1968), no. 39, item 351. English translation with introduction by William E. Butler and John B. Quigley Jr., *The Merchant Shipping Code of the USSR (1968)* (Baltimore: The Johns Hopkins Press, 1970).

the RSFSR by deprivation of freedom up to one year, with or without confiscation of the vessel, and with or without a fine not exceeding the full value of the vessel.[46]

Although the Convention on the High Seas did not enumerate the factors which would constitute a genuine link, Soviet jurists ascribed positive significance to the general principle because it emphasized the necessity for states *not* to grant the right to a flag to vessels which have no basis for a change of flag or nationality. The practice of ships sailing under flags of convenience is attributed by Soviet jurists to the vicious competitive struggle among capitalist ship-owners and to a total lack of concern for the welfare of seamen.[47]

JURISDICTION OF FLAG STATE OVER ITS VESSELS

The jurisdiction which a state may exercise over vessels flying its flag on the high seas has been a source of disagreement among Soviet international lawyers. Tsarist jurists emphasized the territorial character of a vessel on the high seas, considering the vessel to be a part, or a continuation, of the territory of the state whose flag it flies.[48] Martens invoked the principle of territoriality in the *Costa Rica Packet* case, holding that Dutch authorities could not lawfully arrest and prosecute an English vessel and crew for an illegal action on the high seas.[49] This principle was rejected by Keilin as an "obvious legal fiction."[50] Nevertheless, the majority of Soviet jurists have found it convenient to say that a vessel on the high seas is the equivalent of territory, with respect to the effect of the laws and jurisdiction of the flag state on the vessel.[51]

Vereshchetin has suggested that the territorial simile is least accurate for privately owned vessels, especially when they are situated in the territorial waters of a foreign state; indeed, such a concept would endanger the sovereign rights of states. In Vereshchetin's view, the ex-

46. Article 203. Translated in Harold J. Berman and James W. Spindler, *Soviet Criminal Law and Procedure: The RSFSR Codes* (Cambridge: Harvard University Press, 1966), p. 222.
47. Molodtsov, *Mezhdunarodno-pravovoi rezhim otkrytogo moria*, p. 142.
48. Martens, *Sovremennoe mezhdunarodnoe pravo*, II, p. 247; Zakharov, *Kurs obshchago mezhdunarodnogo prava*, p. 171.
49. John Bassett Moore, *History and Digest of International Arbitrations* (Washington D.C.: GPO, 1898), V, p. 4952.
50. Keilin, *Sovetskoe morskoe pravo*, p. 118; Kolodkin has pointed out that the law applicable to hot pursuit and piracy is incompatible with the notion of a vessel as part of territory. Kolodkin, *Pravovoi rezhim territorial'nykh vod*, p. 93.
51. Durdenevskii and Krylov, *Mezhdunarodnoe pravo*, pp. 217–18; Korovin, *Mezhdunarodnoe pravo*, p. 268; Kozhevnikov, *Mezhdunarodnoe pravo*, p. 187; Molodtsov, *Mezhdunarodno-pravovoi rezhim otkrytogo moria*, pp. 160–61.

clusive authority of the flag state over its vessels derives from the equality of rights which all states enjoy on the high seas. The manifestations of any form of jurisdiction by one state over the vessels of another would infringe the rights of the latter.[52] Molodtsov, however, contended that the territorial simile appertains to vessels only while they are on the high seas; the status of the vessel changes when it enters internal or territorial waters.[53] Zhudro conceived of a vessel on the high seas as a "social formation" of the flag state, the legal nature of which is defined by the "legislation and principles" of that state.[54]

The theory of territoriality which influenced the majority of the Permanent Court of International Justice in *The Lotus* case has been criticized by Soviet jurists on both practical and legal grounds.[55] Practically speaking, it was feared that the recruitment of seamen would become more difficult if vessels and their crews were subject to criminal prosecution in foreign courts for violations of law committed while within the jurisdiction of the flag state on board its vessel. The decision was criticized on legal grounds because "each state must respect the sovereignty of another state within the territorial limits of the latter and over the actions of its nationals and juridical persons on this territory irrespective of the consequences of such actions within or beyond the territory." From this statement of what is essentially a territorial principle, Molodtsov concluded that "all events occurring on the high seas and the legal consequences of such events fall within the effect of the laws of the state whose flag the vessel flies."[56]

As a general rule, Soviet doctrine holds that vessels on the high seas are under the exclusive authority of the flag state, and the vessel, its crew, and passengers are subordinate to the laws of the state and enjoy its defense and protection. All Soviet state-owned vessels are, for legal purposes, assimilated to warships in that they are said to enjoy complete immunity from any but flag state jurisdiction. Since Soviet state vessels are state property, enforcement actions with respect to state vessels, whether military or commercial, "as well as bringing such vessels to judicial responsibility without the prior consent of the flag state, is inadmissible from the viewpoint of contemporary international law."[57]

---

52. Vereshchetin, *Svoboda sudokhodstva v otkrytom more,* p. 51.
53. Molodtsov, *Mezhdunarodno-pravovoi rezhim otkrytogo moria,* p. 161.
54. V. M. Koretskii and G. I. Tunkin (eds.), *Ocherki mezhdunarodnogo morskogo prava* (Moscow: Gosiurizdat, 1962), p. 187.
55. Manley O. Hudson (ed.), *World Court Reports* (Washington D.C.: Carnegie Endowment, 1935), II, 20.
56. Molodtsov, *Mezhdunarodno-pravovoi rezhim otkrytogo moria,* p. 145.
57. Vereshchetin, *Svoboda sudokhodstva v otkrytom more,* pp. 48, 58.

The immunity of state-owned merchant vessels has been a highly controversial subject in recent decades. Early in the twentieth century, all state vessels were granted immunity as a matter of general practice. However, as governments began to operate large merchant fleets, the continuing exception of state-owned vessels from attachment and execution while privately owned vessels remained liable to such measures seemed to many to be unfair. Since World War II, in particular, many Western countries have adopted, and international conventions have incorporated, a functional immunity test which denies immunity to state-owned vessels operated for commercial purposes.

Soviet jurists have expressed deep concern over the trend to strip away the shield of immunity from state merchant ships. The immunity of state vessels is described as "one of the oldest, established principles of international law based on the generally-accepted respect for the sovereignty of states: *par in parem non habet imperium.*"[58] Attempts to distinguish between the "public" and the "private" functions of Soviet state vessels were dismissed on the ground that "international merchant shipping is a constituent part of the economic and organizational function of the state. . . . This activity does not pursue and can not pursue private commercial purposes."[59] Moreover, any effort of a judicial agency to determine which functions of a state were exercised in public law and which in private law "would be an inadmissible interference in the domestic affairs of a foreign state," particularly when vessels are state-owned and merchant shipping is a state function.[60]

In response to the argument that immunity for state merchant vessels would be an unfair advantage, Soviet jurists have suggested that legal formulae could be worked out to protect the interests of persons having claims against state vessels while safeguarding the general principle of immunity and the inapplicability of arrest or detention to state vessels. In cases of collision at sea, Soviet steamship authorities have not been pleading the immunity of their vessels when arrested in Dutch territorial waters.[61]

Under Article 9 of the Convention on the High Seas, complete immunity from the jurisdiction of any state other than the flag state is accorded to state-owned or operated vessels only on noncommercial service. In signing the convention, the Soviet government entered a reservation to Article 9 declaring:

58. A. D. Keilin, in *1958 Official Records*, IV, 70.
59. Molodtsov, *Mezhdunarodno-pravovoi rezhim otkrytogo moria*, p. 152.
60. Keilin, *1958 Official Records*, IV, 70.
61. Z. Szirmai and J. D. Korevaar (trans.), *The Merchant Shipping Code of the Soviet Union* (Leyden: Sijthoff, 1960), p. 121.

... the principle of international law, according to which a vessel on the high seas is subject only to the jurisdiction of that state under whose flag it sails, relates without any limitations whatsoever to all state vessels.[62]

The scope of the Soviet reservation to Article 9 is not entirely clear. Vereshchetin has contended that immunity of state-owned vessels applies to every enforcement action of a foreign state, and he criticized Meshera[63] for interpreting such immunity as extending merely to the inviolability of vessels from foreign judicial process.[64]

Soviet legislation tends to support Meshera, for pursuant to Article 20 of the 1968 Merchant Shipping Code of the USSR "vessels owned by the Soviet state may not be subjected to attachment or execution without the consent of the Council of Ministers of the USSR." It has been argued, however, that the reservation of the USSR applies only to the high seas and that, by inference, Soviet merchant vessels in foreign waters are immune only from the civil jurisdiction of the coastal state.[65] This interpretation receives support from Article 77 of the 1968 Merchant Shipping Code, wherein state vessels of foreign powers enjoy immunity from attachment or execution of Soviet authorities on the basis of reciprocity. No distinction is drawn between state merchant vessels carrying commercial or noncommercial cargoes.

EXCEPTIONS FROM THE RULE OF FLAG STATE JURISDICTION

It is a general rule of international law that a vessel on the high seas may not be stopped, detained, attacked, seized, or otherwise subjected to coercive actions by any foreign vessel. Every vessel on the high seas has a duty to refrain from approaching another vessel to prevent the latter from free navigation. Soviet jurists acknowledge that international law provides for certain exceptions to the rule of exclusive flag state jurisdiction, although some would insist that state merchant vessels are not affected by such exceptions.[66]

Hot pursuit. The doctrine of hot pursuit in Soviet legislation and practice has already been discussed.[67] Soviet legislation has codified

---

62. *SDD,* XXII, 222; *SS&D,* VI (1970), 331. Express objections to the Soviet reservation were entered by the United States, the United Kingdom, and Madagascar. Israel objected in general to all reservations and declarations "incompatible with the purposes and objects" of the Convention. *UNTS,* CCCL, 164–67.

63. V. F. Meshera, *Immunitet gosudarstvennykh morskikh sudov SSSR* (Moscow–Leningrad: izd-vo Morskoi transport, 1950), p. 20.

64. Vereshchetin, *Svoboda sudokhodstva v otkrytom more,* p. 58.

65. T. K. Thommen, *Legal Status of Government Merchant Ships in International Law* (The Hague: Nijhoff, 1962), p. 44.

66. Kolodkin, *Pravovoi rezhim territorial'nykh vod,* p. 95.

67. See chapter 2, *supra.*

the provisions governing hot pursuit in Article 23 of the Convention on the High Seas.

The attitudes expressed by Soviet jurists with respect to hot pursuit are highly positive. The principle is considered to be an effective supplemental guarantee of the sovereign rights which states have on land and sea territory.[68] Soviet international lawyers stress, however, that private persons and vessels may not lawfully exercise hot pursuit.[69] The USSR also opposed extending the principle of hot pursuit to violations of the conservation zone contemplated in Article 55 of the draft articles on the regime of the high seas.[70]

Piracy. The act of piracy is commonly described as an "international crime" and the pirate himself as an enemy of the human race (*hostis humani generis*). Any state may seize a pirate ship or aircraft on the high seas or other place beyond the jurisdiction of any state, arrest the culprits, and confiscate the property on board.[71] The pirates may be tried in the courts of the state which carried out the seizure and be punished under the laws of that state.

Traditionally, the penalties for piracy have been severe. Major maritime countries have frequently applied the death penalty. Russia apparently did not regard the offense of piracy with such alarm, for the maximum penalty was fifteen years at hard labor.[72] Although some Soviet jurists defined piracy as occurring both on the high seas and as "attacks from the sea on coastal localities,"[73] Soviet law does not make piracy itself a criminal offense. Vereshchetin considered piracy to be a crime only against the freedom of the seas.[74]

The Soviet doctrine of piracy is distinctive for its exceedingly broad definition of the offense compared to the definition accepted by most states and adopted in Article 15 of the Convention on the High Seas. In the Soviet view it was anachronistic to devote eight articles of the Convention on the High Seas to piracy committed by individuals for private ends, since "in the strict sense piracy is hardly known in

68. Kolodkin, *Pravovoi rezhim territorial'nykh vod,* p. 101.
69. Molodtsov, *Mezhdunarodno-pravovoi rezhim otkrytogo moria,* p. 178.
70. Keilin, *1958 Official Records,* IV, 83; V, 133.
71. Article 19. Convention on the High Seas. *SDD,* XXII, 222; *UNTS,* CCCCL, 82.
72. A. Lokhvitskii, in T. Ortolan, *Morskoe mezhdunarodnoe pravo,* trans. A. Lokhvitskii (St. Petersburg: Tipo. Akademii nauk, 1865), p. 38.
73. Durdenevskii and Krylov, *Mezhdunarodnoe pravo,* p. 239; Korovin, *Mezhdunarodnoe pravo,* p. 292.
74. Vereshchetin, *Svoboda sudokhodstva v otkrytom more,* p. 92. There is no reference to piracy in the Fundamental Principles of Criminal Legislation of the USSR or in the criminal codes of the union republics. Presumably, an individual arrested by Soviet authorities for piracy would have to be tried for other related offenses stipulated in the codes.

modern times."[75] It is the "piracy of warships, or state piracy" which represents a "greater international danger than the piracy of private persons."[76]

Piracy has been defined in Soviet doctrine as an "unlawful act of coercion committed by a vessel or aircraft with respect to other vessels, persons, and property on the high seas or on other territory beyond the jurisdictional limits of any state." Complicity or incitement to piracy is equated to piracy itself. In support of this definition, which does not confine piracy to unlawful actions committed for private ends, it was suggested that piracy has been considered unlawful primarily because piratical actions violated the right of all states to use the high seas on an equal basis, interfered with international navigation and trade, and disturbed international intercourse. Consequently, actions in violation of the principle of freedom of the seas, irrespective of whether they were committed by private or state vessels, may be classified as piracy.[77] Since, as we have seen, Soviet doctrine and practice treat the freedom of the seas as an amorphous, highly politicized principle, the risks for other states in accepting this Soviet definition are rather great.

Vereshchetin admitted that violations by state vessels on the high seas must be significant in order to be classified as piratical, for a violation of the immunity of a state vessel on the high seas could bring serious consequences. Moreover, he recognized that it may be difficult to distinguish between a single piratical action and an act of aggression, although each can arise out of the same tense international conditions.[78] However, no guidelines were offered for making such distinctions.

The Soviet approach to the notion of state piracy has been strongly influenced by Soviet experience since 1917: "Throughout the entire history of the Soviet state, our vessels repeatedly were the objects of the piratical activities of imperialist states."[79] Examples of state piracy cited in Soviet legal media include the sinking of the *Lusitania* by a German submarine during World War I; attacks by German and Italian forces on neutral vessels from 1936 to 1939 during the Spanish Civil War; the attacks by German submarines on neutral passenger, merchant, and fishing vessels in World War II; the sinking of two So-

75. Koretskii, *1958 Official Records*, IV, 32.

76. Molodtsov, *Mezhdunarodno-pravovoi rezhim otkrytogo moria*, p. 172.

77. Vereshchetin, *Svoboda sudokhodstva v otkrytom more*, pp. 84, 93.

78. *Ibid.*, p. 92; Soviet jurists regarded the seizure of the Portuguese vessel *The Santa Maria* in 1961 as a political action and not as piracy *jure gentium*. See Chkhikvadze, *Kurs mezhdunarodnogo prava*, III, p. 254.

79. Vereshchetin, *Svoboda sudokhodstva v otkrytom more*, p. 80. Numerous examples dating from 1921 are cited.

viet vessels by Japan in 1941 and the detention of 178 Soviet merchant vessels between 1941 and 1944 by Japan; attacks by Chinese Nationalist vessels on merchant shipping in the China Seas after 1949.[80] As evidence of the recognition of the concept of state piracy in international law, Soviet jurists cite the resolutions on naval warfare adopted by the Washington Conference of 1922, providing that persons violating the rules of international law, even though acting under superior orders, could be tried for "acts of piracy" (the rules never entered into force); the Nyon Arrangement of 1937; and the order of President Roosevelt in 1940 authorizing American naval forces to fire on German submarines in order to protect American merchant shipping.

It is significant, however, that the concept of state piracy did not become prominent in Soviet international legal literature until late in 1954, when the Soviet Union placed a complaint on the agenda of the United Nations General Assembly concerning violation of the freedom of navigation in the area of the China Seas.

Following the succession to power of a Communist regime on the mainland of China in 1949, Nationalist Chinese forces based on Taiwan harassed foreign shipping destined for mainland Chinese ports. Vessels flying British, Scandinavian, Italian, Panamanian, and East European flags were among the victims. These actions led to vigorous protests and complaints by the powers affected.

On June 23, 1954, the Soviet tanker *Tuapse,* carrying a cargo of kerosene to the People's Republic of China, was seized on the high seas and brought into Taiwan. Nevertheless, as late as November 1954, these incidents were described by a Soviet jurist as violations of "freedom of navigation" and not classified as piracy.[81] However, at

80. *Ibid.;* Molodtsov, *Mezhdunarodno-pravovoi rezhim otkrytogo moria,* p. 167.

81. S. V. Molodtsov, "Nekotorye voprosy territorii v mezhdunarodnom prave," *SGIP,* no. 8 (1954), 71–72. Soviet jurists show a curious ambivalence in treating the legal aspects of blockade, both with regard to the Chinese "closure" of certain ports and later the Cuban quarantine. In June 1949, the Republic of China declared certain regions along the coast and territorial waters of the mainland to be closed to foreign vessels. The United States government was among those powers which denied the validity of the Chinese decree unless an effective blockade were maintained. The Nationalist government in reply distinguished between "closure" and "blockade," emphatically denying that a blockade of the waters in question was contemplated. At this time, Soviet shipping used Port Dairen, far to the north of the area which the Nationalist government attempted to control, and therefore was not materially affected by the closure decree. But even after the seizure of the *Tuapse* on the high seas (and consequently beyond the territorial effect of the Chinese decree), Soviet jurists did not address the question of effective blockade as had their Western counterparts. It may be that the Soviet government considered it unnecessary to become embroiled in the legal intracacies of civil war, belligerency, and blockade in the far east; yet, the slogan of "state piracy" applied to the *Tuapse* incident merely obfuscated the

the ninth session of the General Assembly in December 1954, the Soviet representative categorized the incidents as "systematic attacks" that could "only be described as acts of piracy on the high seas."[82] In 1956 a Soviet representative criticized the draft articles prepared by the International Law Commission on the regime of the high seas for restricting the concept of piracy to acts committed by private vessels or aircraft for private ends.[83]

A Soviet initiative to expand the definition of piracy to include unlawful actions by state vessels on the high seas was unsuccessful at the Geneva Conference on the Law of the Sea, as was a secondary desire to exclude any rules dealing with piracy from the convention if state piracy were not included.[84] As a result, the government of the USSR in signing the Convention on the High Seas entered the following declaration regarding Article 15:

> The definition of piracy given in the Convention does not embrace certain actions which under contemporary international law must be considered piratical and does not respond to the interests of ensuring freedom of navigation on international sea lanes.[85]

Slave trade. The Soviet Union, always a vocal opponent of the slave trade, is a party to the 1956 Supplemental Convention on Slavery.[86] Nevertheless, apprehension has been expressed in Soviet legal media over the scope of Article 22 of the Convention on the High Seas which allows a warship to board a foreign merchant vessel on the high seas if there is reasonable ground for suspecting that the vessel is engaged in the slave trade.

The right to board a suspected vessel "has never been a general norm of international law and was not even when slave trade by sea was carried out on a large scale."[87] In the past, this right of search "had given certain maritime states an opportunity to control shipping in

---

issue, and eight years later, at the time of the Cuban quarantine, Soviet jurists still had not carefully thought through the international law of blockade at sea. One wonders whether the Soviet experience with blockade during the early years of Bolshevik rule has left a permanent scar.

82. Malik, in the Ad Hoc Political Committee, 51st Mtg., United Nations General Assembly (IX), *Official Records,* p. 251. (December 13, 1954); *SS&D,* VI (1970), 333.

83. Morozov, in the Sixth Committee, United Nations General Assembly (XI), *Official Records,* p. 37 (December 3, 1956).

84. Keilin, *1958 Official Records,* IV, 79.

85. *SDD,* XXII, 222; *UNTS,* CCCCL, 82; *SS&D,* VI (1970), 335. Madagascar entered a specific objection to the Soviet declaration.

86. *SDD,* XIX, 146; *UNTS,* CCLXVI, 40.

87. Molodtsov, *Mezhdunarodno-pravovoi rezhim otkrytogo moria,* p. 176.

its own interests,"[88] and its inclusion in the Convention on the High Seas "may be used to infringe on the freedom of navigation on the high seas."[89] Examples of abuse of the right to board suspected vessels, if such have occurred, have not been mentioned in Soviet legal literature.

Performance of international agreements. The Soviet Union is a party to several international agreements which authorize foreign vessels to board and search a Soviet vessel on the high seas under certain conditions in order to verify that the Soviet vessel is acting in conformity with the provisions of the agreement. Examples of such agreements are the Convention for the Protection of Submarine Cables of 1884,[90] the Soviet–Japanese convention on fisheries in the northwest pacific of 1956,[91] and the sealing convention of 1957.[92]

On February 26, 1959, a United States naval vessel placed a boarding party on the Soviet fishing trawler *Novorossiisk* pursuant to Article 10 of the convention of 1884 in order to investigate whether that vessel may have been responsible for damaging one voice and four telegraph transatlantic cables during the previous four days. In an exchange of Notes, it was brought out that the *Novorossiisk* was alone in the immediate vicinity of the breaks on the dates in question, that the vessel possessed gear capable of causing the breaks, that the breaks in the cables were caused by tension through dragging and by man-made cuts, and that lengths of trawling cable apparently broken by a sudden strain were observed on the deck of the vessel. The Soviet government denied that the *Novorossiisk* was responsible for damaging the cable, protested the detention and inspection of the vessel, and suggested the incident was another effort to strain Soviet–American relations.[93] Only the facts were in dispute, however, and the Soviet government did not deny in principle the right of the United States naval vessel to board the *Novorossiisk* pursuant to the 1884 convention.

Verification of flag. If there is a reasonable ground for suspecting that a foreign merchant vessel on the high seas, though flying a foreign flag or refusing to show its flag, is in reality of the same nationality of a warship, the merchant vessel may be stopped and boarded by that warship in order to verify the ship's right to fly its flag. Although this

---

88. Koretskii, *1958 Official Records,* IV, 32.

89. Molodtsov, *Mezhdunarodno-pravovoi rezhim otkrytogo moria,* p. 176.

90. *SDD,* IV, 74; Charles I. Bevans (ed.), *Treaties and Other International Agreements of the United States of America 1776–1949* (Washington D.C.: GPO, 1968), I, p. 89.

91. *SDD,* XVIII, 312; *SS&D,* VI (1970), 359.

92. *SDD,* XIX, 162; *UNTS,* CCCXIV, 105.

93. The exchange of Notes is published in *DSB,* XL (1959), 556; and excerpted in *SS&D,* VI (1970), 337.

rule is included in Article 22 of the Convention on the High Seas, some Soviet jurists suggest that the rule may be applied only to privately owned merchant vessels.[94]

The exercise of this "right of approach" has been the subject of diplomatic protests by the Soviet government. On December 20, 1960, the USSR delivered a Note objecting to dangerous maneuvers allegedly carried out in the Mediterranean Sea which seriously endangered the Soviet ship *Faleshty*. In its reply of January 4, 1961, the United States denied carrying out such provocative measures or endangering the Soviet vessel: ". . . the full extent of the American vessel's action" was to establish mutual identification.[95]

Doctrine of "self-defense" on the high seas. The right of self-defense is believed by many Western jurists to constitute another exception to the general rule of the exclusive jurisdiction of a flag state over its vessels. Pursuant to this right, a state may assert a self-protective jurisdiction when its safety is threatened and arrest a foreign vessel on the high seas. The danger to its safety must be imminent and the conduct of the arrested vessel, gravely suspicious.[96]

The right of self-defense was invoked by the French government in 1958–60 to justify searching the Yugoslav vessel *Slovenia*,[97] the Czechoslovak ship *Lidice*,[98] and the Bulgarian vessels *Nikola Vaptsarov* and *Vasil Levskii*,[99] as well as West German and British vessels.

Soviet jurists are implacably opposed to the doctrine of self-defense in its maritime aspect. Keilin characterized the doctrine as an attempt "to justify willfulness and coercion by imperialist states on the high seas."[100] Vereshchetin contended that the doctrine "never found general recognition in the science and practice of international law." His basic objection to the doctrine was that it created opportunities for naval powers to act willfully on the high seas: ". . . it is a direct infringement on the sovereign rights of states over vessels sailing under its flag and a violation of freedom of navigation on the high seas."[101] Even confining the doctrine to the taking of preventive measures against a direct threat to the security of states is objectionable to Soviet

---

94. Kolodkin, *Pravovoi rezhim territorial'nykh vod,* p. 110.
95. *DSB,* xlvi (1961), 117–18; For other instances of verifications, see Marjorie M. Whiteman, *Digest of International Law* (Washington D.C.: gpo, 1965–), iv, pp. 518–22.
96. Colombos, *International Law of the Sea,* pp. 330–31.
97. *Izvestia,* January 22, 1958, p. 4.
98. *Izvestia,* April 17, 1959, p. 6.
99. Kolodkin, *Pravovoi rezhim territorial'nykh vod,* p. 112.
100. Keilin, *Sovetskoe morskoe pravo,* p. 57.
101. Vereshchetin, *Svoboda sudokhodstva v otkrytom more,* pp. 74–75.

international lawyers unless such an action would meet the requirements of Article 51 of the United Nations Charter.

Safety of Navigation on the High Seas

The Soviet Union is a party to most international agreements regulating safety of navigation on the high seas and has concluded similar multipartite agreements with other socialist countries.

The technical standards for the classification, construction, and repair of Soviet vessels are formulated and supervised by the Registry of the USSR.[102] The unification of such standards received impetus with the conclusion in 1961 of a Convention on Cooperation in Technical Supervision Over Vessels and Their Classification, which has been ratified by eight socialist countries.[103] Bilateral agreements have also been concluded by the Registry with several Western classification agencies.[104]

With regard to collisions, the Soviet Union recognized the 1910 Brussels Convention for the Purpose of Establishing Uniformity in Certain Rules Regarding Collisions of Vessels in February 1926.[105] The USSR is also party to the 1960 Regulations for the Prevention of Collisions of Vessels at Sea[106] and to the 1960 Convention for the Unification of Certain Rules Concerning Liability Arising from a Collision of Vessels of Internal Navigation.[107] Moreover, the Soviet government has ratified the 1930 Agreement on Maritime Signals[108] and the 1930 Agreement concerning Manned Lightships not on their Stations.[109]

In 1926 the USSR recognized the 1910 Brussels Convention Concerning the Establishment of Uniformity in Certain Rules Relating to Assistance at Sea and Salvage.[110] It has ratified the 1960 Convention on Safety of Life at Sea[111] and has concluded agreements with

102. Article 24. Merchant Shipping Code of the USSR. *Vedomosti SSSR* (1968), no. 39, item 351.

103. *SDD*, xxii, 479; *SS&D*, vi (1970), 348.

104. Iu. Kh. Dzhavad (ed.), *Mezhdunarodnye soglasheniia po morskomu sudokhodstvu* (2d ed.; Moscow: izd-vo Transport, 1968), pp. 64–66.

105. *SZ SSSR* (1926), ii, no. 31, item 188; English text in *AJIL Supp.*, iv (1910), 121.

106. Dzhavad, *Mezhdunarodnye soglasheniia*, p. 53.

107. *Diritto Internazionale*, xvi, no. 2 (1962), 32.

108. *SDD*, vii, 117; *LNTS*, cxxv, 95.

109. *SDD*, vii, 113; *LNTS*, cxii, 21.

110. *SZ SSSR* (1926), ii, no. 31, item 188; Bevans, *Treaties and Other International Agreements*, i, p. 780.

111. Dzhavad, *Mezhdunarodnye soglasheniia*, p. 49.

neighboring states concerning cooperation in rescue on the high seas.[112]

Finally, the Soviet Union is a party to the 1930 and 1966 Conventions on Load Line[113] and to conventions with Socialist countries suspending certain load line requirements in the Black Sea and the Baltic Sea.[114]

Prevention of Pollution on the High Seas

The Convention on the High Seas requires states to take steps to combat pollution of the seas by oil and radioactive wastes. Soviet concern with oil pollution is a relatively new development. Although the Soviet Union signed the 1954 London Convention for the Prevention of Pollution of the Sea by Oil, as amended in 1962, ratification was completed only in 1969.[115] Soviet ratification was preceded in 1968 by the enactment of very strict legislation intended to reduce large-scale pollution of the Caspian Sea and its tributaries by oil and industrial wastes.[116] The "zonal" approach to oil pollution adopted in the 1954 convention, which prohibits the discharge of oil by vessels within a specified distance of the coast, was enthusiastically endorsed by Kolodkin as "the first step toward the complete prohibition of pollution of the seas by oil."[117]

Pollution of the sea by radioactive wastes has been a problem with significant political overtones. Prior to the conclusion of the 1963 limited nuclear test ban treaty, Soviet jurists frequently branded the nuclear testing program conducted by the United States unlawful on the ground that radioactive fallout from such tests was poisoning marine life.[118] Efforts of the Soviet Union at the Geneva Conference on the Law of the Sea to include a prohibition against nuclear tests on the high seas in the Convention on the High Seas ultimately resulted only in the ambiguous obligation of Article 25(2) for states "to cooperate

112. Agreements are presently in force with the German Democratic Republic and Poland (*SDD*, XIX, 386); Bulgaria and Rumania (*UNTS*, CCLXVI, 221); North Korea (*SDD*, XIX, 377); Japan (*SDD*, XVIII, 615); Finland (*UNTS*, CCLVIII, 89); Sweden (*UNTS*, CCII, 259); and Norway (*UNTS*, CCLVII, 3).
113. Dzhavad, *Mezhdunarodnye soglasheniia*, pp. 57–60.
114. Agreement between USSR, Bulgaria, and Rumania of July 29, 1960. *SDD*, XXI, 432; *UNTS*, CCCXCII, 69, 84. Agreement between the USSR, German Democratic Republic, and Poland. *UNTS*, CCCCLXXII, 95. Each agreement is open to accession by other states respectively contiguous to the Black or Baltic Seas.
115. *Vodnyi transport,* September 23, 1969, p. 3.
116. *Izvestia,* November 14 and December 24, 1968, p. 2; *SS&D,* VI (1969/70), 197.
117. Kolodkin, *Pravovoi rezhim territorial'nykh vod,* p. 120.
118. See Keilin, *1958 Official Records,* VI, 86.

with competent international organizations in taking measures" to prevent pollution of the seas or airspace above resulting from "activities with radioactive materials or other harmful agents." Nonetheless, the loss of four hydrogen bombs by an American aircraft off the Spanish coast in January 1966 was characterized by the Soviet Government as "having created a real threat of contaminating the high seas . . . in contravention . . . of the principles of freedom of the seas . . . and in violation of the Geneva Convention on the High Seas."[119]

Soviet jurists have, in this same connection, criticized the United States and other countries for disposing of radioactive wastes from peaceful uses of atomic energy at sea in special containers: "In the USSR special methods and devices have been worked out to reprocess and bury radioactive wastes under the earth. . . . But capitalist countries do not wish to use this safe but expensive method."[120]

Nuclear Tests and Military Exercises on the High Seas

For all practical purposes, the 1963 limited nuclear test ban treaty has disposed of the issue of the legality of conducting nuclear tests on the high seas except for a few nonsignatory states (France, the People's Republic of China, etc.). Prior to 1963, however, the unlawfulness of nuclear tests on the high seas was a major theme both in Soviet international legal writing about the high seas and in Soviet diplomacy at the United Nations and the Geneva Conference on the Law of the Sea.[121]

In the Soviet view, nuclear testing on the high seas violated every freedom enumerated in Article 2 of the Convention on the High Seas.[122] Radioactive fallout poisoned or destroyed living resources of the sea, contaminated air space above the high seas, and "brought death and disease to people."[123] Testing also required the closure of large expanses of sea to international navigation; states conducting the tests were "using the high seas as part of their internal waters."[124]

Soviet jurists have also waged a campaign against using the high seas for naval training exercises, maneuvers, and tests:

The view of the high seas as a theater for military maneuvers, for tests of various kinds of military weapons, and for military actions was appropriate

119. *Pravda,* February 18, 1966, p. 2; *SS&D,* VI (1970), 353.

120. Siling, *Narusheniia,* p. 40.

121. E. A. Korovin, "U.S. Violation of the Principle of Freedom of the Seas," *International Affairs* [Moscow], no. 3 (1955), 57–65; V. M. Koretskii, "K voprosu o protivopravnosti ispytanii termoiadernogo oruzhiia v otkrytom more," *Pravovedenie,* no. 1 (1957), 100–6.

122. Koretskii, *1958 Official Records,* IV, 31.

123. Molodtsov, *Mezhdunarodno-pravovoi rezhim otkrytogo moria,* p. 36.

124. Tunkin, *1958 Official Records,* IV, 10.

in the time when war was recognized as a legal means of settling international disputes. At the present time, this view clearly contravenes the purposes and principles of the United Nations Charter and has no legal basis.[125]

A state or group of states which declare zones of the high seas to be dangerous for navigation during the conduct of maneuvers is said to be unilaterally appropriating a portion of the high seas and establishing their authority over it.[126] Examples cited by Soviet diplomats include the use by the United States of the southern portion of the Sea of Japan, the northwest Pacific, the Yellow Sea, and the Caribbean Sea for naval and air force maneuvers. The United Kingdom has been accused of interfering with international shipping during submarine maneuvers in the English Channel during 1957.[127] Joint American–Japanese exercises conducted in 1967 off Soviet coasts in the Sea of Japan were described by the Ministry of Foreign Affairs of the USSR as a "premeditated organized provocative military demonstration" in a Note of May 13, 1967.[128]

Soviet naval maneuvers on the high seas are distinguished from their Western counterparts on the ground that areas of the sea are closed only for a brief period of time and do not interfere with international navigation. However, on July 16, 1961, a Soviet gunboat reportedly detained Finnish, Swedish, French, and British vessels in the southern Baltic for nearly two hours, refusing to give reasons, while Soviet naval training operations were underway in the area.[129]

At the Geneva Conference on the Law of the Sea, the USSR joined Albania and Bulgaria in proposing an amendment to the draft Convention on the High Seas providing that "no naval or air ranges or other combat training areas limiting freedom of navigation may be designated on the high seas near foreign coasts or on international sea routes."[130] It appeared to be the proximity of naval maneuvers rather than the occurrence of exercises which troubled Soviet international lawyers most, as the formulation of the amendment suggests. The Ukrainian delegate at Geneva explained that the amendment referred not to naval training in general but to naval exercises conducted for

125. V. F. Meshera, *Morskoe pravo* (Moscow: izd-vo Morskoi transport, 1959), III, 39.
126. Siling, *Narusheniia*, p. 28.
127. Tunkin, *1958 Official Records,* IV, 10.
128. *Pravda,* May 14, 1967, p. 2; *SS&D,* VI (1970), 355.
129. Anna von Zwanenberg, "Interference with Ships on the High Seas," *International and Comparative Law Quarterly,* X (1961), 797. In April 1970 the Soviet Union held naval maneuvers simultaneously in the Atlantic, Pacific, and Indian Oceans. Also see Uwe Jenisch, *Das Recht zur Vornahme militärischer Übungen und Versuche auf Hoher See in Friedenszeiten* (Hamburg: diss., 1970).
130. Doc. A/CONF.13/C.2/L.32, March 21, 1958. *1958 Official Records,* IV, 124; *SS&D,* VI, (1970), 355.

such prolonged periods that they became tantamount to a sovereign claim over portions of the high seas.[131]

Regulation of Commercial Fishing on the High Seas

Large-scale commercial exploitation of high seas fisheries by the Soviet Union began in the mid-1950's and has continued to expand up to the present day. Soviet fishing vessels began to fish off the coast of the United States in the Bering Sea in 1959, off New England in 1961, in the Gulf of Alaska in 1962, in the Gulf of Mexico and the Caribbean in 1962–63, off Oregon and Washington in 1966, California in 1967, and Hawaii in 1968. Virtually all fishing grounds in the North Atlantic and North Pacific are being exploited by Soviet vessels, and exploratory fishing expeditions have been sent to the Indian Ocean and Latin America. The annual catch of fish by the Soviet Union has grown from 1.49 million tons live weight in 1948 to 4.98 million tons in 1965.[132]

The demand for fish in the USSR is expected to double over the level of 1957–59 by 1970. The design and construction of refrigerated fishing trawlers and large factory ships has made it possible for the Soviet Union to fish in grounds far from home at a level of efficiency for capital investment which exceeds that for domestic meat production.[133] An extensive network of fishery research institutes and organizations has pioneered in basic research and applied techniques to improve the capabilities of the Soviet fishery industry.[134]

Soviet fisheries expansion has been accompanied by greater participation in multilateral and bilateral treaties and conventions which regulate the times, conditions, and places for nations to fish—that is, they lay down ground rules for sharing an exhaustible resource and provide procedures and guidelines for settling disputes among competing nations when such disputes arise. The full extent of Soviet participation in and the successes and failures of such arrangements is a subject beyond the scope of the present inquiry; however, a brief examination of the Soviet Union's divided interests in high seas fisheries is essential to an appreciation of how fisheries influence the overall Soviet attitude toward the high seas.

On its far eastern coast, the Soviet Union has been endeavoring to exclude competitors, principally Japan, whereas in the Atlantic and

131. Pushkin, *1958 Official Records*, IV, 43.
132. Ole A. Mathisen and Donald E. Bevan, *Some International Aspects of Soviet Fisheries* (Columbus, Ohio: Ohio State University Press, 1968), pp. 19–20.
133. Francis T. Christy and Anthony Scott, *The Common Wealth in Ocean Fisheries* (Baltimore: The Johns Hopkins Press, 1965), pp. 122–23, 147.
134. Mathisen and Bevan, *Soviet Fisheries*, pp. 21–27.

Pacific Oceans the USSR is a newcomer to waters traditionally fished by other states.

Japan was effectively kept out of Soviet far eastern coastal fisheries following its defeat in World War II. The so-called "MacArthur Line," promulgated shortly after the Japanese surrender, restricted Japanese fishing to the area immediately surrounding the home islands and the Ryukyus and thence eastward into the Pacific up to the 165th median, while barring the northern waters off Soviet shores. After the signing of the Japanese peace treaty in 1951, several factors obliged Japan to increase its fishing in areas near the USSR. Among these were the 1952 Convention on High Seas Fisheries in the North Pacific, which drastically reduced the annual Japanese catch east of the 175th meridian; the proclamation of the "Rhee Line" by South Korea in 1952 to supersede the MacArthur Line; the nuclear tests in the Pacific which closed off large expanses of sea and inflicted lasting damage on marine life in the area.[135]

Soviet international lawyers interpreted these developments as deliberate attempts to force the Japanese away from the coasts of the Western powers while encouraging the depletion of Soviet fishing stocks.[136] In 1952 the Japanese fishing fleets returned to the Sea of Japan, the Okhotsk Sea, and West Kamchatkan waters, and by late 1955 Japan was rapidly approaching full exploitation of its prewar fisheries in the northern seas.

In February 1956, at a moment when Soviet–Japanese negotiations to terminate the state of war still existing between them had reached an impasse, TASS announced that the Council of Ministers of the USSR had examined the question of the reproduction and protection of far eastern salmon and concluded that "the scale of the catches of Japanese fishermen and the methods they use prevent the passage of fish to their spawning grounds and will inevitably lead in the very near future to the extinction of the far eastern salmon."[137] At about this time the seizures of Japanese fishing vessels for allegedly violating the Soviet fishing zone increased.

On March 21, 1956, the USSR Council of Ministers enacted a decree which established the so-called Bulganin Line for the purpose of protecting fishery stocks and of regulating the salmon catch on the high seas adjacent to the territorial waters of the USSR off the Siberian

135. George Ginsburgs and Scott Shrewsbury, "The Soviet-Japanese Fisheries Problem in the North-West Pacific," *International Studies,* v (1964), 268–71.

136. V. S. Mikhailov, "Mezhdunarodnoe-pravovoe regulirovanie rybolovstva i drugikh morskikh promyslov na tikhom okeane," *Sovetskii ezhegodnik mezhdunarodnogo prava 1960* (Moscow: izd-vo AN SSSR, 1961), pp. 197–99.

137. *Izvestia,* February 11, 1956, p. 1.

coast. Fishing within the prescribed area would be allowed during the spawning season only in conformity with special permits issued by Soviet authorities.[138]

The decree stipulated that these conservation restrictions were provisional and were to remain in force only until "the conclusion of an appropriate agreement with the states concerned." Japan had no recourse but to negotiate, and the result was the Soviet–Japanese fisheries convention of May 14, 1956, which regulated the exploitation of marine resources in an area far larger than that affected by the Soviet decree. The convention provided for the creation of a commission on fisheries, whose annual meetings, after extraordinarily difficult bargaining, have reached decisions on catch quotas, fishing areas, and inspection procedures.[139]

The Soviet Union, it should be added, had a legitimate concern in forcing Japan into the 1956 convention, for pelagic salmon fishing on the high seas dramatically and adversely affected the Soviet salmon catch along Kamchatka and the far eastern coast. Both the Soviet Union and the United States regard high seas fishing for salmon as wasteful because there is no way that salmon runs from a particular river can be allocated rationally once they reach the high seas, and the yield is reduced by the harvesting of fish on the high seas during their growing period. Thus, in effect, the 1956 convention recognized Japanese historical fishing rights in the area.[140]

In areas of the high seas where the Soviet Union had not previously fished, the general pattern has been that the Soviet Union has applied for membership in the relevant international bodies and has acceded to the appropriate international conventions soon after its fishing vessels penetrated the area. The Soviet Union joined the International Council for the Exploration of the Sea in 1955,[141] is a party to the Convention on Fishing in the Northeastern Atlantic Ocean,[142] and is an active member of the Northeast Atlantic Fisheries Commis-

138. *Pravda,* March 21, 1956, p. 1; *SS&D,* vi (1970), 357.
139. *SDD,* xviii, 312. The text of the convention, excerpts from the protocols of the first nine sessions of the Japanese-Soviet Northwest Pacific Fisheries Commission, the provisional rules for the work of the commission, and the Soviet-Japanese agreement regarding the procedure for transferring vessels detained or persons arrested for violations of the convention appear in A. A. Volkov (comp.), *Sbornik mezhdunarodnykh konventsii, dogovorov i soglashenii o rybolovstve i rybokhoziaistvennykh issledovaniiakh* (Moscow: izd-vo zhurnala "Rybnoe khoziaistvo," 1961), pp. 79–114; and A. A. Volkov (comp.), *Sbornik mezhdunarodnykh konventsii, dogovorov i soglashenii, kasaiushchikhsia rybolovstva i rybokhoziaistvennykh issledovanii* (Moscow: izd-vo Pishchevaia promyshlennost', 1966), pp. 9–66.
140. Mathisen and Bevan, *Soviet Fisheries,* p. 36.
141. Volkov, *Sbornik* (1961), p. 9.
142. *Ibid.,* p. 74.

sion.[143] In 1958, the same year 12 large Soviet trawlers fished off the Grand Banks for the first time, the USSR joined the International Commission for the Northwest Atlantic Fisheries.[144] In the western Pacific, a Fisheries Commission composed of the USSR, North Korea, North Vietnam, and Mainland China was formed in 1956 to coordinate oceanographic and marine research.[145] Mongolia joined in 1958, but China withdrew in 1968.[146] A Black Sea fisheries agreement of 1959 between the USSR, Bulgaria, and Rumania established a commission to recommend appropriate fishing methods, conservation measures, etc.[147]

In addition, the USSR is a party to the 1957 convention on north Pacific seals, as amended in 1963,[148] and to a 1957 agreement with Norway on sealing in the northeast Atlantic.[149]

The Soviet Union is one of the few countries still engaging in whaling and is party to the conventions and organizations regulating that activity.[150]

In the 1960's Soviet fishery operations brought the USSR into conflict with countries whose fishing interests are chiefly coastal. Notable examples are Soviet fishing operations off the coasts of the United States and Latin America. In each case, the USSR is a predatory "newcomer" and has tried to strike a balance among its incontestable right to fish on the high seas, its desire not to precipitate unilateral actions by the coastal state restricting fishing, and its desire to minimize conflict.

Consequently, the Soviet government has firmly asserted its right to fish in such areas but has concluded bilateral agreements, particularly with the United States, in which the USSR consents to reduce its catch quota and abstain from fishing certain areas or species at prescribed times in return for the right to conduct loading operations in contiguous fishery zones, to have access to ports under certain condi-

143. *Ibid.,* p. 89; *UNTS,* ccclxxxvi, 157.
144. *SDD,* xx, 519; *UNTS,* cccclxxx, 334.
145. *Izvestia,* June 13, 1956, p. 1; *SDD,* xviii, 347.
146. Kazimierz Grzybowski, *The Socialist Commonwealth of Nations* (New Haven: Yale University Press, 1962), p. 166.
147. *SDD,* xxi, 298; *UNTS,* ccclxxvii, 203. A similar commission has been created by the USSR, Poland, and the German Democratic Republic. Volkov, *Sbornik* (1966), p. 242. Bilateral commissions with Cuba, Ghana, and the United Arab Republic were established in fishery agreements. The statutes of these commissions and protocols of their meetings are collected by Volkov, *ibid.* See also *SS&D,* vi (1970), 394.
148. *SDD,* xix, 162; *UNTS,* ccccxciv, 303.
149. *SDD,* xx, 485; *UNTS,* cccix, 269.
150. *SDD,* xiii, 370; xxi, 296. Douglas M. Johnston, *The International Law of Fisheries* (New Haven: Yale University Press, 1965), pp. 396–411.

tions, and to conduct joint fishery research.[151] In claiming "traditional fishing rights" vis-à-vis coastal states, the USSR seems to have in mind not only actual fishing activity (which in most cases did not occur) but also the historical possibility of such activity.

Symptomatic of the breadth of Soviet fishing interests is the fact that not only does the Soviet government protest indiscriminate fishing off its own coast[152] but also against the detention of Soviet vessels for violating the fishing zones of the United States, Great Britain, and Ghana,[153] as well as against Argentina's excessive assertion of maritime fishery jurisdiction.[154] The wide dispersal of its fishing operations has also impelled the Soviet Union to conclude fishery assistance agreements with Cuba, Yemen, Senegal, Somalia, Bulgaria, Poland, the German Democratic Republic, Iran, Ghana, the United Arab Republic, Indonesia, and others in return for servicing, loading, port, and other privileges essential to support a high seas fishing fleet.[155]

The Soviet Union has never ratified the 1958 Geneva Convention on Fishing and Conservation of the Living Resources of the High Seas, principally because of objections to the compulsory procedure for settlement of fishery disputes provided for by Articles 9–12 of the convention and because reservations to these articles are prohibited. At the Geneva conference, however, the Soviet delegation expressed vigorous opposition to the principle of abstention, "according to which a group of States could announce that a certain species was being exhausted and in that way deprive other States of the right to fish that species. . . ." As a newcomer to high seas fishing, the USSR stressed that "the world was in a dynamic state of development, increasing numbers of new independent states were being formed, and the principle of abstention should not be used to prevent them from cooperating in the exploitation of the high seas."[156]

Soviet delegates were dubious that utilization was truly responsible for reductions in fishery stocks and, in any event, urged that measures to limit the fishing of stocks exploited by more than one state be developed and jointly applied by all the states concerned.[157] In general, the USSR would acknowledge the right of a coastal state to enact unilateral conservation measures only when that state was both

151. *ILM,* viii (1969), 502–15.
152. *Commercial Fisheries Review,* xxix, no. 10 (1967), 38.
153. *Ibid.,* no. 7 (1967), 18–19.
154. *ILM,* viii (1969), 896; *SS&D,* vi (1969), 45.
155. The texts of several such agreements are published in Volkov, *Sbornik* (1966), pp. 207–213; *SS&D,* vi (1970), 377–99.
156. Krylov, *1958 Official Records,* v, 8.
157. Izhevsky, *ibid.,* v, 104.

fishing the stock and had made efforts and sacrifices to increase the reserves of the stock while other states simply exploited the stock without any regard for conservation.[158] This, no doubt, was the manner in which the Soviet Union viewed its unilateral decree of March 21, 1956, against Japanese salmon fishing.

The principle of abstention was eventually rejected by the plenary session of the Geneva conference.[159]

Although the comparatively recent entry of the Soviet Union into the ranks of major fishing powers has already had a significant impact upon world fishery production, the development of fishery technology, the acquisition of marine biological data, the growth of fishing fleets and the congestion of certain fishing grounds, and other aspects of fisheries, the Soviet Union has had little perceptible effect upon the international law of fisheries. Except for the dispute settlement procedure in the Convention on Fishing and Conservation of the Living Resources of the High Seas, the Soviet government has been able to accept without change the constitutional and conventional structures of the various international organizations, commissions, and treaties regulating fishing.

One must hasten to add that international fishery arrangements have not, as yet, placed onerous burdens on their participants. Catch quotas are negotiated by all members, and, although the efficiency of fishing gear is limited in order to protect immature fish stocks, there are virtually no obstacles, except economic, to an expanded fleet or greater efforts or to shifting fishing emphasis from species to species. The general scheme of national enforcement of these conventions and of nationally directed research into fishery problems is wholly compatible with Soviet preferences in such matters. As an example of Soviet cooperation on the international level and as an example of Soviet observance of international obligations, the fisheries industry is probably without peer. It would not be unreasonable to speculate that Soviet fishery interests will eventually find the dispute settlement procedures of the Convention on Living Resources of the High Seas acceptable.

Right to Lay Submarine Cables

The basic provisions of international law governing submarine cables under the high seas are embodied in the 1884 convention for the protection of submarine cables. The Soviet Union acceded to that

158. Krylov, *ibid.,* v, 58.
159. A. Savel'ev, "Mezhdunarodnaia konferentsiia po morskomu pravu," *Morskoi flot,* no. 8 (1958), 25.

convention in 1926.[160] The 1958 Convention on the High Seas devoted three articles to submarine cables in order to ensure that states would enact legislation to protect submarine cables, pipelines, or power lines from damage and to ensure the payment of compensation for any losses inflicted and the costs of repairs.[161]

Article 205 of the 1960 Criminal Code of the RSFSR provides that the negligent damaging of a marine telegraph cable, if it has resulted or could result in an interruption of telegraph communication, may be punished by the imposition of correctional tasks for a term not exceeding 3 months or by a fine not exceeding 100 rubles.[162] Although the Criminal Code does not contain special provisions on the protection of marine telegraph cables, the intentional destruction of such a cable would be classified as the intentional destruction or damaging of state property under Article 98 of the code, or, if committed by a Soviet official, under Chapter VII of the code, which deals with official crimes.[163]

There are no special provisions in Soviet legislation relating to the damaging of submarine pipelines.

Pacific Blockade

Pacific blockade originated as a form of reprisal in the nineteenth century and was frequently applied by the major powers against smaller states. Russia participated in the first significant use of pacific blockade in 1827, when Britain, France, and Russia blockaded Turkish coasts to compel the Porte to accept their program for the independence of Greece. In 1886 Greece was again blockaded by Russia

160. *SZ SSSR* (1926), II, no. 31, item 190.
161. Keilin, *1958 Official Records*, IV, 89.
162. Berman and Spindler, *Soviet Criminal Law and Procedure*, p. 223.
163. B. S. Nikiforov (ed.), *Nauchno-prakticheskii kommentarii ugolovnogo kodeksa RSFSR* (Moscow: Gosiurizdat, 1963), p. 440. In 1969 the USSR established special zones at sea for the protection of submarine cables within Soviet territorial waters and issued instructions concerning the navigation of all vessels near such zones. Masters of either Soviet or foreign vessels are subject to criminal prosecution for violation of the instructions. See *IM* (1970), no. 18. On October 17, 1969, the following article was added to the Criminal Code of the RSFSR:

> *Article 205–1. Violation of rules for protection of communication lines.* The violation of rules for the protection of communication lines, causing damage to a cable line of intercity communication and resulting in an interruption of communication, shall be punished by deprivation of freedom for a term not exceeding one year or by correctional tasks for the same term or by a fine not exceeding two hundred rubles.

Vedomosti RSFSR (1969), no. 43, item 1291.

and other powers, as was Crete in 1897. The majority of Russian international lawyers, including Martens and Kamarovskii, did not support the concept of pacific blockade.[164]

Prior to the imposition of the Cuban "quarantine" by the United States in October 1962, Soviet jurists treated the notion of pacific blockade descriptively, as a form of reprisal, "which does not conceal the dictate of capitalist states with respect to small states, since it can only be effective with regard to the latter."[165] Lisovskii seemed to be even less critical of pacific blockade in the second edition of his international law textbook issued in 1961.[166] Thus, the Cuban quarantine found the Soviet international legal community without a firmly established position on the question of pacific blockade.

Soviet jurists immediately rejected as artificial any distinction between a quarantine and a blockade: "The American Government . . . established in peacetime an actual blockade of Cuban coasts."[167] Nevertheless, Soviet representatives in the United Nations Security Council presented a legal case for the Soviet position only in very general terms of "piratical" actions in derogation of international law and of the United Nations Charter.

In an article published in December 1962, slightly more than a month after the quarantine was lifted, Korovin argued that the blockade violated the freedoms of the seas enumerated in Article 2 of the Convention on the High Seas and several provisions of the United Nations Charter, to wit: the obligations "to live together in peace with one another as good neighbors" (preamble); "to settle international disputes by peaceful means" (Article 2[3]); to respect the principle of equal rights and self-determination of peoples and to take appropriate measures to strengthen international peace (Article 1[2]); to be guided by the principle of "sovereign equality of all its members" (Article 2[1]). Korovin further contended that the quarantine was an unlawful threat or use of force in contravention of Article 2(4) of the charter in a matter "essentially within the domestic jurisdictions" of Cuba and the Soviet Union (Article 2[7]). Responsibility for these alleged violations was not placed on the president of the United States, but on the pentagon and "U.S. militarists and their accomplices."[168]

In a more substantive legal analysis of the quarantine, A. L.

164. Martens, *Sovremennoe mezhdunarodnoe pravo*, II, p. 512.
165. Korovin, *Mezhdunarodnoe pravo*, p. 500.
166. Lisovskii, *Mezhdunarodnoe pravo* (2d ed.), p. 405.
167. A. D. Keilin, "Aktual'nye voprosy sovremennogo mezhdunarodnogo morskogo i rechnogo prava," *Sovetskii ezhegodnik mezhdunarodnogo prava 1962* (Moscow: izd-vo Nauka, 1963), pp. 108–9.
168. E. A. Korovin, "International Law Through the Pentagon's Prism," *International Affairs* [Moscow], no. 12 (1962), 3–7.

Kolodkin criticized the general use of pacific blockade as a reprisal wholly incompatible with the United Nations Charter, unless invoked by the United Nations itself in pursuance of Articles 39, 41, and 42, by an individual state for the purpose of self-defense during wartime, or in the event of an armed attack upon a United Nations member within Article 51 of the charter. Applying these principles to the Cuban quarantine, Kolodkin concluded that it "openly violated the United Nations Charter"; force was applied despite the injunction of Article 2(4) and the peaceful settlement obligation of Article 2(3). Article 51 was alleged to have been breached because compulsory measures were taken in the absence of an armed attack, and Article 53 because compulsory measures were taken pursuant to a regional arrangement without the necessary authorization of the Security Council. In addition, Kolodkin alleged that the principle of sovereignty in Article 1 of the Inter–American Treaty of Reciprocal Assistance and Articles 1, 15, 16, and 102 of the Charter of the Organization of American States were violated. Consequently, the Cuban quarantine was an aggressive act on the high seas against Cuba and "third countries."[169]

Lisovskii had written in 1961 that in the event of a pacific blockade:

... a vessel of a third state (with regard to the given conflict) does not have a right of passage to the blockaded coast. Thus, for example, if one state blockades the coast of another, then a vessel belonging to a third state does not have a right to pass through to the blockaded coast of this state.[170]

This statement was interpreted by Kolodkin to mean that a Soviet jurist had supported the view that the vessel of a third state may not even approach the blockaded area: "the legality of detaining vessels of third states is proclaimed under pacific blockade."[171] In rejecting Lisovskii's view as unsound, Kolodkin had to resort exclusively to Western international law treatises to prove that the weight of opinion supported the rights of third states. Siling has since characterized pacific blockade as "aggression."[172]

One can only speculate whether the existence of a firm Soviet view opposing the legality of pacific blockade prior to 1962 could have stiffened Soviet resistance to the Cuban quarantine. The lack of a well-defined position may have made it easier to accede to American pressures during the crisis.

169. A. L. Kolodkin, "Morskaia blokada i sovremennoe mezhdunarodnoe pravo," *SGIP*, no. 4 (1963), 92–103.
170. Lisovskii, *Mezhdunarodnoe pravo* (2d ed.), p. 405.
171. Kolodkin, "Morskaia blokada," p. 96.
172. Siling, *Narusheniia*, p. 25.

CONCLUSION

Broadly speaking, the development of Soviet attitudes toward the international law of the sea falls into three distinct periods; we may be on the verge of yet a fourth.

From the October revolution of 1917 until about 1948, neither the Soviet doctrine nor practice of public maritime law departed fundamentally from that of nonsocialist states. Even though Soviet foreign policy and the status of Soviet Russia in the international system had changed drastically from that of Tsarist Russia, the common thread of vulnerable sea frontiers and naval weakness made prerevolutionary theory and practice of maritime law appropriate, in the eyes of the Bolshevik leadership, for a revolutionary government. Soviet legislation concerning coastal jurisdiction was modeled expressly on Tsarist laws and asserted the same pattern and kinds of claims to authority. Particularly noteworthy was the decision of the Soviet government to follow the Tsarist practice of distinguishing sharply the regulation of fisheries in the far east from the creation of an exclusive fishery zone along the northern Arctic coast. The Soviet government also preserved the requirement found in Tsarist legislation that not more than three foreign warships may simultaneously visit Soviet ports in the absence of special permission. State monopolization of the coasting trade also was a feature of Tsarist law.

In diplomatic correspondence and at international conferences the Soviet government espoused the position of its predecessors in denying the existence of a rule of international law fixing the breadth of territorial waters. However, in practice the Soviet government conformed to the policies of other states by creating contiguous zones of varying breadths for the purpose of exercising limited coastal jurisdiction. Even the most controversial of these claims, the 12-mile fishery zone, was ameliorated through international agreements and concession contracts with those states adversely affected.

Customary international law of the sea was accepted in large measure by the Soviet government, even though custom theoretically was anathema to a Marxist approach to international law. The right of innocent passage for all vessels was recognized in theory and practice, and the Soviet government repeatedly invoked international custom when objecting to unauthorized visits of foreign warships to Soviet ports. Nor was the Soviet attitude toward the regime of the high seas especially distinctive during this period.

These attitudes toward the law of the sea were generally compatible with, and doubtless a product of, Soviet foreign and maritime policy during this era. Dependent upon foreign shipping to carry seaborne trade, possessing modest naval forces suitable at best for coastal defense, and striving to attain diplomatic recognition, expanded foreign trade, and greater international acceptance, the Soviet government was neither disposed nor in a position to challenge effectively the public order of the oceans.

As East-West relations worsened after 1946, Soviet attitudes toward the law of the sea were significantly transformed. Exercising the perogatives of a great power, the USSR began to enforce vigorously its 12-mile fishing zone against the Scandinavian countries and Japan. It became exceedingly hard to extract concessions by treaty to fish up to within 3 miles of the Soviet coast. In international forums the Soviet government continued to insist that international law did not establish a maximum limit for coastal jurisdiction at sea.

It is especially noteworthy that the hardening of Soviet attitudes occurred within the general framework of legislation and practice dating from the interwar period. This pattern remained more or less constant until 1960, so that with the exception of fishery jurisdiction Soviet maritime practice continued essentially unchanged during the first 43 years of Soviet statehood.

Soviet international legal doctrine regarding the law of the sea was quite another matter. As a land power possessing no merchant, fishing, or naval fleets of consequence, the immense sea frontier of the USSR seemed especially vulnerable and the prevailing law of the sea especially charitable to powerful naval adversaries. Commencing in 1948, Soviet diplomats and jurists—without exception and in striking contrast to legal doctrine of the prewar period—sought to create a legal basis for broad claims over coastal waters and expanded jurisdiction on the high seas.

Those Soviet jurists who prior to 1940 had interpreted Soviet legislation as creating contiguous zones were criticized for their harmful and mistaken views. It was now insisted that the USSR had always claimed a 12-mile limit, supposedly fixed by Tsarist Russia in 1909. Some jurists went so far as to question the existence in international law of a "right" of innocent passage. Stimulated in part by references in Soviet diplomatic correspondence, the historic waters and closed sea doctrines were introduced into Soviet doctrine. With regard to the high seas, the principle of freedom of the seas was redefined in a manner more favorable to Soviet interests, and the concept of state piracy was militantly defended in legal media.

Each of these theories was a substantive departure from customary international law and from previous Soviet attitudes; all reflected an obsession with encirclement and national security. However, the strenuous efforts of the Soviet delegation to the Conferences of the Law of the Sea to incorporate these ideas in the four conventions adopted by the 1958 conference were unsuccessful. The postwar period culminated in 1960, when the Soviet Union ratified three of the four Geneva conventions and enacted legislation implementing their provisions. In certain instances where the conferences were unable to achieve a consensus (breadth of territorial waters, innocent passage for warships), the Soviet government felt justified in acting unilaterally to protect its position.

The importance of postwar Soviet doctrinal innovations in the law of the sea lies not only in their substance and in the reasons for which they were advanced. The style of seeking change in legal norms also was characteristic of the Soviet system. One must suppose that in the late 1940's a decision was made in high party and government circles to develop a concerted campaign in support of expanded coastal sovereignty over adjacent waters. In fulfilling this task, Soviet international lawyers resorted to a technique commonly used in Communist political dialogue: they reinterpreted Soviet legislation and practice and argued that the traditional rules were not binding because they had not been recognized by the USSR. Since Tsarist and Soviet Russia were on record as having favored the kind of change which Soviet jurists said had already been accomplished, it was easy for Western observers to confuse the advocacy of a change in policy with the adoption of such change by the Soviet government. Thus, Soviet international legal doctrine is often more important for insights into contemporary policy trends or preferences than as a reliable guide to modern state practice.

It is impossible to know at this point whether the 1960's should be looked upon as a distinct period of transition in Soviet maritime law or as part of a longer era whose end is still undetermined. Shortly after enacting a 12-mile limit into law, thereby achieving an objective long sought by Russian governments, the Soviet Union began to re-examine its postwar attitudes toward the law of the sea. To be sure, there will be no retreat from the 12-mile limit; however, as the Soviet Union recognized the legal implications of its newly attained status of major maritime power, changes in doctrine and practice became perceptible.

The decision to acquire a large merchant fleet has been accompanied by greater Soviet acceptance of Western merchant shipping law, as illustrated by the recently enacted 1968 Merchant Shipping Code of the USSR. A more dramatic manifestation has been the legal consequences of the shift in Soviet focus from coastal security to the efficient acquisition of high-protein food supply from the sea at a lower cost than land-raised meat. The Soviet high seas fishing fleet is one of the world's largest and most sophisticated, and its foraging activities have encouraged an expansionist attitude toward the sea comparable in many respects to that of other leading technological powers. On questions of fishery policy, the USSR has become more internationally minded. Claims of less advanced powers to fishery jurisdiction beyond 12 miles have been protested as illegal by the Soviet government. One can reasonably anticipate that the Soviet approach to fisheries will increasingly be dominated by functionally oriented, rational policy considerations.

The growth of the Soviet navy has also contributed to the transition from the protective, security-oriented maritime jurisprudence of the postwar era to a greater interest in freedom of navigation on the high seas. The Soviet attitude toward the archipelago theory, for example, has shifted from lukewarm approval to thinly veiled disapproval. Soviet jurists have revised their previous view that a state may fix the limits of its territorial waters in accordance with its historical, economic, or security interests by stipulating a maximum breadth of 12 miles. The right of innocent passage for merchant and fishing vessels has been reaffirmed in law and practice. The closed sea doctrine shows signs of being abandoned or at least diluted to a less restrictive notion, and the list of Soviet historic waters has been significantly abbreviated. At the United Nations, Soviet diplomats have opposed expansive claims to the continental shelf or deep seabed, while insisting upon adequate guarantees for observance of the freedoms of the seas.

It is difficult to identify a distinctively Marxist–Leninist ideological approach to the substantive issues of the law of the sea examined in this study. Soviet legislation and state practice have differed from that of other states only in minor detail. On the whole, Soviet practice reveals a pattern of realistic, rather traditional, often sensitive appraisals of the existing state of international law by Soviet authorities. The "zonal" approach to coastal jurisdiction, the assertion of fishery jurisdiction in the prerevolutionary model, the exercise of civil and criminal jurisdiction, and the restraint in making or recognizing claims to the continental shelf were all undertaken in a cautious, nonideological manner. Enforcement of Soviet maritime legislation, at least in form, has been carefully based upon statutory language. Diplomatic notes of the Soviet government alleging violations of state frontiers either invoked the language of legislation in force or were studiously vague about asserting claims inconsistent with such legislation.

Thus, when the doctrinal writings of Soviet jurists are placed in proper perspective, differences between "socialist" and "bourgeois" approaches to the law of the sea do not appear to be inherently incapable of resolution. Whether the international community is capable of reconciling other competing economic, military, political, and technological interests, more tangible and divisive in nature, remains for the future.

SELECTED BIBLIOGRAPHY

Akty istoricheskie, sobrannye i izdannye arkheograficheskoiu kommissieiu. 5 vols. St. Petersburg, 1841.

Aleksandrov, B. A. "Pravo rybolovstva v territorial'nykh vodakh v zakonodatel'stvo i mezhdunarodnykh dogovorakh soiuza SSR," *Mezhdunarodnaia zhizn'*, No. 9–10 (1928), 94–99.

Alekseev, A. "Important Initiative for Disarmament," *International Affairs* [Moscow], No. 9 (1968), 7–11.

Alexander, Lewis M. (ed.). *The Law of the Sea: Offshore Boundaries and Zones.* Columbus, Ohio: Ohio State University Press, 1967.

Andreev, Iu. A., and Astrakhanskii, I. N. "Amerikanskie piraty na morskikh i okeanskikh putiiakh," *Morskoi sbornik*, No. 1 (1961), 10–16.

Armstrong, Terence. *The Northern Sea Route: Soviet Exploitation of the North East Passage.* New York: n.p., 1952.

Bakhov, A. S. (ed.). *Voenno-morskoi mezhdunarodno-pravovoi spravochnik.* Moscow: Voengiz, 1956.

Barabolia, P. D. *et al. Voenno-morskoi mezhdunarodno-pravovoi spravochnik.* Moscow: Voenizdat, 1966.

Barabolia, P. D., and Lesnikov, N. D. "Novoe polozhenie ob okhrane gosudarstvennoi granitsy soiuza SSR," *Morskoi sbornik,* No. 2 (1961), 11–19.

Barabolia, P. D., and Tsyganov, V. T. "Territorial'nye vody pribrezhnykh gosudarstv," *Morskoi sbornik,* No. 8 (1966), 69–73.

Barnes, Kathleen. "Fisheries: Mainstay of Soviet-Japanese Friction," *Far Eastern Survey,* IX (1940), 75–80.

Barov, P. D. "Razgranichenie morskikh vod i kontinental'nogo shel'fa v finskom zalive," *Morskoi sbornik,* No. 8 (1966), 79–80.

Belli, V. A. (ed.). *Voenno-morskoi mezhdunarodno-pravovoi spravochnik.* 2 vols. Moscow-Leningrad: izd-vo NKVMF, 1939–40.

Berman, Harold J. *Justice in the U.S.S.R.* Rev. ed. Cambridge: Harvard University Press, 1966.

Berman, Harold J., and Spindler, James W. (trans.). *Soviet Criminal Law and Procedure: The RSFSR Codes.* Introduction by Harold J. Berman. Cambridge: Harvard University Press, 1966.

Bernfeld, Seymour S. "Developing the Resources of the Sea—Security of Investment," *The International Lawyer,* II (1967), 67–76.

Bevans, Charles I. (ed.). *Treaties and Other International Agreements of the United States of America 1776–1949.* Washington D.C.: Government Printing Office, 1968–.

Bilmanis, Alfred. *The Baltic States and the Problem of Freedom of the Baltic Sea.* Washington D.C.: The Latvian Legation, 1943.

Böhmert, Viktor. "Die russische Fischereigrenze," *Zeitschrift für Volkerrecht,* XXI (1937), 441–96; XXII (1938), 257–306.

Borgstrom, Georg. "The Atlantic Fisheries of the U.S.S.R.," *Atlantic Ocean Fisheries,* ed. Georg Borgstrom and Arthur J. Heighway. London: Fishing News Ltd., 1961, pp. 282–315.

Borisov, S. "Mezhdunarodnyi sud o territorial'nykh vodakh," *Sovetskoe gosudarstvo i pravo,* No. 8 (1952), 52–54.

Bouchez, Leo J. *The Regime of Bays in International Law.* Leyden: Sijthoff, 1964.

Brock, John R. "Archipelago Concepts of Limits of Territorial Seas," *Naval War College Review,* XIX, No. 4 (1966), 34–97.

Burke, William T. *International Legal Problems of Scientific Research in the Oceans.* Washington D.C.: National Council on Marine Resources and Engineering Development, 1967.

Butler, William E. "American Research on Soviet Approaches to International Law," *Columbia Law Review,* LXX (1970), 218–35.

———. (trans. & ed.). *Customs Code of the USSR.* Washington D.C.: Hazen Publications, 1966.

———. "Foreign Fishing in Soviet Waters," *Commercial Fisheries Review,* XXX, No. 11 (1968), 33–36.

———. "The Harvard Text of the Zinov'ev Letter," *Harvard Library Bulletin,* XVIII (1970), 43–62.

———. *The Law of Soviet Territorial Waters: A Case Study of Maritime Legislation and Practice.* New York: Frederick A. Praeger, 1967.

———. "The Legal Regime of Russian Territorial Waters," *American Journal of International Law,* LXII (1968), 51–77.

———. "Recent Developments in Soviet Maritime Law," *The International Lawyer,* IV (1970), 695–708.

———. "The Soviet Association of Maritime Law," *Journal of Maritime Law and Commerce,* I (1970), 313–15.

———. "Soviet Concepts of Innocent Passage," *Harvard International Law Journal,* VII (1965), 113–30.

———. (ed. & trans.). "Soviet Maritime Law," *Soviet Statutes and Decisions,* VI (1969/70), 1–415.

———. "Soviet Territorial Waters," *World Affairs,* CXXX (1967), 17–25.

———. "The Soviet Union and the Continental Shelf," *American Journal of International Law,* LXIII (1969), 103–107.

Butler, William E., and Quigley, John B. "Apropos the 1968 Soviet Maritime Code," *San Diego Law Review,* VI (1969), 412–27.

———. (trans. & ed.). *The Merchant Shipping Code of the USSR (1968).* Baltimore: The Johns Hopkins Press, 1970.

Carusi, C. F., and Kojouharoff, C. D. "The First Armed Neutrality," *National University Law Review,* IX, No. 1 (1929), 1–69.

Cheprov, I. I. "Mezhdunarodno-pravovoi rezhim morskogo dna," *Sovetskoe gosudarstvo i pravo,* No. 10 (1968), 80–86.

————. *Novye problemy mezhdunarodnogo prava.* Moscow: izd-vo Mezhdunarodnye otnosheniia, 1969.

Chkhikvadze, V. M. *et al.* (eds.). *Kurs mezhdunarodnogo prava v shesti tomakh.* 6 vols. Moscow: izd-vo Nauka, 1967–.

Christy, Francis T. "A Social Scientist Writes on Economic Criteria for Rules Governing Exploitation of Deep Sea Minerals," *The International Lawyer,* II (1968), 224–42.

Christy, Francis T., and Scott, Anthony. *The Common Wealth in Ocean Fisheries.* Baltimore: The Johns Hopkins Press, 1965.

Colombos, C. John. *The International Law of the Sea.* 6th ed. London: Longmans, 1967.

Cooper, Dennis A. *The Air Code of the U.S.S.R.* Charlottesville: Michie Company, 1966.

Corbett, Percy E. *Law and Society in the Relations of States.* New York: Harcourt, Brace & Co., 1951.

Cowen, R. *Frontiers of the Sea.* Garden City, N.Y.: Random House, 1961.

Creamer, Robert A. "Title to the Deep Seabed: Prospects for the Future," *Harvard International Law Journal,* IX (1968), 205–31.

Crocker, Henry G. *The Extent of the Marginal Sea.* Washington D.C.: Government Printing Office, 1919.

Davydov, A. P. "Mezhdunarodno-pravovoe regulirovanie rybolovstva v otkrytom more," *Morskoe pravo i praktika: sbornik materialov,* XXXI (1966), 3–10.

Dean, Arthur. "The Geneva Conference on the Law of the Sea: What Was Accomplished," *American Journal of International Law,* LII (1958), 611.

Dokumenty vneshnei politiki SSSR. Moscow: Gospolitizdat, 1957–.

Dranov, B. A. *Chernomorskie prolivy: mezhdunarodno-pravovoi rezhim.* Moscow: Iurizdat, 1948.

Durdenevskii, V. N., and Krylov, S. B. (eds.). *Mezhdunarodnoe pravo.* Moscow: Iurizdat Ministerstva iustitsii SSSR, 1947.

Durdenevskii, V. N., and Vereshchetin, V. S. "Frantsuzskii mezhdunarodnik o sovetskoi kontseptsii morskogo prava," *Sovetskoe gosudarstvo i pravo,* No. 10 (1960), 134–35.

Dzhavad, Iu. Kh. (ed.). *Mezhdunarodnye soglasheniia po morskomu sudokhodstvu.* 2d ed. Moscow: izd-vo Transport, 1968.

Egor'ev, V. V. "Gaagskaia konferentsiia po territorial'nym vodam," *Morskoi sbornik,* No. 7 (1930), 80–91.

Egor'ev, V. V. *et al. Zakonodatel'stvo i mezhdunarodnye dogovory Soiuza SSR i soiuznykh respublik o pravovom polozhenii inostrannykh fizicheskikh i iuridicheskikh lits.* Moscow: Iurizdat NKIU RSFSR, 1926.

Egorov, K. F., and Shmigel'skii, G. L. *Pravovye voprosy okazaniia pomoshchi i spasaniia na more.* Moscow: izd-vo Morskoi transport, 1961.

Eikhel'man, O. O. *Khrestomatiia russkago mezhdunarodnago prava.* 2 vols. Kiev: St. Vladimir University, 1887–89.

————. *Zametki iz lektsii po mezhdunarodnomu pravu.* Kiev: Tipo. zavadskago, 1889.

Ely, Northcutt. "American Policy Options in the Development of Undersea Mineral Resources," *The International Lawyer,* II (1968), 215–23.

Fulton, Thomas W. *The Sovereignty of the Sea.* Edinburgh: Wm. Blackwood & Sons, 1911.

Gidel, Gilbert. *Le Droit Public de la Mer.* 3 vols. Paris: Recueil Sirey, 1932–34.

Ginsburgs, George, and Shrewsbury, Scott. "The Postwar Soviet-Japanese Fisheries Problem in the North-West Pacific," *Orbis,* VII (1963), 596–616.

————. "The Soviet-Japanese Fisheries Problem in the North-West Pacific," *International Studies,* V (1964), 259–80.

Glaser, E. "International Cooperation for the Exploitation for Peaceful Purposes of the Natural Resources of the Sea-Bed and the Ocean Floor, and the Subsoil Thereof," *Revue Roumaine d'Etudes Internationales,* No. 3–4 (1968), 57–87.

Glenn, Gene. "The Swedish-Soviet Territorial Sea Controversy in the Baltic," *American Journal of International Law,* L (1956), 942–49.

Golder, F. A. *Russian Expansion on the Pacific 1641–1850.* Cleveland, Ohio: Arthur H. Clark Co., 1914.

Golubev, V. P. "Sovremennoe opredelenie territorial'nago moria," *Iuridicheskii vestnik,* Nos. 3–4 (1914), 35–48.

Goriainov', S. *Bosfor' i dardanelly.* St. Petersburg: Tipo. Skorokhodov, 1907.

Gorovtsev', A. M. *Slovar' kratkoi entsiklopedii mezhdunarodnogo prava.* St. Petersburg: Tipo. Trenke i Friuso, 1909.

Grabar, V. E. "Beregovoe more," *Novyi entsiklopedicheskii slovar'.* St. Petersburg: Brokganz & Efron, [1916].

————. *Materialy k istorii literatury mezhdunarodnogo prava v Rossii (1647–1917).* Moscow: izd-vo Akademii nauk SSSR, 1958.

Gray, Whitmore, and Stults, Raymond. (trans.). *Soviet Civil Legislation.* Ann Arbor: University of Michigan Law School, 1965.

Grzybowski, Kazimierz. *The Socialist Commonwealth of Nations.* New Haven: Yale University Press, 1962.

————. "The Soviet Doctrine of Mare Clausum and Politics in Black and Baltic Seas," *Journal of Central European Affairs,* XIV (1955), 339–53.

————. *Soviet Public International Law: Doctrines and Diplomatic Practice.* Leyden: Sijthoff, 1970.

Harben, William N. "Soviet Positions Concerning Maritime Waters," *JAG Journal,* XV (1961), 149–54, 160.

Hartingh, France de. *Les Conceptions Soviétiques du Droit de la Mer.* Paris: Pichon, 1960.

Hazard, John N. "Cleansing Soviet International Law of Anti-Marxist Theories," *American Journal of International Law,* XXXII (1938), 244–52.

Herrick, Robert W. *Soviet Naval Strategy: Fifty Years of Theory and Practice.* Annapolis, Md.: U.S. Naval Institute, 1968.

Higgins, A. P., and Colombos, C. John. *Mezhdunarodnoe morskoe pravo,* ed. S. B. Krylov. Moscow: izd-vo Inolit, 1953.

Howard, Harry N. *The Problem of the Turkish Straits.* Washington D.C.: Government Printing Office, 1947.

Hudson, Manley O. (ed.). *World Court Reports.* 4 vols. Washington D.C.: Carnegie Endowment, 1935.

Hurewitz, J. "Russia and the Turkish Straits: A Reevaluation of the Origins of the Problem," *World Politics,* xiv (1962), 605–32.

Imenitov, G. I. *Sovetskoe morskoe i rybolovnoe pravo.* Moscow: Gosiurizdat, 1951.

Ivanashchenko, L. A. "Mezhdunarodnaia konferentsiia po morskomu pravu," *Morskoi sbornik,* No. 5 (1959), 67–79.

Ivanov, F. "Chetvertaia sessiia komisii mezhdunarodnogo prava OON," *Sovetskoe gosudarstvo i pravo,* No. 11 (1952), 72–79.

Ivanov F., and Volodin S. "Piataia sessiia Komisii mezhdunarodnogo prava OON," *Sovetskoe gosudarstvo i pravo,* No. 7 (1953), 88–100.

Ivanov, I. V. "Mezhdunarodnye soglasheniia v oblasti regulirovaniia pravovovogo rezhima regional'nogo moria," *Pravovedenie,* No. 1 (1966), 111–19.

———. "Osnovy pravovoi klassifikatsii morei," *Morskoe pravo i praktika: sbornik materialov,* xxx (1965), 3–12.

Jenisch, Uwe. *Das Recht zur Vornahme militärischer Übungen und Versuche auf Hoher See in Friedenszeiten.* Hamburg: diss., 1970.

Jessup, Philip C. *The Law of Territorial Waters and Maritime Jurisdiction.* New York: G. A. Jennings Co., 1927.

———. "The United Nations Conference on the Law of the Sea," *Columbia Law Review,* lix (1959), 234–68.

Johnston, Douglas M. *The International Law of Fisheries.* New Haven: Yale University Press, 1965.

Kalinkin, G. F. "Ob ispol'zovanii morskogo dna iskliuchitel'no v mirnykh tseliakh," *Sovetskoe gosudarstvo i pravo,* No. 10 (1969), 117–22.

Kalinkin, G. F., and Ostrovskii, Ia. A. *Morskoe dno: komu ono prinadlezhit?* Moscow: izd-vo Mezhdunarodnye otnosheniia, 1970.

Kamarovskii, L. A., and Ul'ianitskii, V. A. *Mezhdunarodnoe pravo po lektsiiam.* Moscow: Universitetskaia tipo., 1908.

Katchenovsky, D. I. *Prize Law: Particularly with Reference to The Duties and Obligations of Belligerents and Neutrals,* trans. F. T. Pratt. London: Stevens & Sons, 1867.

Kawakami, Kenzo. "Outline of the Japanese-Soviet Fishery Talks," *Japanese Annual of International Law,* vii (1963), 24–29.

Kazanskii, P. E. *Uchebnik mezhdunarodnogo prava.* Odessa: n.p., 1902.

Keilin, A. D. "Aktual'nye voprosy sovremennogo mezhdunarodnogo morskogo i rechnogo prava," *Sovetskii ezhegodnik mezhdunarodnogo prava 1962.* Moscow: izd-vo Nauka, 1963, pp. 78–113.

————. "Maritime Law in the Light of International Relations Today," *Current Digest of the Soviet Press,* XXI, No. 12 (April 9, 1969), 10–12.

————. *Sovetskoe morskoe pravo.* Moscow: izd-vo Vodnyi transport, 1954.

Keilin, A. D., and Tsarev, V. F. "Kontinental'nyi shel'f i ego granitsy," *Sovetskoe gosudarstvo i pravo,* No. 1 (1970), 98–102.

Keilin, A. D., and Vinogradov, P. P. *Morskoe pravo.* Moscow: izd-vo Morskoi transport, 1939.

Kerner, Robert J. *The Urge to the Sea: The Course of Russian History.* Berkeley: University of California Press, 1946.

Koers, Albert W. *The Debate on the Legal Regime for the Exploration and Exploitation of Ocean Resources: A Bibliography for the First Decade, 1960–1970.* Kingston: Law of the Sea Institute, 1970.

Kolbasov, O. S. (comp.). *Okhrana prirody: sbornik zakonodatel'nykh aktov.* Moscow: Gosiurizdat, 1961.

Kolodkin, A. L. "Morskaia blokada i sovremennoe mezhdunarodnoe pravo," *Sovetskoe gosudarstvo i pravo,* No. 4 (1963), 92–103.

————. "Novoe polozhenie ob okhrane gosudarstvennoi granitsy SSSR i rezhim sovetskikh morskikh vod," *Morskoe pravo i praktika: sbornik materialov,* LXVII (1961), 3–9.

————. *Pravovoi rezhim territorial'nykh vod i otkrytogo moria.* Moscow: izd-vo Morskoi transport, 1961.

————. "Territorial Waters and International Law," *International Affairs* [Moscow], No. 8 (1969), 79–81.

Kolodkin, A. L., and Kibirevskii, S. "Printsipy deiatel'nosti gosudarstv po ispol'zovaniiu morskogo dna," *Sovetskoe gosudarstvo i pravo,* No. 6 (1970), 95–100.

Kolotinskaia, E. N. *Pravovaia okhrana prirody v SSSR.* Moscow: izd-vo MGU, 1962.

Koretskii, V. M. "K voprosu o protivopravnosti ispytanii termoiadernogo oruzhiia v otkrytom more," *Pravovedenie,* No. 1 (1957), 100–6.

————. "Novoe v razdele 'otkrytogo moria' (Vopros o kontinental'nogo shel'fa)," *Sovetskoe gosudarstvo i pravo,* No. 8 (1950), 54–61.

Koretskii, V. M., and Tunkin, G. I. (eds.) *Ocherki mezhdunarodnogo morskogo prava.* Moscow: Gosiurizdat, 1962.

Korovin, E. A. "International Law Through the Pentagon's Prism," *International Affairs* [Moscow], No. 12 (1962), 3–7.

————. (ed.). *Mezhdunarodnoe pravo.* Moscow: Gosiurizdat, 1951.

————. *Sovremennoe mezhdunarodnoe publichnoe pravo.* Moscow: Gosizdat, 1926.

————. "SSSR i poliarnye zemli," *Sovetskoe pravo,* No. 3 (1926), 46.

————. "U.S. Violation of the Principle of Freedom of the Seas," *International Affairs* [Moscow], No. 3 (1955), 57–65.

Kozhevnikov, F. I. (ed.). *International Law,* trans. Dennis Ogden. Moscow: Foreign Languages Publishing House, [1961].

————. (ed.). *Kurs mezhdunarodnogo prava.* 2d ed. Moscow: izd-vo IMO, 1966.

————. (ed.). *Mezhdunarodnoe pravo.* Moscow: Gosiurizdat, 1957.

————. (ed.). *Mezhdunarodnoe pravo.* Moscow: izd-vo IMO, 1964.

————. *Russkoe gosudarstvo i mezhdunarodnoe pravo.* Moscow: Iurizdat Ministerstva iustitsii SSSR, 1947.

————. *Sovetskoe gosudarstvo i mezhdunarodnoe pravo.* Moscow: Iurizdat Ministerstva iustitsii SSSR, 1948.

Krylov, S. B. "Angliia i vopros o shirine territorial'nykh vod (pis'mo k redaktsiiu)," *Sovetskoe gosudarstvo i pravo,* No. 3 (1959), 125.

Krypton, Constantine. *The Northern Sea Route and the Economy of the Soviet North.* New York: Frederick A. Praeger, 1956.

Kucherov, Samuel A. "Das Problem der Kustenmeere und die Sowjetunion," *Osteuropa Recht,* v (1959), 15–24.

Lakhtin, V. L. *Prava na severnye poliarnye prostranstva.* Moscow: Litizdat NKID, 1928.

Lakhtin, V. L. "Rights Over the Arctic," *American Journal of International Law,* XXIV (1930), 703–17.

Lapenna, Ivo. *Conceptions Soviétiques de Droit International Public.* Paris: Pedone, 1954.

Leonard, L. Larry. *International Regulation of Fisheries.* Washington D.C.: Carnegie Endowment, 1944.

Levin, D. B., and Kaliuzhnaia, G. P. (ed.). *Mezhdunarodnoe pravo.* Moscow: Gosiurizdat, 1960; 2d ed., 1964.

Levine, R. "La Pêche japonaise dans les eaux russes," *L'Asie Française,* II (1937), 46–48.

Lisitsyn, A. P., and Udintsev, G. B. "Sostoianie i zadachi geologii Mirovogo okeana," *Vestnik Akademii nauk SSSR,* No. 7 (1963), 21–32.

Lisovskii, V. I. *Mezhdunarodnoe pravo.* Kiev: izd-vo Kievskii universitet, 1955; 2d ed., 1961.

————. *Mezhdunarodnoe pravo.* Moscow: izd-vo Vysshaia shkola, 1970.

McDougal, Myres S., and Burke, William T. *The Public Order of the Oceans: A Contemporary International Law of the Sea.* New Haven: Yale University Press, 1962.

Malinin, S. A. "K voprosu o pravovoi klassifikatsii vodnykh prostranstv," *Morskoe pravo i praktika,* XLVI (1960), 13–19.

Malloy, William M. (ed.). *Treaties, Conventions, International Acts, Protocols, and Agreements Between the United States and Other Powers.* Washington D.C.: Government Printing Office, 1910.

Martens, F. F. "Le Tribunal d'Arbitrage de Paris et la Mer Territoriale," *Revue Générale de Droit International Public,* I (1894), 32–43.

————. (ed.). *Sobranie traktatov' i konventsii, zakliuchennykh' Rossieiu s' inostrannymi derzhavami.* 15 vols. St. Petersburg: Tipo. A. Benke, 1874–1909.

————. *Sovremennoe mezhdunarodnoe pravo tsivilizovannykh narodov'.* 5th ed. 2 vols. St. Petersburg: Tipo. A. Benke, 1904–05.

Martens, G. F. von. *Recueil de Traités d'Alliance* . . . Gottingen: Librairie de Dieterich, 1818–.

Masterson, William E. *Jurisdiction in Marginal Seas with Special Reference to Smuggling.* New York: Macmillan Co., 1929.

Mathisen, Ole A., and Bevan, Donald E. *Some International Aspects of Soviet Fisheries.* Columbus, Ohio: Ohio State University Press, 1968.

Meshera, V. F. *Immunitet gosudarstvennykh morskikh sudov SSSR.* Moscow-Leningrad: izd-vo Morskoi transport, 1950.

————. *Morskoe pravo.* 7 vols. Moscow: izd-vo Morskoi transport, 1958–59.

————. (ed.). *Normativnye dokumenty po morskomu pravu.* Moscow: izd-vo Transport, 1965.

Meyer, C. B. V. *The Extent of Jurisdiction in Coastal Waters.* Leiden: Sijthoff, 1937.

"Mezhdunarodno-pravovoi rezhim baltiiskikh prolivov (Dissertatsiia S. V. Molodtsova)," *Sovetskoe gosudarstvo i pravo,* No. 5 (1950), 61–63.

Mikhailov, S. V. *Mirovoi okean i chelovechestvo.* Moscow: izd-vo Ekonomika, 1969.

Mikhailov, V. S. "Mezhdunarodno-pravovoe regulirovanie rybolovstva i drugikh morskikh promyslov na tikhom okeane," *Sovetskii ezhegodnik mezhdunarodnogo prava 1960.* Moscow: izd-vo AN SSSR, 1961, pp. 189–205.

Miller, Margaret. *The Economic Development of Russia, 1905–1914.* 2d ed. London: Frank Cass & Co., 1967.

Mitchell, Mairin. *The Maritime History of Russia 848–1948.* London: Sidgwick & Jackson, 1949.

Molodtsov, S. V. "Kodifikatsiia i dalneishee razvitie mezhdunarodnogo morskogo prava," *Sovetskii ezhegodnik mezhdunarodnogo prava 1958.* Moscow: izd-vo AN SSSR, 1959, pp. 327–45.

————. *Mezhdunarodno-pravovoi rezhim otkrytogo moria i kontinental'nogo shel'fa.* Moscow: izd-vo AN SSSR, 1960.

————. "Nekotorye voprosy regulirovaniia pravovogo rezhima otkrytogo moria," *Sovetskii ezhegodnik mezhdunarodnogo prava 1959.* Moscow: izd-vo AN SSSR, 1960, pp. 327–41.

————. "Nekotorye voprosy territorii v mezhdunarodnom prave," *Sovetskoe gosudarstvo i pravo,* No. 8 (1954), 71.

————. "Problema kontinental'nogo shel'fa," *Morskoi flot,* No. 10 (1958), 28–29.

Moore, John Bassett. *History and Digest of International Arbitrations.* 6 vols. Washington D.C.: Government Printing Office, 1898.

Mouton, M. A. *The Continental Shelf.* The Hague: Nijhoff, 1952.

Movchanovskii, B. F., and Orlov, V. A. *Ocherki sovetskogo morskogo prava.* Moscow: Gostransizdat, 1931.

Nikiforov, B. S. (ed.). *Nauchno-prakticheskii kommentarii ugolovnogo kodeksa RSFSR.* Moscow: Gosiurizdat, 1963.

Nikolaev, A. N. "Obsuzhdenie rezhima territorial'nykh vod," *Morskoi flot,* No. 10 (1958), 28–29.

————. "O zalive Petra Velikogo," *Mezhdunarodnaia zhizn',* No. 2 (1958), 50–57.

————. *Problema territorial'nykh vod v mezhdunarodnom prave.* Moscow: Gosiurizdat, 1954.

————. *Territorial'noe more: kodifikatsiia mezhdunarodno-pravovykh norm po probleme territorial'nykh vod.* Moscow: izd-vo Mezhdunarodnye otnosheniia, 1969.

————. "Zhenevskaia konferentsiia po morskomu pravu," *Sovetskoe gosudarstvo i pravo,* No. 9 (1958), 51–60.

Nussbaum, Arthur. "Frederick de Martens: Representative Tsarist Writer on International Law," *Nordisk Tidsskrift for International Ret,* XXII (1952), 51–66.

Oda, Shigeru. *International Control of Sea Resources.* Leyden: Sijthoff, 1963.

Ohira, Zengo. "Fishery Problems Between Soviet Russia and Japan," *Japanese Annual of International Law,* II (1958), 1–19.

Ortolan, T. *Morskoe mezhdunarodnoe pravo,* trans. A. Lokhvitskii. St. Petersburg: Tipo. Akademii nauk, 1865.

Ovchinnikov, I. "Territorial'noe more," *Morskoi sbornik,* CCXC, No. 1 (1899), 49–86.

————. "Treteiskii sud po delu o zakhvat amerikanskikh shkun russkimi kreiserami," *Morskoi sbornik,* CCCXXIX, No. 8 (1905), 45–72; CCCXXX, No. 10 (1905), 111–45; CCCXXXV, No. 8 (1906), 59–84; CCCXXXVI, No. 9 (1906), 93–116; No. 10 (1906), 73–103; CCCXXXVII (1906), 71–92.

Ovchynnyk, Michael M. "Development of Some Marine and Inland Russian Fisheries, and Fish Utilization," *Atlantic Ocean Fisheries,* ed. Georg Borgstrom and Arthur J. Heighway. London: Fishing News Ltd., 1961, pp. 267–81.

Pashukanis, E. B. *Ocherki po mezhdunarodnomu pravu.* Moscow: izd-vo Sovetskoe zakonodatel'stvo, 1935.

Pazukin, A. A. (ed.). *Sbornik gramot' i dogovorov' o prisoedinenii tsarstv' i oblastei k' gosudarstvu rossisskomu v XVII–XIX v'kakh.* Petersburg: Gosizdat, 1921.

Petrow, Richard. *Across the Top of Russia: The Cruise of the USCGC Northwind into the Polar Seas North of Siberia.* New York: David McKay, 1967.

Pharand, Donat. "Soviet Union Warns United States Against Use of Northeast Passage," *American Journal of International Law,* LXII (1968), 927–35.

Phillipson, Coleman, and Buxton, Noel. *The Question of the Bosporus and Dardanelles.* London: Stevens & Haynes, 1917.

Pogodin, A. "Bonn's Strategic Plans in the Baltic," *International Affairs* [Moscow], No. 9 (1961), 33–37.

Przetacznik, Franciszek. "La Déclaration sur le Plateau Continental de la Mer Baltique et le Droit International," *Revue belge de droit international,* VI (1970), 462–83.

Ramundo, Bernard A. *Peaceful Coexistence: International Law in the Building of Communism.* Baltimore: The Johns Hopkins Press, 1967.

————. *The (Soviet) Socialist Theory of International Law.* Washington D.C.: George Washington University, 1964.

Reinkemeyer, H. A. *Die sowjetische Zwölfmeilenzone in der Ostsee und die Freiheit des Meeres.* Köln: Heymann, 1955.

"Reply of the Union of Soviet Socialist Republics," League of Nations, Conference for the Codification of International Law, *Bases of Discussion Drawn Up for the Conference by the Preparatory Committee: Supplement to Volume II—Territorial Waters.* Geneva: League of Nations, 1929.

Riesenfeld, Stefan A. *Protection of Coastal Fisheries Under International Law.* Washington D.C.: Carnegie Endowment, 1942.

Romanov, V. "Zaliv Petra Velikogo—vnutrennie vody sovetskogo soiuza," *Sovetskoe gosudarstvo i pravo,* No. 5 (1958), 47–55.

Rozental', E. F. (ed.). *Morskoe pravo SSSR.* Moscow: Vneshtorgizdat, 1932.

Rubinshtein, N. L. *Vneshniaia politika sovetskogo soiuza v 1921–1925 godakh.* Moscow: Gospolitizdat, 1953.

Savel'ev, A. "Mezhdunarodnaia konferentsiia po morskomu pravu," *Morskoi flot,* No. 8 (1958), 25–26.

Sbornik deistvuiushchikh dogovorov, soglashenii i konventsii zakliuchennykh SSSR s inostrannymi gosudarstvami. Moscow: Gospolitizdat, 1924–.

Sbornik diplomaticheskikh dokumentov, kasaiushchikhsia peregovorov po zakliucheniiu Rybolovnoi konventsii mezhdu Rossiei i Iaponiei, avgust 1906–iul' 1907. St. Petersburg: Tipo. V. Kirshbauma, 1907.

Schapiro, Leonard B. "The Limits of Russian Territorial Waters in the Baltic," *British Year Book of International Law,* xxvii (1950), 439–48.

Scott, James Brown. (ed.). *The Armed Neutralities of 1780 and 1800: A Collection of Official Documents Preceded by the Views of Representative Publicists.* New York: Oxford University Press, 1918.

Semyonov, Yuri. *Siberia: Its Conquest and Development.* Baltimore: Helicon Press, 1963.

Serbov, S. "Shestaia i sedmaia sessii Komissii mezhdunarodnogo prava," *Sovetskoe gosudarstvo i pravo,* No. 8 (1955), 108–12.

Shalowitz, Aaron L. *Shore and Sea Boundaries.* 2 vols. Washington D.C.: Government Printing Office, 1962–64.

Shapiro, Leonard. (ed.). *Soviet Treaty Series: 1917–1939.* 2 vols. Washington D.C.: Georgetown University Press, 1950–55.

Sheptovitskii, M. Ia. *Morskoe pravo.* Leningrad: Gostransizdat, 1936.

Shmigel'skii, G. L., and Iasinovskii, V. A. *Osnovy sovetskogo morskogo prava.* Moscow: izd-vo Morskoi transport, 1959; 2d ed., 1963.

Shotwell, James T., and Déak, Francis. *Turkey at the Straits: A Short History.* New York: Macmillan Co., 1940.

Shparlinskii, V. M. *The Fishing Industry of the U.S.S.R.* Jerusalem: Israel Program for Scientific Translations, 1964. (U.S. Department of Commerce Publication ots 63–11122).

Siling, A. N. *Morskoe pravo.* Moscow: izd-vo Transport, 1964.

———. *Narusheniia imperialisticheskimi gosudarstvami svobody moreplavaniia i rybolovstva v otkrytom more.* Moscow: Gosiurizdat, 1963.

Sivers, V. *Glavneishie svedeniia po morskomu mezhdunarodnomu pravu.* St. Petersburg: n.p., 1902.

Slouka, Zdenek J. *International Custom and the Continental Shelf.* The Hague: Nijhoff, 1968.

Smith, H. A. (ed.). *Great Britain and the Law of Nations: A Selection of Documents Illustrating the Views of the Government of the United Kingdom Upon Matters of International Law.* 2 vols. London: P. S. King Ltd., 1932–35.

Sørenson, Max. "Law of the Sea," *International Conciliation,* No. 520 (November 1958).

Spirin, V. G. "Problema territorial'nykh vod v praktike latinoamerikanskikh stran," *Sovetskoe gosudarstvo i pravo,* No. 7 (1956), 118–22.

State Duma Commission on Fisheries. "Doklad po zakonoproektu ob uporiadochenii rybnago promysla v Arkhangel'skoi gubernii," *Prilozheniia k stenograficheskim otchetam gosudarstvennoi dumy. Tretii sozyv'. Sessiia chetvertaia. 1910–1911 gg.,* v, No. 592, III/4. St. Petersburg, 1911.

Stefanova, S. *Mezhdunarodnopraven rezhim na otkritoto more.* Sofia: Nauka i izkustvo, 1965.

Stoianov, A. N. *Ocherki istorii i dogmatiki mezhdunarodnogo prava.* Kharkov: Universitetskoi tipo., 1875.

Strohl, Mitchell P. *The International Law of Bays.* The Hague: Nijhoff, 1963.

Sugiyama, Shigeo. "The Japanese-Soviet Tangle Collection Agreement of 1963," *Japanese Annual of International Law,* VIII (1964), 75–98.

Svirin, E. "Baltic Continental Shelf," *New Times,* No. 47 (1968), 6–7.

Swarztrauber, Sayre A. *The Three-Mile Limit of Territorial Seas: A Brief History.* Washington D.C.: American University, unpublished Ph.D. diss., 1970.

Syatauw, J. G. *Some New Established Asian States and the Development of International Law.* The Hague: Nijhoff, 1961.

Szirmai, Z., and Korevaar, J. D. (trans.). *The Merchant Shipping Code of the Soviet Union.* Leyden: Sijthoff, 1960.

Taracouzio, T. A. *Soviets in the Arctic.* New York: Macmillan Co., 1938.

———. *The Soviet Union and International Law.* New York: Macmillan Co., 1935.

Thomas, Benjamin Platt. *Russo-American Relations 1815–1867.* Baltimore: The Johns Hopkins Press, 1930.

Thommen, T. K. *Legal Status of Government Merchant Ships in International Law.* The Hague: Nijhoff, 1962.

Tikhmenev, P. A. *Istoricheskoe obozr'nie obrazovaniia Rossiisko-amerikanskoi kompanii i d'istvii eia do nastoiashchago vremeni.* 2 vols. St. Petersburg: E. Veimar, 1861–63.

Tomilin, Iu. "Keeping the Sea-Bed Out of the Arms Race," *International Affairs* [Moscow], No. 1 (1970), 41–45.

Törnudd, Klaus. *Soviet Attitudes Towards Non-Military Regional Co-operation.* Helsinki: Centraltryckeriet, 1961.

Tunkin, G. I. *Ideologicheskaia bor'ba i mezhdunarodnoe pravo.* Moscow: izd-vo IMO, 1967.

―――. "Zhenevskaia konferentsiia po mezhdunarodnomu morskomu pravu," *Mezhdunarodnaia zhizn',* No. 7 (1958), 63–70.

Ul'ianitskii, V. A. *Lektsii po mezhdunarodnomu pravu.* Moscow: Obshchestvo rasprostraneniia poleznykh knig, 1900.

―――. *Mezhdunarodnoe pravo.* Tomsk: Tipo. Sibir. t-va. pechatnogo dela, 1911.

USSR Naval Hydrographic Office. *Izveshcheniia moreplavateliam.* Leningrad: serial published weekly.

United Nations. *Yearbook of the International Law Commission.* New York: United Nations, 1954–58.

United Nations Conference on the Law of the Sea, Geneva, 1958. *Official Records.* London: United Nations, 1958. 7 vols.

―――. 2d, Geneva, 1960. *Official Records.* New York: United Nations, 1962. 2 vols.

United States Department of State. *Sovereignty of the Sea.* Washington D.C.: Government Printing Office, 1969. (Geographic Bulletin No. 3).

Uustal', A. T. "Iskhodnaia liniia territorial'nykh vod Estonskoi SSR," *Sovetskoe pravo* [Tallin], No. 2 (1969), 103–108.

―――. *Mezhdunarodno-pravovoi rezhim territorial'nykh vod.* Tartu: izd-vo Tartuskogo gos. univ., 1958.

―――. "Osnovnye voprosy pravovogo rezhima territorial'nykh vod," *Sovetskoe gosudarstvo i pravo,* No. 6 (1957), 71–79.

Vanin, I. I. "Morskoe dno i pentagon," *SShA: ekonomika, politika, ideologiia,* I, No. 1 (1970), 68–70.

Vasil'ev, I. *O turetskom "neitralitete" vo vremia vtoroi mirovoi voiny.* Moscow: Gospolitizdat, 1951.

Vereshchetin, V. S. "K voprosu o territorial'nykh vodakh," *Mirovaia ekonomika i mezhdunarodnye otnosheniia,* No. 12 (1958), 117–19.

―――. *Svoboda sudokhodstva v otkrytom more.* Moscow: izd-vo IMO, 1958.

Veshniakova, V. I. *Rybolovstvo i zakonodatel'stvo.* St. Petersburg: Trenke & Fiusnu, 1894.

Vinogradov, L. G., and Neiman, A. A. "Organizmy kontinental'nogo shel'fa, sostavliaiushchie gosudarstvennym sobstvennost' SSSR," *Rybnoe khoziaistvo,* No. 3 (1969), 6–7.

Volkov, A. A. "Mezhdunarodnopravovye voprosy ekspluatatsii zhivykh resursov kontinental'nogo shel'fa," *Sovetskii ezhegodnik mezhdunarodnogo prava 1964–1965.* Moscow: izd-vo Nauka, 1966, pp. 213–29.

―――. *Morskoe pravo.* Moscow: izd-vo Pishchevaia promyshlennost', 1969.

―――. "Pravovoi rezhim rybolovnykh zon," *Sovetskii ezhegodnik mezhdunarodnogo prava 1963.* Moscow: izd-vo Nauka, 1965, pp. 204–18.

————. (comp.). *Sbornik mezhdunarodnykh konventsii, dogovorov i soglashenii, kasaiushchikhsia rybolovstva i rybokhoziaistvennykh issledovanii.* Moscow: izd-vo Pishchevaia promyshlennost', 1966.

————. (comp.). *Sbornik mezhdunarodnykh konventsii, dogovorov i soglashenii o rybolovstve i rybokhoziaistvennykh issledovaniiakh.* Moscow: izd-vo Pishchevaia promyshlennost', 1961.

Vyshnepol'skii, S. A. "Freedom of the Seas in the Epoch of Imperialism," *Current Digest of the Soviet Press,* I, No. 16 (1949), 3–12.

————. "K probleme pravovogo rezhima arkticheskoi oblasti," *Sovetskoe gosudarstvo i pravo,* No. 7 (1952), 36.

————. *Mirovye morskie puti i sudokhodstvo.* Moscow: Geografgiz, 1953.

Waultrin, René. "La Question de la Souveraineté des Terres Arctiques," *Revue Générale de Droit International Public,* XV (1908), 78–125, 185–209, 401–423.

Wells, R. D. "The Icy 'Nyet,' " *United States Naval Institute Proceedings,* XCIV (1968), 73–79.

Wertheim, Barbara. "The Russo-Japanese Fisheries Controversy," *Pacific Affairs,* VIII (1935), 185–98.

Westlake, John. *International Law.* 2d ed. 2 vols. Cambridge: The University Press, 1910.

Whiteman, Marjorie M. (ed.). *Digest of International Law.* Washington D.C.: Government Printing Office, 1965–.

Woodward, David. *The Russians at Sea.* London: William Kimber, 1965.

Young, Richard. "The Geneva Convention on the Continental Shelf: A First Impression," *American Journal of International Law,* LII (1958), 733–38.

Zakharov, N. A. *Kurs obshchago mezhdunarodnogo prava.* Petrograd: Veisbrut, 1917.

Zakharov, V. K. *Morskaia lotsiia.* 2d ed. Moscow: izd-vo Morskoi transport, 1969.

Zenkevitch, L. *Biology of the Seas of the U.S.S.R.,* trans. S. Botcharskaya. New York: Interscience Publishers, 1963.

Zhitinskii, N. S., and Tarkhanov, I. E. "Svoboda otkrytogo moria i pravovoi rezhim poletov samoletov," *Morskoi sbornik,* No. 10 (1966), 26–31.

Zhudro, A. K. "K voprosu o razgranichenii territorial'nykh vod i vnutrennykh vod gosudarstv v arkhipelagakh," *Morskoe pravo i praktika: sbornik materialov,* XCVII (1963), 3–9.

————. (ed.). *Morskoe pravo.* Moscow: izd-vo Transport, 1964.

————. "Zhenevskaia konferentsiia organizatsii ob'edinennykh natsii po mezhdunarodnomu morskomu pravu," *Morskoe pravo i praktika: sbornik materialov,* XXXIV (1958), 3–18.

Zhudro, A. K., and Kolodkin, A. L. *Some Legal Aspects of Using the Sea-Bed.* Rome: Istituto Affari Internazionali, 1969. Mimeo.

Zwanenberg, Anna von. "Interference with Ships on the High Seas," *International and Comparative Law Quarterly,* X (1961), 785–817.

TABLE OF STATUTES AND ORDERS

Boldface numbers in brackets indicate page numbers.

217

1869

March 10: Edict Granting Certain Exemptions and Privileges to a Company for Industrial and Trade Undertakings Along the Ob and Enesei Rivers and the Coasts of the Arctic Ocean   **[120]**
————: Rules on Prizes and Recaptures   **[28]**

1882

————: Regulation on far eastern fisheries (?)   **[87]**

1892

————: Customs Code   **[28, 74, 80, 81]**

1893

Feb. 12: Rules for Seal Fisheries   **[88]**

1895

March 27: Statute on Maritime Prizes   **[28]**

1901

————: Fishery Regulations for the Maritime Province (?)   **[110]**

1909

Dec. 10: Customs Statute   **[25, 31–33, 39, 40, 46, 81]**

1911

May 29: Rules on Marine Commercial Fishing in the Priamur General-Gubernatorstvo   **[31–33, 46, 49, 89, 120]**

1914

————: Statute on Maritime Prizes   **[28]**

UNION OF SOVIET SOCIALIST REPUBLICS

1923

Sept. 7: Statute on the Protection of the Boundaries of the USSR   **[34]**

1924

Jan. 31: Constitution of the USSR   **[24]**
July 5: Instruction for the Navigation of Vessels in Coastal Waters Within Artillery Range of Shore Batteries in Peacetime   **[34, 35, 51, 52, 59, 60]**

1925

July 3: Statute on Fisheries   **[98]**

1926

April 16: Decree on the Proclamation of Lands and Islands Located in the Northern Arctic Ocean as Territory of the USSR   **[112, 139]**

1927

June 15: Statute on the Protection of the State Boundaries of the USSR **[21, 24, 25, 34, 39–41, 46, 52, 60, 75]**

1928

July 24: Decree on Use of Wireless Radio Equipment by Foreign Vessels During Their Sojourn in Waters of the USSR   **[35, 78–80]**

1929

Feb. 14: Instruction Concerning the Application of the Decree of July 24, 1928, on Use of Wireless Radio Equipment by Foreign Vessels During Their Sojourn in Waters of the USSR   **[79]**
June 14: Merchant Shipping Code of the USSR   **[35, 83, 84]**

1930

Aug. 3: Decree on the Water Expanse of the Gulf of Finland to Which the Authority of Agencies of the USSR and RSFSR Extends   **[36, 46]**

1931

March 28: Provisional Rules for Foreign Warships Visiting Waters of the USSR   **[60, 62–64]**
Aug. 23: Decree on the Sanitary Protection of the Boundaries of the USSR   **[35, 82]**

1935

Aug. 7: Air Code of the USSR   **[24, 25, 35]**
Sept. 25: Decree on the Regulation of Fishing and the Conservation of Fishery Stocks   **[24, 25, 39, 40, 76, 98]**

1936

Dec. 5: Constitution of the USSR   **[24]**
————: Rules for the Entrance of Vessels into Areas of Restrictive Movement   **[52]**

1940

April 15: Statute on the Procedure of Investigation of Maritime Average [**73**]

1944

Sept. 14: Rules for Vessels Being Conducted by Icebreakers Through Ice [**78**]

1954

Aug. 10: Decree on Conservation of Fishery Stocks and the Regulation of Fishing in Waters of the USSR   [**37, 38, 98**]

1956

March 21: Decree on the Conservation of Stocks and the Regulation of Salmon Fishing on the High Seas in Areas Adjacent to the Territorial Waters of the USSR in the Far East   [**100, 190, 191, 194**]

1957

July 21: Decree on Peter the Great Bay   [**108**]

1958

Sept. 15: Statute on the Conservation of Fishery Stocks and the Regulation of Fishing in Waters of the USSR   [**37, 38, 98**]

Dec. 25: All-Union Fundamental Principles of Criminal Legislation of the USSR and Union Republics   [**71, 179**]

Dec. 25: Law on Criminal Responsibility for Crimes Against the State [**77**]

1960

June 25: Rules for Visits by Foreign Warships to Territorial Waters and Ports of the USSR   [**52, 53, 64, 65, 70, 78, 84**]

Aug. 5: Statute on the Protection of the State Boundary of the USSR   [**22, 44, 46, 48, 52–54, 57, 58, 64, 65, 70, 72, 73, 75, 77, 80, 82, 83, 98, 102, 106, 107, 114**]

1961

Jan. 16: Instruction on the Navigation Procedure for Vessels of the Commercial Fishing Fleet of the USSR, the Conduct by Them of Commercial Fishing on the High Seas, and the Duties of Executive Personnel With Regard to its Fulfillment   [**59**]

June 27: Flight Rules for Foreign Civil Aircraft Within the Territory of the USSR (as amended)   [**100**]

Aug. —: Instruction Concerning Foreign Submarines in Soviet Territorial Waters **[65]**
Dec. 8: All-Union Fundamental Principles of Civil Legislation of the USSR and Union Republics **[73]**
Dec. 26: Air Code of the USSR **[100]**

1963

Oct. 29: Statute on State Sanitary Supervision in the USSR **[82]**

1964

May 5: Customs Code of the USSR **[59, 69, 80]**

1968

Feb. 6: Edict on the Continental Shelf of the USSR **[22, 144, 145, 148–50]**
Sept. 17: Merchant Shipping Code of the USSR **[77, 78, 82–84, 102, 174, 178, 185, 201]**
Sept. 23: Decree on Measures Relating to the Prevention of Pollution of the Caspian Sea **[138, 186]**
Oct. 29: List of Living Organisms Which Are Natural Resources of the Continental Shelf of the USSR **[148]**

1969

July 18: Decree on the Procedure for Conducting Work on the Continental Shelf of the USSR and the Protection of its Natural Resources **[150]**

1970

Dec. 10: Fundamental Principles of Water Legislation of the USSR and Union Republics **[22, 50]**

RUSSIAN SOVIET FEDERATED SOCIALIST REPUBLIC

1918

May 15: Decree on the Establishment of the Border Guard **[24, 33, 46, 81, 89]**
July 10: Constitution of the RSFSR **[89]**

1921

May 24: Decree on the Conservation of Fish and Furbearing Animals in the Northern Arctic Ocean and the White Sea **[33, 34, 38, 90, 91, 94, 95, 98]**

May 31: Decree on the Fishing Industry and Fisheries   [**90**]

1923

Jan. 16: Decree Relating to Rules for the Use of Wireless Radio Equipment by Foreign Vessels While Off the Shores or in the Internal Waters of the RSFSR and Constituent Republics   [**35**]

March 2: Decree on the Procedure for the Exploitation of Commercial Fisheries and Marine Furbearing Animals in the Far East   [**34, 96–98**]

1926

Nov.22: Criminal Code of the RSFSR   [**79**]

1927

May 24: Decree on Making Arrests on Foreign Merchant Vessels   [**71**]

1960

Oct. 27: Criminal Code of the RSFSR   [**71, 72, 79, 84, 98, 99, 174, 175, 195**]

1964

June 11: Civil Code of the RSFSR   [**74**]

ARMENIAN SOVIET SOCIALIST REPUBLIC

1927

Sept. 18: Criminal Code of the Armenian SSR   [**79**]

AZERBAIDZHAN SOVIET SOCIALIST REPUBLIC

1927
Dec. 3: Criminal Code of the Azerbaidzhan SSR   [**79**]

GEORGIAN SOVIET SOCIALIST REPUBLIC

1928

March 26: Criminal Code of the Georgian SSR   [**79**]

TURKMEN SOVIET SOCIALIST REPUBLIC

1927

Sept. 28: Criminal Code of the Turkmen SSR   [**79**]

UKRAINIAN SOVIET SOCIALIST REPUBLIC

1927

June 8: Criminal Code of the Ukrainian SSR   [**79**]

TABLE OF TREATIES

Boldface numbers in brackets indicate page numbers.

1780

Feb. 28: Declaration of the Empress of Russia Concerning the Principles of Armed Neutrality   [**8, 117, 125, 168**]

July 9: Convention for an Armed Neutrality between Russia and Denmark and Norway, signed at Copenhagen   [**117, 125, 168**]

Aug. 1: Convention for an Armed Neutrality between Russia and Sweden, signed at St. Petersburg   [**117, 125, 168**]

1781

Jan. 4: Act by Which the Netherlands Accedes to the Convention for Armed Neutrality between Russia and Denmark and Norway, and Russia and Sweden, signed at St. Petersburg   [**117, 125, 168**]

May 19: Convention between Russia and Prussia for the Maintenance of the Freedom of Neutral Commerce and Navigation, by Which Prussia Accedes to the System of Armed Neutrality, signed at St. Petersburg   [**117, 125, 168**]

Oct. 9: Act of Accession of the Emperor of the Romans to the System of Armed Neutrality, signed at Vienna   [**117, 125, 168**]

1782

May 2: Swedish Note to Prussia regarding Swedish Accession to the Convention of May 19, 1781, between Russia and Prussia, for the Maintenance of Freedom of Neutral Commerce and Navigation   [**117, 125, 168**]

July 24: Convention between Russia and Portugal for the Maintenance of the Freedom of Neutral Commerce and Navigation, by Which Portugal Accedes to the System of Armed Neutrality, signed at St. Petersburg   [**117, 125, 168**]

1786

Dec. 31: Treaty of Navigation and Commerce between France and Russia, signed at St. Petersburg   [**26, 168**]

1787

Jan. 6: Treaty of Commerce between Russia and The Kingdom of the Two Sicilies, signed at Tsarskoe Selo   [**26, 168**]

Dec. 9: Treaty of Commerce between Portugal and Russia, signed at St. Petersburg   [**26**]

1798

Dec. 27: Treaty of Friendship, Navigation, and Commerce between Russia and Portugal, signed at St. Petersburg   [**168**]

1800

Dec. 16: Convention between Russia and Denmark and Norway for the Reestablishment of an Armed Neutrality, signed at St. Petersburg [**117, 125, 168**]

Dec. 16: Convention between Russia and Sweden for the Reestablishment of an Armed Neutrality, signed at St. Petersburg [**117, 125, 168**]

Dec. 18: Convention between Russia and Prussia for the Reestablishment of an Armed Neutrality, signed at St. Petersburg [**117, 125, 168**]

1801

March 1: Treaty of Friendship, Commerce, and Navigation between Sweden and Russia, signed at St. Petersburg [**26, 168**]

1809

Sept. 5: Treaty of Peace between Sweden and Russia, signed at Friedrichshahm [**168**]

1813

Oct. 12: Treaty of Perpetual Peace and Friendship between Russia and Persia, signed at Gulistan [**119**]

1824

April 5: Convention between Russia and the United States as to the Pacific Ocean and Northwest Coast of America, signed at St. Petersburg [**27, 86**]

1825

Feb. 16: Convention between Great Britain and Russia, signed at St. Petersburg [**27, 86**]

1828

Feb. 22: Treaty of Peace and Friendship between Russia and Persia, signed at Turkmanchai [**119**]

1829

Jan. 15: Declaration between Russia and Denmark Concerning the Salute at Sea, signed at Copenhagen [**168**]

1833

July 8: Treaty of Defensive Alliance between Russia and Turkey, signed at Constantinople [**123**]

1841

July 13: Convention Respecting the Dardanelles and Bosporus, signed at London   [**123**]

1856

March 30: Convention Relating to the Dardanelles and Bosporus Straits, signed at Paris   [**9, 17**]
April 16: Declaration Respecting the Principles of International Maritime Law, signed at Paris   [**8**]

1857

March 14: Convention and Protocol for the Redemption of the Sound Dues, signed at Copenhagen   [**117, 125**]

1871

Jan. 17: Annex to the Protocol of the Conference between Great Britain, Austria, France, Germany, Italy, Russia, and Turkey, Relative to the Inviolability of Treaties, signed at London   [**9**]

1875

May 7: Treaty between Russia and Japan for the Mutual Cession of Territory, signed at St. Petersburg   [**88**]

1884

March 14: Convention on the Protection of Submarine Cables, signed at Paris   [**183, 194**]

1893

May: Agreement between Great Britain and Russia relative to Seal Fisheries, signed at ?   [**88**]

1894

May 4: Agreement between the United States and Russia for a *Modus Vivendi* in Relation to the Fur-seal Fisheries in the Bering Sea and the North Pacific Ocean, signed at Washington D.C.   [**88**]

1899

July 29: Convention for the Pacific Settlement of International Disputes, signed at The Hague   [**9**]
July 29: Convention with Respect to the Laws and Customs of War on Land, signed at The Hague   [**9**]

1905

Aug. 23: Peace Treaty between Russia and Japan, signed at Portsmouth
[**88**]

1907

July 15: Fishery Treaty between Japan and Russia, signed at St. Petersburg   [**88, 89, 96, 97**]
Oct. 16: Convention between Rumania and Russia Relating to the Fisheries in the Waters of the Danube and the Pruth, signed at Bucharest
[**89**]

1910

Sept. 23: Convention for the Purpose of Establishing Uniformity in Certain Rules Regarding Collisions of Vessels at Sea, signed at Brussels
[**185**]
Sept. 23: Convention for the Unification of Certain Rules with Respect to
Assistance and Salvage at Sea, signed at Brussels   [**185**]

1911

July 7: Convention for the Preservation and Protection of Fur Seals,
signed at Washington D.C.   [**88**]

1920

Feb. 2: Treaty of Peace between the RSFSR and Estonia, signed at Tartu
[**51**]
Aug. 11: Treaty of Peace between Russia and Latvia, signed at Riga   [**51**]
Oct. 14: Treaty of Peace between Finland and the RSFSR, signed at
Dorpat   [**36, 37, 46, 51, 89, 90**]

1921

Feb. 26: Treaty of Friendship between the RSFSR and Persia, signed at
Moscow   [**101**]
March 16: Trade Agreement between the RSFSR and the United King-
dom, signed at London   [**92**]

1922

Oct. 21: Convention between Finland and the RSFSR Regarding Fishing
and Sealing in the Territorial Waters of the Arctic Ocean, signed at
Helsinki   [**90**]

1923

July 24: Convention on the Regime of the Straits, signed at Lausanne
[**121**]

1924

Feb. 7: Treaty of Commerce and Navigation between the Soviet Union and Italy, signed at Rome   [51]

March 15: Treaty of Commerce between the Soviet Union and Sweden, signed at Stockholm   [51]

April 6: Provisional Agreement between the Soviet Union and Japan Concerning Fisheries, signed at ?   [96]

Aug. 8: [General Treaty between the Soviet Union and the United Kingdom], signed at London   [93]

1925

Jan. 20: Convention between the Soviet Union and Japan Concerning General Principles of Mutual Relations, signed at Peking   [96]

Aug. 19: Convention Concerning the Suppression of Contraband Traffic in Alcoholic Products, signed at Helsinki   [40, 75, 81]

Aug. 19: Agreement between the Soviet Union, Estonia, and Finland Defining the Areas Subject to Control Under the Convention of August 19, 1925, Concerning the Suppression of Contraband Traffic in Alcoholic Products, signed at Helsinki   [75, 81]

Oct. 12: Treaty between the USSR and Germany, signed at Moscow   [51, 95]

Dec. 15: Treaty of Commerce and Navigation between Norway and the Soviet Union, signed at Moscow   [36, 51, 95]

1926

April 22: Protocol between the Soviet Union, Estonia, and Finland Defining the State Boundaries Under the Agreement of August 19, 1925, Supplementary to the Convention of the Same Date Concerning the Suppression of Contraband Traffic in Alcoholic Products, signed at Moscow   [75]

1927

March 11: Treaty of Commerce and Navigation between the Soviet Union and Turkey, signed at Ankara   [51]

Oct. 1: Treaty of Nonaggression and Neutrality between the Soviet Union and Persia, signed at Moscow   [101]

Oct. 1: Agreement between the Soviet Union and Persia Concerning Exploitation of Fisheries on the Southern Shores of the Caspian Sea, signed at Moscow   [102]

1928

Jan. 23: Convention on Fisheries between the Soviet Union and Japan, signed at Moscow   [47, 48, 97, 110]

1929

April 13: Convention between the Soviet Union and Finland Concerning Customs Supervision in the Gulf of Finland, signed at Moscow [**37, 75, 81**]

1930

May 22: Provisional Agreement between the Soviet Union and the United Kingdom Concerning the Regulation of Fisheries in Waters Contiguous to the Northern Coasts of the USSR, signed at London [**36, 48, 93, 94, 99**]

July 5: International Load Line Convention, signed at London [**186**]

Oct. 23: Agreement Concerning Maritime Signals, signed at Lisbon [**185**]

Oct. 23: Agreement Concerning Manned Lightships Not on Their Stations, signed at Lisbon [**185**]

1932

Aug. 13: Agreement Concerning Fisheries Questions between the Soviet Union and Japan, signed at Moscow [**97, 98**]

1936

May 25: Protocol Extending the Fishery Convention of January 23, 1928, between the Soviet Union and Japan, signed at Moscow [**97, 98**]

July 20: Convention Concerning the Regime of the Black Sea Straits, signed at Montreux [**121, 130**]

Dec. 28: Protocol Extending the Fishery Convention of January 23, 1928, between the Soviet Union and Japan, signed at Moscow [**97, 98**]

1937

Sept. 14: The Nyon Arrangement, signed at Nyon [**173, 181**]

Sept. 17: Agreement Supplementary to the Nyon Arrangement, signed at Geneva [**173, 181**]

Dec. 29: Protocol Extending the Fishery Convention of January 23, 1928, between the Soviet Union and Japan, signed at Moscow [**97, 98**]

1939

April 2: Protocol Extending the Fishery Convention of January 23, 1928, between the Soviet Union and Japan, signed at Moscow [**97**]

Dec. 31: Protocol Extending the Fishery Convention of January 23, 1928, between the Soviet Union and Japan, signed at Moscow [**97, 98**]

1940

March 12: Treaty of Peace between the Soviet Union and Finland, signed at Moscow   [**44, 50**]

March 25: Treaty of Commerce and Navigation between the Soviet Union and Iran, signed at Teheran   [**102**]

Oct. 11: Agreement between Finland and the Soviet Union Concerning the Demilitarization of the Aaland Islands, signed at Moscow   [**37**]

1941

Jan. 21: Protocol Extending the Fishery Convention of January 23, 1928, between the Soviet Union and Japan, signed at Moscow   [**97, 98**]

1944

March 30: Protocol Extending the Fishery Convention of January 23, 1928, between the Soviet Union and Japan for a Period of Five Years, signed at Moscow   [**97–99**]

1945

June 26: Charter of the United Nations, signed at San Francisco   [**185, 188, 196, 197**]

1946

Dec. 2: International Convention on the Regulation of Whaling, signed at Washington D.C.   [**192**]

1947

Sept. 2: Inter-American Treaty of Reciprocal Assistance between the United States and Other American Republics, signed at Rio de Janeiro   [**197**]

1948

April 30: Charter of the Organization of American States, signed at Bogotá   [**197**]

1951

May 25: International Sanitary Regulations—World Health Organization Regulations No. 2, adopted at Geneva   [**82**]

Sept. 8: Treaty of Peace with Japan, signed at San Francisco   [**129, 190**]

1952

May 9: International Convention for High Seas Fisheries of the North Pacific Ocean, signed at Tokyo   [**190**]

1954

May 12: International Convention for the Prevention of Pollution of the Sea by Oil, signed at London   [186]

Sept. 29: Agreement between the Soviet Union and Sweden on Cooperation in Saving Lives on the Baltic Sea, signed at Moscow   [186]

1956

May 14: Convention Concerning Fishing on the High Seas in the Northwest Pacific Ocean between Japan and the Soviet Union, signed at Moscow   [40, 100, 148, 183, 191]

May 14: Agreement between the Soviet Union and Japan on Cooperation in Saving Persons in Distress at Sea, signed at Moscow   [186]

May 25: Agreement between the Soviet Union and the United Kingdom Concerning Fisheries, signed at Moscow   [41, 99]

June 12: Agreement on Cooperation in Conducting Fishery, Oceanological, and Limnological Research in the Western Pacific Ocean, signed at Peking   [192]

July 3: Agreement between the Soviet Union and North Korea on Cooperation in Saving Lives and Rendering Aid to Vessels or Aircraft in Distress at Sea, signed at Moscow   [186]

Sept. 7: Supplemental Convention on the Abolition of Slavery, the Slave Trade, and Institutions and Practices Similar to Slavery, signed at Geneva   [182]

Sept. 11: Agreement between the Soviet Union, Bulgaria, and Rumania on Cooperation in Saving Lives and Rendering Aid to Vessels or Aircraft in Distress on the Black Sea, signed at Moscow   [186]

Oct. 19: Agreement between the Soviet Union and Norway on Cooperation in Saving Persons in Distress and Searching for Lost Persons on the Barents Sea, signed at Oslo   [186]

Dec. 7: Agreement between the Soviet Union and Finland on Cooperation in Saving Lives on the Baltic Sea, signed at Helsinki   [186]

Dec. 12: Agreement between the Soviet Union, German Democratic Republic, and Poland on Cooperation in Saving Lives and Rendering Aid to Vessels or Aircraft in Distress on the Baltic Sea, signed at Moscow   [186]

1957

Feb. 9: Interim Convention for the Protection of Fur Seals in the North Pacific Ocean, signed at Washington D.C.   [183, 192]

Feb. 15: Agreement between Norway and the Soviet Union Concerning the Sea Frontier between Norway and the USSR in the Varangerfjord, signed at Oslo   [50]

Nov. 22: Agreement between the Soviet Union and Norway on Measures to Regulate Sealing and the Conservation of Seals in the Northeastern Atlantic Ocean, signed at Oslo   [192]

1958

March 18: Protocol between Poland and the Soviet Union Concerning the Delimitation of Polish and Soviet Territorial Waters in the Gulf of Gdansk of the Baltic Sea, signed at Warsaw   [**50**]

April 29: Convention on the Territorial Sea and the Contiguous Zone, signed at Geneva   [**15, 22, 24, 25, 43, 44, 48, 52, 56–59, 64–66, 70, 73, 74, 78, 107, 147**]

April 29: Convention on the High Seas, signed at Geneva   [**69, 70, 75, 171, 172, 174, 175, 177–79, 182–84, 186, 187, 195, 196**]

April 29: Convention on Fishing and Conservation of the Living Resources of the High Seas, signed at Geneva   [**165, 193, 194**]

April 29: Convention on the Continental Shelf, signed at Geneva   [**144–53, 162**]

1959

Jan. 24: Convention on Fishing in the Northeastern Atlantic Ocean, signed at London   [**191, 192**]

Feb. 21: Agreement between Finland and the Soviet Union Regarding Fishing and Sealing, signed at Moscow   [**99**]

July 7: Agreement between the Soviet Union, Bulgaria, and Rumania on Fishing in the Black Sea, signed at Varna   [**192**]

1960

March 15: Convention for the Unification of Certain Rules Concerning Liability Arising from a Collision of Vessels of Internal Navigation, signed at Geneva   [**185**]

June 17: International Convention on Safety of Life at Sea, signed at London   [**185**]

June 17: Regulations for the Prevention of Collisions of Vessels at Sea, signed at London   [**185**]

July 29: Agreement between the Soviet Union, Bulgaria, and Rumania on the Load Line for Vessels Sailing under the Flags and between the Ports of the USSR, Bulgaria, and Rumania on the Black Sea, signed at Moscow   [**186**]

1961

Dec. 15: Convention on Cooperation in Technical Supervision Over Vessels and Their Classification, signed at Warsaw   [**185**]

1962

April 16: Agreement on Fishing between the Soviet Union and Norway, signed at Moscow   [**99**]

June 6: Agreements on the Regulation of Pelagic Whaling in Antarctica, signed at London   [**192**]

July 28: Agreement between the Soviet Union, German Democratic Republic, and Poland on Cooperation in Marine Fishing, signed at Warsaw   [**192, 193**]

Aug. 3: Protocol between the Soviet Union and Cuba on Rendering Technical Aid to Cuba Without Compensation by the Soviet Union for the Development of Commercial Fishing, signed at Havana   [**192, 193**]

Sept. 15: Exchange of Notes between the Soviet Union and Iran Regarding the Obligation of Iran to Prevent the Creation of Foreign Missile Bases on its Territory   [**103**]

Sept. 25: Agreement between the Soviet Union and Cuba on the Construction of a Fishing Port in Cuba, signed at Havana   [**192, 193**]

Sept. 25: Agreement between the Soviet Union and Cuba on Cooperation in the Development of Marine Fisheries, signed at Havana   [**192, 193**]

1963

June 7: Agreement between the Soviet Union, German Democratic Republic, and Poland on the Load Line for Vessels Sailing under the Flag and between the Ports of the USSR, GDR, and Poland on the Baltic Sea, signed at Moscow   [**186**]

June 10: Agreement between the Great Japan Fisheries Association and the USSR Ministry of Fisheries Concerning the Collection of Sea Kale in Areas Around Kaigara Island by Japanese Fishermen, signed at Moscow   [**40, 100**]

July 27: Agreement between the Soviet Union and Iran on Economic and Technical Cooperation, signed at Teheran   [**193**]

Aug. 5: Treaty Banning Nuclear Weapons Tests in the Atmosphere, in Outer Space, and Under Water, signed at Moscow   [**186, 187**]

Oct. 28: Agreement on the System of International Supervision Over Whaling Bases Engaged in Pelagic Whaling in Antarctica, signed at London   [**192**]

Dec. 9: Agreement on Rendering Technical Assistance by the Soviet Union to Bulgaria in the Catching of Fish on the Oceans, signed at Moscow   [**192, 193**]

Dec. 20: Agreement between the Soviet Union and Ghana on Cooperation in Marine Fisheries, signed at Accra   [**192, 193**]

1964

Feb. 27: Agreement between the Soviet Union and the United Arab Republic on Cooperation in Developing Marine Fisheries, signed at Cairo   [**192, 193**]

July 15: Agreement between the Soviet Union and Indonesia on Cooperation in Fishing, signed at Moscow   [**193**]

Sept. 12: Convention on the International Council for the Exploration of the Sea, signed at Copenhagen   [**191**]

Oct. 18: Protocol on Mutual Cooperation in Marine Fisheries between the Soviet Union and Yemen, signed at Sana   [**193**]

Dec. 14: Agreement between the United States and the Soviet Union Relating to Fishery Operations in the Northeastern Part of the Pacific Ocean, signed at Washington D.C.   [**193**]

1965

Feb. 5: Agreement between the Soviet Union and the United States Relating to Fishing for King Crabs, signed at Washington D.C.   [**149, 193**]

May 20: Agreement between Finland and the Soviet Union Regarding the Boundaries of Sea Waters and the Continental Shelf in the Gulf of Finland, signed at Helsinki   [**44, 50, 146**]

May 20: Protocol Regarding Extension of the Finnish-Soviet Agreement of February 21, 1959, Regarding Fishing and Sealing in the Area of the Gulf of Finland to the East of Suursaari Island, signed at Helsinki   [**99**]

Oct. 9: Agreement between the Soviet Union and Denmark Concerning Salvage Operations Within Danish and USSR Territorial Waters, signed at Moscow   [**83**]

1966

April 5: Convention on Load Line, signed at London   [**186**]

1967

April 5: Protocol-Description of the Sea Boundary Line between Finland and the Soviet Union in the Gulf of Finland to the Northeast of Gogland Island, signed at Helsinki   [**146**]

May 5: Agreement between the Soviet Union and Finland Regarding the Boundary of the Continental Shelf between the Soviet Union and Finland in the Northeastern Part of the Baltic Sea, signed at Helsinki [**146**]

Nov. 25: Agreement between the United States and the Soviet Union on Certain Fishery Problems on the High Seas in the Western Areas of the Middle Atlantic Ocean, signed at Moscow   [**193**]

1968

Oct. 23: Declaration of the Soviet Union, Poland, and the German Democratic Republic on the Continental Shelf of the Baltic Sea, signed at Moscow   [**15, 134, 146, 147, 149, 150**]

Dec. 13: Agreement between the United States and the Soviet Union on Certain Fishery Problems on the High Seas in the Western Areas of the Middle Atlantic Ocean, signed at Washington D.C.   [**193**]

1969

Jan. 31: Agreement on Extending the Validity of the Agreement of February 5, 1965, between the United States and the Soviet Union Relating to Fishing for King Crabs, signed at Washington D.C. **[193]**

Jan. 31: Agreement on Extending the Validity of the Agreement of February 13, 1967, between the United States and the Soviet Union on Certain Fishery Problems in the Northeastern Part of the Pacific Ocean off the Coast of the United States, signed at Washington D.C. **[193]**

Jan. 31: Agreement between the United States and the Soviet Union Relating to the Agreement of December 14, 1964, signed at Washington D.C. **[193]**

June 13: Agreement between the Soviet Union and Finland Regarding Fishing and Sealing, signed at Moscow **[99]**

Aug. 28: Agreement between the Soviet Union and Poland Concerning the Course of the Continental Shelf Boundary in the Gulf of Gdansk and the Southeastern Part of the Baltic Sea, signed at Warsaw **[146]**

INDEX

THE JOHNS HOPKINS PRESS

Designed by James C. Wageman

*Composed in Times Roman text and display
by Typoservice Corporation*

*Printed on 60-lb. Sebago, MF
by Universal Lithographers, Inc.*

*Bound in Columbia Riverside Linen, RL-3478
by L. H. Jenkins, Inc.*